D1220885

SMITH, Susan J. Crime, space and society. Cambridge, 1986. 228p bibl index 86-
6858. 42.50 ISBN 0-521-264561. HV 6947. CIP

Smith's study is a geographer's contribution to understanding the nature of crime in
Britain. The author begins with a spatial analysis of a sample area in Birmingham,
where she finds the inner city to have the highest incidence of crime and victims. She
then examines sociologically the influence of crime on the living patterns and social
values of inner-city people, concentrating on the fears of victims who are unable to find
political redress. Smith's study also links her sample to national crime patterns and to
the role of the police. All this is firmly set within the existing scholarship on crime,
especially that on the US, where the conclusions Smith has drawn for British crime
patterns have already been formulated. Her work should be of interest across the social
sciences at the upper-division undergraduate level and above.—*M.J. Moore, Appala-
chian State University*

Cambridge Human Geography

CRIME, SPACE AND SOCIETY

Cambridge Human Geography

CRIME, SPACE AND SOCIETY

SUSAN J. SMITH

Research Fellow
Centre for Housing Research, University of Glasgow

673857

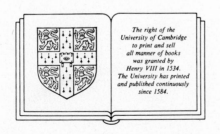

The right of the
University of Cambridge
to print and sell
all manner of books
was granted by
Henry VIII in 1534.
The University has printed
and published continuously
since 1584.

CAMBRIDGE UNIVERSITY PRESS

Cambridge
London   New York   New Rochelle
Melbourne   Sydney

Published by the Press Syndicate of the University of Cambridge
The Pitt Building, Trumpington Street, Cambridge CB2 1RP
32 East 57th Street, New York, NY 10022, USA
10 Stamford Road, Oakleigh, Melbourne 3166, Australia

First published 1986

Printed in Great Britain at the University Press, Cambridge

British Library cataloguing in publication data

Smith, Susan, 1956–
Crime, space and society. – (Cambridge human geography)
1. Crime and criminals – Social aspects – Great Britain
I. Title   364'.941   HV6947

Library of Congress cataloguing in publication data

Smith, Susan, 1956–
Crime, space and society.
(Cambridge human geography)
Bibliography.
Includes index.
1. Crime and criminals – Great Britain.
2. Victims of crime – Great Britain. 3. Crime and criminals – England –
Birmingham (West Midlands)
I. Title.   II. Series.
HV6947.S55   1986   364'.941   86–6858
ISBN 0 521 264561

BO

To my parents

Contents

Tables

Acknowledgments

I am indebted to many individuals in a variety of agencies who allowed me access to their crime data. Particular thanks are due to Chief Superintendent Tony Butler of the West Midlands Police, and to Mike Hough, who introduced me to the first British Crime Survey. A congenial and constructive research environment provided by colleagues at the University of California, Los Angeles, and at Brunel University, was much appreciated. I am especially grateful for three months as an Urban Studies Research Fellow at the University of Glasgow, which provided me with ideas, friendship and much-needed writing time. Some of my original research was carried out under the supervision of Clyde Mitchell and Ceri Peach in Oxford. Their help and support has been invaluable. Finally, I should like to thank Mike Summerfield for his patience and encouragement.

Permission to reproduce tables and to draw upon text, previously published in the following articles by the author, is gratefully acknowledged: 'Race and reactions to crime', *New Community*, 10: 233–42; 'Victimisation in the inner city – a British case study', *British Journal of Criminology*, 22: 386–402; 'Negotiating ethnicity in an uncertain environment', *Ethnic and Racial Studies*, 7: 360–73; 'Crime and the structure of social relations', *Transactions, Institute of British Geographers* New Series 9: 427–42; 'News and the dissemination of fear' in J. Burgess and J. Gold, eds. *Geography, the media and popular culture* (1985, London), pp. 229–53.

Preface

This book was conceived as an attempt to integrate theoretically the study of crime with recent developments in our understanding of social organisation and change. Criminological research has tended (in practice if not by design) to abstract crime from its broader social context. A magnificent fund of knowledge has been created, but contemporary social theory has often developed in advance of, or in isolation from, shifts in criminological thought. Based on the groundwork of others, my aim is to introduce a much broader perspective on crime. I view it as one facet in a wider structure of social relations. As such, crime, like any other form of human interchange, can be understood in terms of the differential distribution of rewards and life chances in society, and in terms of the rules of social reproduction which sustain inequality.

Many commentators acknowledge that the nature of deviance has varied historically, but few explore locational variations in its meaning, causes and consequences. I shall argue that the impact and social significance of crime *does* vary locationally, even within a single nation or region. It varies not only because the environmental opportunities for crime and the economic circumstances of potential offenders vary in space, but also because crime and the fear of crime are bound up with the distribution of power and its realisation in the form of social relations amongst differently positioned social and economic groups.

For reasons amplified in the text, this book focusses on crime in Britain's inner cities generally, and on a case study in Birmingham in particular. Reflecting the extent and persistence of social and residential segregation in this country, the inner cities are areas in which the effects of crime and the quality of race relations intermingle, and much of my theoretical argument attempts to explain why this is so.

I would like to explain my use of the terms 'race' and 'culture', and my avoidance of the term 'ethnicity' in this volume. 'Race' refers to a *social* category, based on perceptions of physical differences between groups of people. The notion of race in a genetic sense is not legitimated by modern biological science, and its use in this context is racist. 'Race' is a valid object of enquiry only in so far as racist discourse and thought persist to give conceptions of racial difference their contemporary social (political and economic) significance. Part of my concern in this book is to account for the continuing significance of racial differences in the form of local social relations.

'Culture' is regarded as a system of shared meanings shaped by a group's history and its material conditions of existence. I reject idealist interpretations of culture as the pregiven 'informing spirit' of a way of life, preferring to regard it as a signifying system, expressing shared experiences and aspirations. I suspect that this definition of culture leaves 'ethnicity' redundant (when it refers to linguistic or religious minorities) or racist (when it describes cultural groups defined in terms of racial criteria). My suspicion has prompted me to avoid the appelation 'ethnic' (though I have used it without such reservations in earlier publications) for the time being.

This book draws together the very diverse interests which a geographical education has allowed me. Such eclecticism is not favoured by the specialisation that has accompanied an academic division of labour, but it encourages the openness and scepticism that feeds research. I have tried, therefore, to be wide-ranging in exploring the relationships between crime and society, although I often reject comprehensiveness in favour of theoretical coherence (particularly when considering the role of crime in the reproduction of local social relations). My success in combining speculative social theory with statements on public policy has been variable. The technical interests of planners sit uneasily with the practical and critical interests of professional academia. Nevertheless, the theoretical concerns of chapters 5 and 7 complement some of the more descriptive and policy orientated chapters which precede them; and the practical recommendations of chapter 6, although political in implication, are faithful to a wide range of empirical evidence. I do not pretend, then, to offer any grand theory of crime and society. What I suggest is a broader view of criminological research than has hitherto been usual: one that is in tune with recent developments in geography and sociology; and one whose scope I can only begin to explore in the chapters which follow.

May 1985   SUSAN J. SMITH

1

An introduction to criminological research

This book is not a conventional geography of crime. It does not thoroughly review the spatial organisation of criminal behaviour, the properties of defensible space or the distribution of victims. These important areas of analysis are well represented in the literature. My aim is to use them as the basis of an attempt to link the study of crime with the study of society, theoretically informed by a geographical perspective, in so far as this draws time and space into an appreciation of the structure of social relations.

As an introduction, a critique of the history of the analysis of deviance serves to illustrate the extent to which criminological knowledge has expressed the interests held by analysts (both tacitly and self-consciously) during specific historical periods in particular national contexts. This provides some insight into the strengths and weaknesses of a variety of approaches to criminological enquiry; it also provides a touchstone against which to appreciate the different combinations of perspectives adopted in subsequent chapters. The introduction is organised in sympathy with Habermas's (1968) account of knowledge as constituted (only) through human interests. I acknowledge that many have quibbled with his view, but find it nonetheless illuminating in its interpretation of criminological research over the last century and a half.

Habermas formulated his theory of knowledge-constitutive interests from a concern that scientific (positivistic) knowledge tends, in seeking out the 'laws' of society, to misrepresent as natural and eternal that which is historically specific and alterable. Such knowledge, he argues, can only perpetuate the status quo and all relations of domination and subordination based upon it. Habermas's theory challenges what he terms the 'false objectivism' of positivistic science, arguing that the object domain of forms of knowledge, and the criteria by which such knowledge is validated, are constituted by human interests. These interests define the limits of the possible applications of the knowledge to which they give rise

(Keat 1981: 66). Habermas identifies three knowledge-constitutive interests, which he links with the human projects of communication or interaction, labour and domination. He describes the interests as practical, technical and emancipatory (respectively) and argues that they are expressed through three distinct domains of enquiry – historical-hermeneutic science, empirical-analytical science and critical theory.

The discussion below begins by exploring the empirical-analytical perspective which has dominated most spatial studies of crime. The approach gained ascendency in the affluent 1960s, accompanying increasing crime rates and a rediscovery of the problems of the inner city. A quantitative, positivistic criminology developed, aiming to predict and control the level of crime in modern democracies. This technical interest manifested itself in a variety of perspectives fundamentally informed by the philosophical presuppositions of direct or naive realism.* These perspectives range from biological definitions of criminal 'types' to a host of multivariate areal and ecological analyses of crime; from functionalist analyses of deviance to deterministic interpretations of the relationship between crime and environment. Direct realism takes crime rates as 'given', in that they are regarded as an empirical rather than a theoretical problem. Consequently, the empirical-analytical tradition contains 'a moral imperative which gears academic analysis to the eradication of crime', although it creates an intellectual climate in which 'a critique of law or law enforcement has been effectively denied' (Lowman 1982: 310). Additionally, the approach has allowed analysts to perform their tasks in contexts far removed from the subjective lifeworlds of those practising and affected by crime.

Fortunately, as the chapter goes on to show, there are long periods in the history of criminological enquiry during which an oral tradition has prevailed. Life histories and vivid ethnographic descriptions bear witness to academia's attempts to understand and communicate the essence of deviant behaviour to a broad readership. This kind of experiential knowledge, grounded in the methods of historical-hermeneutic science, is constituted by what Habermas terms a practical interest in intersubjectivity. Through this medium, a world of traditional or 'folk' meanings may be disclosed and imparted to those unable or disinclined to participate in it themselves.

---

* This philosophy assumes that the objects of enquiry exist independently of an observer, and that the reality of these objects is at least partially present in their appearance (i.e. in the analyst's experience of them). Johnston (1980) bases his discussion of human geography on the presuppositions of direct realism.

Most recently, various 'radical' criminologies have emerged. Notwithstanding the diversity of these critical approaches, they have in common the view that crime is inseparable from the institutionalised norms it violates, and they share the aim of making explicit, and of questioning, the values embedded within such norms. The interest here is emancipatory: critical criminology forms part of a self-reflective movement towards a more rational society based on explanatory understanding rather than on interpretative or causal analysis. This is the third theme explored below.

Habermas's thesis leaves many questions unanswered and poses a philosophical problem in that it fails to specify the *origins* of the three sets of interests. But the issue of whether they arise from the material conditions of society (which Habermas does not favour), or from something intrinsic to human nature or the mind, is largely beyond the scope of this book. Those who wish to explore such questions further are referred to McCarthy's (1978) detailed critique of Habermas's ideas, and to the work of Apel (1981), who has begun to construct a firmer philosophical basis for these ideas by re-examining Charles Peirce's pragmatic theory of truth.

Habermas's scheme, then, is neither complete, nor unassailable as a theory of knowledge. What it does offer is an intellectual framework in which the forms of knowledge or domains of enquiry that have so far been pursued in criminological research can be identified in terms of the human interests they embody. Interests other than the three identified by Habermas might be possible, but this trichotomous distinction is sufficient to guide the following selective account of the recent history of criminological thought.

The empirical-analytical tradition

A technical interest in crime control was first systematically evinced in the work of the so-called 'cartographic criminologists' of nineteenth-century Europe. Scholars such as Alison (1840), Fletcher (1849), Glyde (1856), Guerry (1833), Quetelet (1842) and Rawson (1839) sought to match spatial (usually regional) patterns of crime and offender rates with variations in 'moral' statistics (including literacy, population density, wealth, occupation, nationality and the home environment) and with physical phenomena (such as climate).

Guerry, aided by the geographer Adriano Balbi, noted that offender rates in France between 1825 and 1830 were related to criminals' age and sex, and to season. He tested three popular explanations of crime (based on the criminogenic effects of poverty, poor education and high population density) and found them all wanting. Rawson subsequently concentrated on the role of employment, dividing England into agricultural, manufacturing, mining and metropolitan areas and tracing out the links between urban industrialism and crime rates. Quetelet went a step further, arguing, in a similar vein to many modern analysts, that there could be no simple relationship between crime and wealth in France or England, but that high crime rates would occur where economic inequalities were most marked within small areas (i.e. where both the opportunities for crime and the predisposition to offend were present). Others, again pre-empting the thrust of modern studies, focussed on the relationship over time between changes in crime rates and fluctuations in business cycles. Clay (1855), for example, showed that in nineteenth-century England times of economic hardship tended to be accompanied by an increase in crime.

The nineteenth-century studies are summarised in greater detail by Morris (1957: 37–64) and by Phillips (1972). In favouring socio-economic explanations of the crime rate these early works usually provided a more rational and objective basis for pioneer reformism than did preceding biblical notions of good and evil. Retrospectively, their findings also seem more enlightened than Lombroso's biological theories of criminality that succeeded them. Yet, despite their initial appeal, nineteenth-century ecological and sociological initiatives in the study of crime *were* soon eclipsed by theories favouring biological/physiological explanations for individuals' criminality (a demise discussed in some detail by Morris (1957)).

Europe's empirical-analytical tradition was rediscovered in early twentieth-century Chicago. Ogburn and Thomas (1922), for instance, correlated business cycles with convictions over a fifty-year period between 1870 and 1920. The greatest strides, however, were made by Clifford Shaw and Henry McKay, who pursued the spatial study of crime at an intra-urban scale. They aimed to locate the origins and correlates of deviance with a view to reforming the adverse social and environmental conditions of crime-prone neighbourhoods. These authors stressed that their approach to crime was strictly sociological, 'an attempt to relate behavior to the social and cultural setting in which it arises' (Shaw 1929: 9, see also Shaw and McKay 1931, 1942); and this had a striking geographical dimension, undetected in earlier research informing the psychological and biological theories which linked crime with individual pathology.

Finestone's (1976) account of the Chicago School's epidemiological research draws out an important parallel with the earlier European studies: both discover an association in space between delinquency and economic indices. The consistency and significance of this link was to elude a generation of factorial ecologists before re-emerging in the late 1970s. Nevertheless, as the 1930s proceeded, the association became increasingly prominent in the writings of the Chicago criminologists. Whereas Shaw and McKay had originally interpreted delinquency in terms of cultural and social change, increased mobility and excessive 'disorganisation' (factors that had seemed to affect successive waves of European immigrants), as the depression worsened (and migration and residential mobility became sluggish) their interpretations increasingly rested on economic criteria:

From an emphasis upon social change and social process they had moved to an emphasis upon social structure. From stress upon personal and primary group relationships – that is, upon the local milieu – they had moved to attribute priority to the impersonal pressures originating in the larger social systems. The conceptual primacy of local community was replaced by that of social class. (Finestone 1976: 93)

Shaw and McKay's widely quoted conclusion that crime and delinquency follow the physical structure and social organisation of the city stimulated an innovative approach to neighbourhood crime control in Chicago, and precipitated a long series of areal and ecological studies of crime in the academic literature. These have been condemned as atheoretic and positivistic, but the best are inspired by the sound philosophical presuppositions of direct realism.

Areal analyses of crime are concerned primarily with describing spatial distributions. A first stage in dealing with crime and criminals is to discover where they are. Most intra-urban research of this type has focussed on the location of offenders' homes, following the lead of Shaw and McKay (1942), who discovered an enduring tendency for known offenders to cluster within the inner city, and for offender residence rates to decrease outwards following the familiar distance decay curve. In Britain, too, Bagot (1941) found that the homes of convicted juvenile delinquents clustered disproportionately into three central wards of Liverpool on the banks of the river Mersey. Later, however, Morris (1957) observed in Croydon that offenders were also segregated in peripheral council-housing estates (a tendency also apparent from the mid-1950s in Hobart, Tasmania (Scott 1965)).

Timms (1965) sustained this areal tradition with a study in Luton, but perhaps the most thorough contemporary British studies of offender residence have been completed in Sheffield (Baldwin and Bottoms 1976; Bottoms and Xanthos 1981; Mawby 1979b), and in Cardiff (Evans 1980; Herbert 1976a). In Sheffield, the majority of offenders live between one and three miles from the city centre and cluster: (a) in the 'twilight' areas with high proportions of Irish and New Commonwealth immigrants; (b) in some enumeration districts adjacent to the main areas of heavy industry; and (c) on some council estates, especially those built in the inter-war years. In Cardiff, a similar pattern emerges of high offender rates in the inner-city terraces, the middle-ring rooming houses and suburban local authority estates. Here, the main aim of the areal analyses has been to preface a series of ecological and behavioural studies attempting to clarify the concept of 'delinquency areas'. However, the range of centrographic techniques employed by Rose and Deskins (1980), in their examination of offenders' and victims' residential patterns in Detroit, might anticipate the extended use of spatial statistics in the analysis of offender data (see also Stephenson 1980).

Simple areal analyses of *offences* have been less prominent in the literature. Harries (1973, 1974, 1976b, 1980) examined inter-city areal variations in North America, drawing attention particularly to the high incidence of violence (especially murder) in the south. Rengert and Müller (1972) traced the diffusion of drugs down the urban hierarchy in New York state; and there are also areal studies of prostitution, offering a novel view of the geographies of San Francisco and Nevada (Shumsky and Springer 1981; Symanski 1974). Phillips (1972) has probably produced one of the most detailed intra-urban areal studies of crime to date, in Minneapolis, where he identified a 'centralised' distribution of car theft, business robbery and business burglary, various 'ghettoised' clusters of assaults, property damage, street robbery and purse snatching, and a 'partially dispersed' pattern of residential burglary.

Ultimately, however, the depth of insight to be gleaned from areal studies is limited, since it is an approach which takes no account of population, land use or other features of the urban environment which affect the pattern of crime by constraining the distribution of opportunities. Far more interest within the empirical-analytical tradition has thus focussed on *ecological* analysis, which Herbert (1976a) defines as the correlation in space of areally aggregated crime rates and measurable indices of the social and physical environment.

Historically, four broadly distinct phases in the ecological analysis of crime can be discerned. The first two movements have already been mentioned. They are Europe's nineteenth-century 'cartographic criminology' and the pioneering intra-urban studies of deviance completed in early twentieth-century Chicago. Amongst more recent developments, it is relevant to distinguish the theoretically weak factorial ecologies of the 1960s from the more rigorous econometric studies of the last decade.

During the 1960s, a variety of numerically sophisticated but theoretically weak factorial ecologies was published, exploring the empirical associations between crime rates and socio-economic indicators. Despite authors' intentions, the practical application of results has often been limited, since many studies were crudely positivistic and held few insights for planners and policy-makers. It would therefore be superfluous to itemise and evaluate the results of every application of social-area analysis, factor analysis, principal-components analysis and related techniques for comparing the incidence of crime with that of other social phenomena, particularly since a number of critical reviews already exist. Gordon's (1967) discussion of papers by Lander (1954) and Chilton (1964), for instance, serves to illustrate some methodological pitfalls of multivariate techniques, while their theoretical shortcomings are amply documented in Baldwin's (1975) critique of ecological research in Britain. In this, and in other critical reviews Baldwin (1974a, 1979) is distressed by the blurred objectives of quantitative ecological analyses; by the fact that their conceptual difficulties and ambiguities are often overlooked; and by the tendency for results to be presented as if the use of technically sophisticated methods had obviated the need for careful explanations.

These reservations notwithstanding, the best of the studies, and the fruits of the Crime Prevention Through Environmental Design movement (stimulated by the discovery of consistent empirical associations between crime and the built environment, and introduced more fully in chapter 3) provide a ready basis for the quick 'solutions' to the crime problem that modern politicians require. There are, moreover, three persistent, if controversial, themes that have endured throughout the stormy history of ecological analyses of urban crime. They are the quixotic condition of 'social disorganisation', the association between crime rates and various measures of density or crowding, and the elusive relationship between deviance and economy. The practical and theoretical significance of these themes for future research is discussed in chapter 2.

The 1970s witnessed a more promising series of ecological studies of crime published by economists. They are usually based on North American data, and they draw attention to the relationship between crime rates and economic indicators at several spatial scales: the census tract (Beasley and Antunes 1974; Bechdolt 1975; Kvolseth 1977); the city or SMSA (Allison 1972; Flango and Sherbenous 1976; Hoch 1974; Phillips and Votey 1975); and the state (Nagel 1978). These studies are reviewed in detail by Berger (1980). The link they identify between crime rates and economic trends, and the implications of such a link for the monetarist economies of the 1980s, may be the most fruitful discovery of a generation of often inconclusive quantitative analyses.

For the most part, then, the empirical-analytical approach to criminological research takes as its task the statistical comparison of measurable crime patterns with the incidence of factors possibly associated with their genesis. In so far as strong association might be indicative of causality, the aim of such studies has been to find some basis for controlling the crime rate. Definitions of crime are usually taken from official statistics and treated as the starting point for analysis rather than as the end point of law-enforcement practices. Consequently, an understanding of the *meaning* of crime has rarely proved integral to research in this tradition.

The main thrust of today's spatial studies of crime, however, is indebted to the work of the Chicago School, and the spirit of the North American research was that of direct realism rather than atheoretic positivism (the distinction is clarified by Keat and Urry 1975: 9–40). The ecologists were not primarily concerned with causal connections between spatially coincident variables. Their aim was not to predict crime and delinquency by eliciting 'laws' which would link deviance with substandard housing, poverty, population change, foreign-born populations, cultural minorities, tuberculosis, mental disorder and the many other persistent crime correlates. It was, rather, to offer *explanations* for these enduring links. 'To explain things is not merely to show that they are instances of well-established regularities. Instead we [the realist] must discover the necessary connections between phenomena, by acquiring knowledge of the underlying structures and mechanisms at work' (Keat and Urry 1975: 5).

In Chicago, this knowledge was secured through the use of life histories and participant observation in a research environment which refused to separate empirical-analytical techniques from the insights of oral-ethnographic study. Large-scale areal analyses were used instrumentally to illuminate high-delinquency areas; small-scale in-depth study explored, experienced and interpreted this localisation. But since the 1950s, the ecological and hermeneutic traditions have progressively been divorced. Rising crime rates, sensationalism in the mass media, and the elevation of law and order to an election issue in many countries, placed the emphasis of research firmly on crime control. This emphasis continues, and the popularity of empirical-analytical research seems assured. An appropriate form for such research, if it is to avoid theoretically weak positivism and capitalise on the strengths of direct realism, is discussed in chapter 2. The interpretative tradition survived, however, and since its contribution to the geography of crime has been so limited, its merits are worth considering at some length.

The oral-ethnographic tradition

Direct observations, life histories, unpublished documents and other first-hand data sources have fuelled enough research to produce an extensive and compelling literature grounded in the oral-ethnographic tradition. Fulfilling a communicative role and offering a vivid glimpse of the human consequences of crime and deviance, this tradition can be traced across three-and-a-half centuries. It provides an important commentary on the effects of socio-economic change on the structure of social relations, and it bears witness to the rich theoretical insight to be gained when the study of crime is integrated with a broader appreciation of the social context in which deviance arises.

Crime and the urban poor in nineteenth-century Britain

Friedrich Engels made an important statement about the experience of life in late eighteenth- and early nineteenth- century Britain in *The condition of the working class in England* (1845). It is not an ethnographic document based on Engels's own extensive experience (he had spent only twenty months as a visitor to the country when he wrote it), but it is sensitively compiled from contemporary reports, pamphlets and newspapers, and from the vivid impact of a personal acquaintance with the growing industrial cities of the north.

Engels interpreted crime as a rational reaction to relative deprivation – a consequence of the unequal distribution of the material rewards of the industrial revolution:

The worker lived in poverty and want, and saw that other people were better off than he was. The worker was not sufficiently intelligent to appreciate why he, of all people, should be the one to suffer – for after all he contributed more to society than the idle rich, and sheer necessity drove him to steal in spite of his traditional respect for private property. (Engels 1845: 242)

Similarly,

Acts of violence committed by the working classes against the bourgeoisie and their henchmen are merely frank and undisguised retaliation for the thefts and treacheries perpetrated by the middle classes against the workers. (Engels 1845: 242)

Criminality was observed by Engels not only in the deprived working classes, but also among the 'surplus population' of casual workers, street sweepers, beggars, prostitutes and peddlars, who were provoked by their acute distress to wage open warfare against the bourgeosie. While deviance could not be regarded as an organised or effective class action, part of the importance of crime for Engels is its potential for feeding into such actions. In this view, 'the criminal is an unconscious and premature social rebel' (Marcus 1974: 224).

That Engels chose to intepret his raw material, rather than merely describe it for the reader, is both a strength and a weakness. It is a strength in that the author's values are self-consciously exposed and unequivocal. As Henderson and Chaloner (1958: xxii) point out, 'Engels cast himself in the role of counsel for the prosecution against capitalists. He did not pretend to be an impartial observer.' It is clear what selective principles must have been invoked in compiling the work, and the value judgements that all writers must make are anything but tacit. The weakness of this approach is that the immediacy of first-hand experience can easily be displaced by the message of a specific interpretation of that experience. As a political treatise, *The condition of the working class in England* is a monumental work; as a source of intimate knowledge about the commonsense understandings of the people it is less illuminating than the subsequent writings of reformers such as Henry Mayhew and Charles Booth. In relating the incidence of crime to the growth of the working class, and in identifying a link between increasing crime rates and urban industrialism, Engels did, however, recognise the spatial dimension of crime, and in relating this to the process of economic development he raised a theoretical question whose significance has scarcely been acknowledged by modern analysts.

Henry Mayhew, novelist, dramatist, journalist and scientist, was born in 1812, the son of a solicitor and one of seventeen children. Although he was not especially concerned with the study of crime, he is a major figure amongst those 'shadow criminologists' whose pre-theoretical observations provide a body of research clearly anticipating the more formal conceptualisations of deviance that were to follow: 'It ['shadow criminology'] contains much that is repetitive, conjectural, and fanciful. It also contains a great deal of valuable material and sensible observation. Properly read, it may be recognized as an anticipation of the theorizing that now passes for the sociology of deviance' (Downes and Rock 1982: 51).

Mayhew is best known (and, even then, curiously neglected) for his vivid 'street biography', which was initially published between 1849 and 1850 as a series of bi-weekly articles on England's industrial poor, and later expanded into four volumes on *London labour and the London poor* (1862). Known crime in England steadily increased during the first half of the nineteenth century and, through his detailed observations, Mayhew almost incidentally pioneered its study within the interpretative tradition. His writing is sprinkled with descriptions of deviance as experienced by ordinary people, and with passages based on delinquents' oral histories. These criminological vignettes are not grouped together for analytical convenience; rather, 'they appear here and there, as crime itself appears from time to time in some people's lives' (Bennett 1981: 272). Deviance is skilfully integrated within its appropriate socio-economic context, and its significance can be gauged by readers as they are introduced to London's lodging houses, vagrant gatherings and street sellers.

From Mayhew's ethnography, the dominant impression is that poverty and decrepit living environments, together with the transmission of deviant values between deprived children in the ragged schools, were at the root of urban crime in nineteenth-century Britain. Environment and economy appeared to explain intra- and inter-urban patterns of crime. However, as Bennett (1981) points out, from the work which includes Mayhew's most direct discussion of delinquency (and which does not include detailed ethnography) a different opinion emerges. In *The criminal prisons of London and scenes of prison life* (1862), Mayhew and Binney reject poverty, overcrowding, vagrancy and aspirations for material wealth as the causes of delinquency, blaming instead inadequate parental control of juveniles and

that innate love of a life of ease, and aversion to hard work, which is common to all natures, and which, when accompanied with lawlessness of disposition as well as disregard for the rights of our fellow creatures and a want of self-dignity, can but end either in begging or stealing the earnings and possessions of others. (Mayhew and Binney 1862: 84)

Mayhew never explained this incongruity between the inferences of his street biography and those of his work amongst convicted criminals, but this does not undermine his main achievement, which was to establish the viability and value of an observational-interpretative approach to the study of delinquency. He rejected analytical categorisation in favour of data secured in terms meaningful to those he observed, so evincing that disciplined selflessness required of analysts seeking to understand and faithfully represent the lives of the public.

Like Mayhew, Charles Booth belonged to an era in which it was believed that political differences, or different opinions regarding the best solution to a problem, could be resolved by discovering more relevant facts. Yet, although Booth presided over the Royal Statistical Society (founded in 1834), he was suspicious of decontextualised quantitative data abstracted from sample surveys, particularly when they revealed that poverty had spread to an extent incommensurate with his conservative views.* In 1886, in order to elicit enough facts to judge the condition of the labouring classes, Booth began a massive enquiry into the circumstances of London's poor, which was to take seventeen years to complete. His aims were reformist rather than narrowly academic, and he attempted to gather both qualitative and quantitative data, reasoning that 'the statistical method was needed to give bearings to the results of personal observations and personal observation to give life to statistics' (Booth, cited in Simey and Simey 1960: 78).

As Booth's concern for the obvious problems of poverty in the midst of plenty developed, his early fears of prejudicing 'objective' findings by subjective impression diminished, and the amount of experiential fieldwork increased. The result, a treatise on *Life and*

---

* Booth's major enquiry was prompted partly by his disbelief of the Social Democratic Federation's suggestion in 1885 (on the basis of a sample survey) that 25% of London's workers could not live adequately on their wages. It is ironic that he was forced in his own study to recognise that over 30% of the population were at all times more or less deprived in material and financial terms.

labour of the people in London (1902–3) ran to seventeen volumes and contains a wealth of observational detail. As in Mayhew's writings, crime is carefully integrated with the environment and lifestyles of specific social milieux. The reader is offered no grand theory, nor even a broad conceptual interpretation of the problem. Only in the final summary volume does Booth develop the 'general but implicit hypothesis that social isolation was a major factor in producing decay and disorganization on both individual and community levels – an isolation that was more often than not physical [environmental] in its inception' (Pfautz 1967: 78).

By refusing to abstract crime from the social, environmental and locational context in which it occurred, by integrating deviance with the life and work of both perpetrators and victims, Booth (like Mayhew) conveys to his readers the impression that deviance is a *social* problem, rather than an individual, pathological condition. Thus, despite Booth's links with the quantitative origins of British sociology, in later years his methodological innovation seemed otherwise to an energetic American journalist, philosopher and sociologist seeking to make sense of American urbanism from his vantage point in Chicago. The man most responsible for ethnography's twentieth-century revival claims:

It was not, however, Booth's statistics, but his realistic descriptions of the actual life of the occupational classes – the conditions under which they lived and labored, their passions, pastimes, domestic tragedies, and the life-philosophies with which each class met the crises peculiar to it – which made these studies a memorable and permanent contribution to our knowledge of human nature and society. (Park 1929: 7)

Delinquency and urbanisation in early twentieth-century Chicago

Robert Park's contribution to the hermeneutic sciences has been discussed elsewhere (see Jackson and Smith 1984; Smith 1981a; 1984b). His leadership in Chicago University's department of sociology inspired numerous interpretative, humanistic studies of the wide range of problems encountered in North America's rapidly growing cities. His students investigated homelessness and suicide, drunkenness and vice, professional crime and juvenile delinquency. Given Chicago's reputation as the crime capital of the world, it is hardly surprising that crime became an important focus of research for Park and his colleagues who were, after all, working in the home town of Al Capone.

The Chicago School rarely treated delinquency as a problem to be isolated from the lifestyle of individuals, or from the organisation of society as a whole (although analysts did focus almost exclusively on the offenders rather than the victims of crime). Most published work corroborates a generalisation about the social origins and consequences of crime that can be traced back to the writings of Mayhew and Booth, and Booth's concern to determine the differential criminogenic effects of the physical and social structure of the city can be seen reiterated throughout the writings of the Chicago School. Thrasher's (1927) account of juvenile delinquency and gang formation, and Landesco's (1929, 1933) venture into the world of organised crime are particularly good examples.

From the mid-1920s onwards, the major statements on crime in Chicago issued from the work of Shaw and McKay at the Illinois Institute for Juvenile Research. While Park's infamous dot maps, locating anything from immigrants to taxi dance halls, no doubt gave impetus to the ecological studies produced by the Institute, the humanistic aspects of Park's philosophical thought were carried there by Ernest Burgess (Park's junior by twenty-two years), whose courses first interested Shaw in delinquency. Burgess had much greater reforming zeal than Park, though the two colleagues shared commitment to the empathetic understanding of delinquency and both favoured social rather than psychological interpretations of deviance. Significantly, it is in the work of Shaw and McKay that the practical, communicative interests of the historical-hermeneutic sciences, and the technical policy orientated interests of the empirical-analytical sciences, most nearly meet.

Although the names Shaw and McKay are inextricably linked in the history of criminological thought, it is Shaw who preferred interpretative, experiential approaches to the analysis of delinquency.

McKay was the professional scholar and gentleman – polite, kind, thoughtful – an academic out to prove his position with empirical evidence. Shaw was the more emotional practitioner, a professional administrator and organizer – talkative, friendly, personable, persuasive, energetic, and quixotic – out to make his case through action and participation. (Snodgrass 1976: 3)

Shaw began collecting delinquents' life histories in the early 1920s, amassing hundreds more during the 1930s. Although he did concern himself with methodology (e.g. Shaw 1926), Shaw's technique is best revealed in the stories of Stanley and Sidney told in *The jack-roller*

(1930) and *The natural history of a delinquent career* (1931), and in the fortunes of five siblings detailed in *Brothers in crime* (1938).*

Shaw (1930: 3) claims that his life histories are especially valuable in exposing these facets of deviant behaviour: they emphasise the point of view of the delinquent; they illuminate the social and cultural situations to which an offender is responsive; and they allow crime commission to be understood in terms of its position in a sequence of life events experienced by a delinquent. Again, therefore, crime is portrayed as a contingency of the social organis-ation of specific communities. Retrospectively, it is clear that such a perspective focussed too much on the immediate community as the seedbed of delinquency, and too little on the political economy of a wider society. In the 1930s, however, when the majority of prison inmates were classed as psychopathic, Shaw's work marked a welcome and innovative shift in the conceptualisation of delinquency, emphasising its import as a social problem rather than interpreting it as a reflection of individual pathology.

Drawing from the interpretative case studies encouraged by Park, and the life histories collated by Shaw, the oral-ethnographic tra-dition in Chicago came as near as it ever would to having a practical application. The Chicago Area Project, implemented during the 1930s and 1940s, was an almost legendary experiment in community based crime prevention, which represented the first systematic applied challenge by sociologists to the psychiatric treat-ment of delinquency (cf. Schlossman and Sedlak 1983). Enlightened by the ethnographers' vivid accounts of urban culture, and moved by the grim (if sometimes romanticised) realities of deviants' life histories, community organisations based in the Institute for Juvenile Research mobilised local volunteers to begin changing, at neighbourhood level, those aspects of the physical and social environment thought to provoke delinquency.

The project aimed to increase understanding and co-operation between individuals and institutions. The public was acquainted with 'scientific' opinions about the sociological origins of delin-quency, dialogue between neighbourhood residents and institutions was encouraged, and volunteers attempted to reconcile the adult members of communities with their delinquent youth (see Finestone 1976: 116–50). Yet, although some of the community committees set up to deal with individual offenders still exist, for the

---

* The career of Stanley, the jack-roller, is pursued in a recently published sequel to Shaw's original (Snodgrass 1982), which retains much of the charm and eloquence of the earlier work.

most part the reforming intentions of those devoted to experiential research were to be frustrated:

Periodically we witness sensational exposés of some aspect of the city's life – political corruption, festering slums, sweatshop exploitation, vice, crime. The cry goes up from press and pulpit for reform. Militant organizations spring up over night. Repressive legislation is proposed and too frequently enacted. The sentimental and idealistic device [sic] new forms of 'uplift' which makes more work for the police. Then public interest flags. Little is actually accomplished. Yet the next exposé of city life creates the same demand for reform. (Zorbaugh 1929: 268–9)

The interpretative approach developed in Chicago seemed destined to fulfil an essentially communicative role. Acute observation and empathetic understanding provided a rich source of information about urban life in early twentieth-century Chicago, but the practical implications of such knowledge tended to ignore the constraints of financial viability and political expedience. It soon became obvious that the insights of experiential research could rarely be cast in a form appropriate to the needs of planners and policy-makers.

Such research undoubtedly had, and still has, theoretical import, and it fulfils a social function in providing for power-brokers a vivid image of the conditions in which the powerless exist. However, most findings were based on semi-formulated fieldwork set within a philosophical framework opposed to the notion of any structured 'reality' capable of organising vast stores of observational detail.* The work of the Chicago criminologists is certainly more systematic and intellectually refined than that which preceded it but, eschewing holistic theories, their interpretations of delinquency can be criticised for exaggerating social disorganisation and for failing to explore the links their observations expose between delinquency and industrial expansion (see Snodgrass 1976). Limitations notwithstanding, however, the ethnographic tradition was to persist and become the symbolic interactionism of the 1960s.

Interpretative criminology: problems and prospects

The conscious development of symbolic interactionism marked a new surge of interest in experiential data collection, which can best

* The Chicago School brought together the pragmatism of John Dewey, William James and George Herbert Mead, and Georg Simmel's neo-Kantian formalism. Pragmatism focusses on the dynamic processes giving rise to an emergent, unpredictable world; formalism admits to a multiplicity of 'realities' accountable to no *a priori* theory. The consequences of this for the study of crime and society are discussed by Rock (1979) and Smith (1984b).

be understood as a reaction to the abstract quantification of urban pathologies (discussed above) that dominated criminological research during the 1950s and 1960s. Symbolic interactionism moved away from the early ethnographers' concern with offenders' life histories and criminogenic social settings, when, inspired by Howard Becker's monograph *Outsiders* (1963), observers began to explore inconsistencies in the labelling of criminals. It was, therefore, through the oral-ethnographic tradition, with its primary interest in interaction, communication and symbolic meanings, that the role of outsiders in the production of deviance began to be appreciated, and this, as Downes and Rock (1982: 152) point out, significantly enlarged the task and complexity of criminological research.*

Of course, earlier researchers had noticed injustices in the enforcement of laws. Mayhew and Binney listed a string of petty offences for which youngsters had been imprisoned, condemning the fact as 'a scandal to the nation which permits the law-officers of the country so far to outrage justice and decency'. In their view, it reflected 'a savage love of consigning people to prison for faults that cannot even be classed as immoral, much less criminal' (Mayhew and Binney 1862:42). Similarly enraged, Saul Alinsky left his job with Shaw and McKay at the Institute for Juvenile Research, sacrificing ethnographic observation for political action against the injustice he felt discriminated against powerless urban communities.

In the majority of their work, however, the founders of interactionism were so caught up in documenting the social setting of known offenders and the environment of crime that they did not dwell upon inequities in the administration of justice. Later researchers compensated amply for this omission, often to the extent that the identity of offenders was sacrificed to the career of their delinquent label. The main analytical foci became the differential distribution of power in society; the selective use of this power to criminalise; and the effects of this labelling procedure on peoples' propensity to offend. Moreover, several writers attest to the importance of location in this process, drawing attention to the detrimental effects on residents of the labelling of neighbourhoods such as Wine Alley (Damer 1974) and Luke Street (Gill 1977).

This new emphasis on the power of public officials to criminalise

---

* Rock (1979) offers a penetrating account of interactionist sociology; its application to the study of deviance is further discussed by Athens (1974, 1977, 1980) and by the authors of a collection of papers edited by Rubington and Weinberg (1968).

and stigmatise drew the oral-ethnographic tradition into an 'institutionalist' approach to deviance. From this perspective, crime and criminals are viewed as an aspect or product of social organis- ation. Criminal statistics cannot therefore be wrong or incomplete (so obviating the realist's search for a dark figure of crime), although they might contain evidence of a biased or unjust system of defining criminality. Thus institutionalists' concerns centre on the extent to which peoples' dispensation at the hands of the criminal justice system can be affected more by the interaction of organisational processes with personal or population attributes than by the charac- teristics of the (criminal) events in which people are involved.

Three approaches to this type of analysis are discussed in some detail by Bottomley (1979). The first involves the study of differences of judgement and action between individual decision-makers (be they policemen or judges), assuming that the responsibility for any disparity in the treatment of offenders rests with individual members of the judiciary rather than with the organisation of the criminal justice system or the structure of society. A second approach monitors the extent to which the short-term organ- isational goals of the separate units of the law-enforcement system 'displace' justice in favour of administrative efficiency. Finally, a third approach examines the bargaining for justice which takes place between different levels of a bureaucratic criminal justice system. These three analytic strategies have been variously employed to study most aspects of the criminal process, and the implications of results for future research are discussed in the next chapter.

By focussing primarily upon the power exercised by public officials within an hierarchical authority structure, institutionalism often neglected to trace out the effects of crime *within* communities, and the subtleties of power relations exercised through more general processes of social labelling escaped analysis (an omission which chapter 7 begins to remedy). In many cases, the merits of earlier researchers' attempts to integrate crime into a wider struc- ture of social relations were lost, and in general the pursuit of the oral-ethnographic tradition into the realms of labelling 'theory' has been difficult and frustrating. Nevertheless, the approach has remained appealing and potentially powerful in its capacity to reveal the meaning of deviance for those affected by crime, or the fear of crime. At their best, the interpretative studies of both the 1920–30s and those of the 1960–70s evince a rigorous commitment on the part of their authors to 'enter the worlds of native persons so as to render those worlds understandable from the standpoint of a theory that is grounded in the *behaviors, language, definitions, attitudes* and *feelings* of those studied' (Denzin 1974: 273).

Judged according to these criteria, the achievements of the oral-ethnographic tradition are considerable. Its finest and most notable accomplishment (and one not unexpected given the presumed relationship between knowledge and interests) is its efficacy as a communicative device. Mayhew's journalistic forays into the poorest streets of London must have been a revelation to the majority of his wealthier readers at a time when social classes were extremely polarised; the Chicago ethnographers provided a touchstone against which to comprehend the complexities of unprecedented urban growth and social change in North America; later twentieth-century institutionalism has exposed the inequities of the criminal justice system to the liberal middle classes who rarely experience it. The message of Mayhew and Booth was that, properly understood, the 'dangerous classes' might be regarded less as a threat and more as an unfulfilled social responsibility; the Chicagoans showed crime to be less a pathological human deficiency and more a sociologically explicable contingency of urban indus-trialism; labelling theories warn that the criminal statistics which fuel moral indignation are not untainted by the bureaucratic procedures that produce crime and criminals. That the graphic detail of well-executed interpretative research appeals to a wider non-academic, non-professional audience can only add to its communicative role, perhaps offering the non-expert a glimpse of the true character of a phenomenon more usually encountered through the bias and exaggeration of the mass media.

The interactionist tradition has also been a rich source of new theoretically promising ideas, especially during times of intellectual stagnation. As Becker (1966: xii) observes in his new introduction to *The jack-roller*, when a discipline has 'pursued the investigation of a few variables with ever-increasing precision but has received dwin-dling increments of knowledge from the pursuits', then experiential research allows analysis to 'suggest new variables, new questions, and new processes, using the rich though unsystematic data to provide a needed reorientation of the field'. Bennett (1981: 254) suggests that this procedure of exploration and enrichment has underlain most crucial turning points in criminological thought, partly because it gives scope to range widely and innovate freely, and partly because the authors of life history or ethnography can use vivid emotive detail to 'convert' readers to their ways of thinking and theorising.

The chapters which follow thus draw inspiration freely from the hermeneutic tradition: the importance of integrating crime with specific social and environmental milieux is emphasised through-out, though the (actual and potential) victims of crime receive greater attention than has been usual in ethnographic studies; interpretative methods allow an appreciation of crime as it both reflects and affects a wider structure of social relations; ethno-graphic research allows the stark realities of crime in an ailing economy supporting high rates of unemployment to be examined in terms meaningful to those it affects.

The knowledge generated by humanistic research, committed to interpretative understanding, nevertheless seems limited in its application by the practical interests expressed in the analyst's quest for intersubjectivity. Often, the whole notion of crime and deviance is challenged, so that interpretative research stops short of inform-ing crime-control policy; offering insights into the world of deviance but failing to pass judgement on offenders and unable to prescribe policy-relevant action. It is perhaps for this reason that applied geographers have favoured the empirical-analytical tradition of criminological research: not only is it more obviously spatial; it also promises to make geography more useful. This assurance, however, is one which reckons without the advent of critical theory which has turned criminology's conventional presuppositions on their head.

Critical criminology

A critical approach to the analysis of deviance seeks to expose the tacit assumptions and biases of research in which the definition and meaning of crime appears unproblematic. In part, this may be read as a logical extension of the interactionists' labelling theories. Fundamentally, however, critical criminology marks a significant break with the historical-hermeneutic tradition, seeking a holism in its analysis of crime and society that is quite at odds with the presup-positions of classical ethnography and life-history research as discussed earlier. Interactionism acknowledges many realities and claims a monopoly on none. Its world is emergent and capricious, defined and structured only through direct experience. Critical theory attempts to transcend the limits of experience, addressing directly the *a priori* conditions of possible knowledge. From the out-set, critical criminology demanded that 'Laws and rules, rather than defining the boundaries of criminology, now had to be included within criminological explanations. Criminology was forced to encompass the political nature of deviance and its control, and so examine the relationship between theory and ideology' (Wiles 1976: 17). If interactionism's labelling perspective appears to speak the same language as critical theory, it is probably because 'criminology began to develop a radical vocabulary before it had developed radical theories' (Wiles 1976: 9). The more sceptical interactionists may have sown the seeds of critical criminology, but those who followed brought with them a quite different set of interests.

Taylor, Walton and Young (1975) argue that critical criminology should be normatively committed to the abolition of inequalities in wealth and power, with the aim of creating 'the kind of society in which the facts of human diversity are not subject to the power to criminalize' (Taylor et al. 1975: 44). The interest they express is emancipatory: freeing analysts to question the (legal) norms which, in the broadest sense, create crime; freeing those most likely to be processed by the criminal justice system to help define the kinds of behaviour that should be outlawed. Notwithstanding the wide variety of radical and critical perspectives, a major shared priority is to reconceptualise the definition of crime in terms of the violation of human rights. This is a move which Taylor et al. (1975) see as increasingly urgent as the law is extended to control essentially political acts with the consequence that the potentially criminal population is widened.

Critical theorists are divided, however, as to the point of departure for their radical, usually socialist, critiques. Young (1979) identifies two strong currents within this literature: left idealism and reformism. Left idealism identifies the law as an expression of ruling-class interests. As such, the law is necessarily violated by working-class behaviour which expresses 'proletarian' interests at odds with those of the lawmakers. According to this perspective, crime is normal (i.e. not 'deviant'), since 'a society which is predicated on the unequal right to the accumulation of property *gives rise to* the legal and illegal desire to accumulate property as rapidly as possible' (Taylor et al. 1975: 34).

Geography's critical spokesman on criminological research, Richard Peet, adopts the perspective of left idealism (see Peet 1975, 1976). For Peet, crime is the surface expression of discontent deeply embedded within a social system. The incidence of crime mirrors the geography of the class system; the directedness of offending reflects the spatial dynamics of class conflict. Peet's view, like that of other left idealists, is that crime is a proto-revolutionary flicker of class consciousness, challenging the property relations set up under capitalism. But his conclusions are naive and empirically questionable:

When property and possessions are allocated extremely unequally, yet everyone is taught to value them, we can expect informal devices to develop by which the poor attempt to even up the distribution. Thus, the potential arises for illicit flows of possessions from areas of surplus to areas of want. Interclass crime is a way of freeing property so that it can flow across space. (Peet 1976:99)

The too-appealing assumption of left idealism is that crime reflects the extent to which the distribution of property is accepted or rejected by the working class. This political explanation is easily criticised since most empirical evidence shows that the majority of crime occurs between people with *similar* socio-economic characteristics. Peet's neat geography of crime does not exist, and it seems inconceivable that crime – which is, after all, a socially defined phenomenon, recognised well before the advent of capitalism – would be eradicated in a fully socialist world. A second approach within critical criminology tempers the easily questioned idealism of such a position and offers a more fruitful way forward.

The view of the critical reformists is broader and more plausible than that of the idealists. The reformists accept that deviance will occur in any social order, even though its present excessive rate might be attributable to a particular stage in the development of national and international economies. Amongst geographers, perhaps Lowman (1982) has come closest to expressing this view. It is a civil libertarian perspective which might be seen as an extension of what Taylor et al. (1975) term 'exposé criminology'. This latter movement first challenged the degree to which crime committed by middle- and upper-class offenders went undetected. The early research was not fully critical in that moral indignation often replaced analytical argument: amazement at the double standards of those in authority produced a literature laced with emotive rhetoric and unable to address the critical questions of reform or transformation. Today, however, socialist reformism recognises crime as a problem for all social classes, both privileged and underprivileged, arguing that a rational response to this problem is denied by flaws in legal administration (which currently discriminates against the least powerful). Most energy on the part of the reformists, therefore, is devoted to the quest for an equitable distribution of justice, on the assumption that this might be achieved through changes in law enforcement policy and practice.

Left idealists and socialist reformists both identify a gap between the theory and practice of law enforcement; both expose a bias in the criminal justice system against the poor. The idealists' solution is to create a society in which criminal law is unnecessary. Reformists advocate, rather, that the content of the law should be re-evaluated and reformulated so that it no longer reinforces the inequalities that permeate class-based societies. Young (1979) argues that neither solution is wholly adequate and that truly critical theory should strive for even more fundamental changes in the form of the law. He believes that a critical perspective should indicate ways in which present legal norms could be transcended to allow legislation to be addressed to new, more radical principles, such as the allocation of collective responsibilities for deviance.

The emphasis of a still-developing critical tradition has thus moved away from the analysis of crime towards a critique of the law which defines it (and which may be used to wield power and exercise control). The consequences of this for geographical studies of deviance are hinted at by Lowman (1982). Critical criminology recognises that the organisation of intellectual activity is shaped by historically specific social forces, and asserts that valid enquiry requires these forces to be self-consciously exposed and written into the analysis. This is why Booth, Mayhew and Alinsky could not be described as critical, even though they were all aware of the class bias of legal injustice. A fully critical criminology is free to ask questions concerning the origins and legitimacy of authority; it must explore the relationships between law and politics; it is free to challenge the law when it serves the interests of some groups rather than others.

Prospectus

In this book, I do not offer a critique of the institutionalised norms that define criminal behaviour, although it is as well that the reader remains alert to the fact that definitions of crime and criminals are relative, negotiable and frequently questionable. I do, however, aim to expose some of the socio-economic inequalities reflected in the incidence of crime, and I will argue that these same inequalities in the distribution of power and wealth help to account for the effects of fear and the nature of social responses to perceived deviance.

Primarily, my concern is to resolve some of the differences between critical theory and hermeneutic enquiry by examining how structural factors influencing the distribution of crime and criminal sanctions are translated into the daily life of a general public. This process could not, however, be appreciated without taking full account of contemporary empirical-analytical studies, since these work with the data that inform public policy and provide the basis of crime's 'social reality'.

I attempt in this book to set crime in its widest social context, treating it, wherever possible, as one of a number of local problems, as one element in a multifaceted structure of social relations, as one medium through which the uncertainties of modern urban life are experienced. For, despite its current isolation in the academic division of labour, the notion of criminality is one of the most pervasive and enduring elements of civilisation: it reflects and affects the very substance of the built and social environments.

Deviance is everywhere and it leaves its traces everywhere. It marks those who report it, those who attempt to control it, those who gain from it, those who suffer from it, those who imaginatively describe it, and the contexts in which it is accomplished. Properly read, almost every man-made environment can be interpreted as a record of the effects and responses which deviance produces. (Downes and Rock 1982: 410)

Assenting to the importance of integrating analyses of crime and deviance with an appreciation of the structure and meaning of social relations, chapter 2 begins by examining the directives for future research to be gleaned from the three interest-related modes of enquiry considered above. So far, the realist tradition of areal and ecological analysis has not produced any coherent theoretical explanation of the relationships between crime, space and society. At the city scale, spatial perspectives often provide only a geometric framework for the arrangement of criminal statistics, constructed with a view to controlling the form rather than grasping the meaning of crime in society. On the other hand, those perspectives which expose the theoretical limitations of these empirical-analytical studies have rarely been considered in terms of their spatial dimensions. A juxtaposition of the work of geography's 'direct realists' with that of criminology's phenomenological 'institutionalists' is fruitful, however, since the practical recommendations of both schools regarding progress in the analysis of deviance are similar: both stress the importance of specifying the political and economic context of enquiry; both demand that greater attention be paid to the small-scale behaviour patterns and relationships that contribute to the construction of larger-scale patterns of deviance. These two directives guide the development of chapters 3 to 7.

Chapter 3 establishes that the residents of Britain's inner cities experience the highest rates of crime, whether measured by police statistics or victimisation surveys. Certainly, these high rates cannot be portrayed merely as an artifact of official crime figures. Acknowledging that there are working-class areas with high crime rates throughout urban Britain (including a number of peripheral council housing estates), I use the example of Britain's inner cities generally, and of a neighbourhood in north central Birmingham in particular, to illustrate the causes and consequences of crime at a declining edge of the British economy. My argument is that these areas express most acutely some of the less desirable effects of current socio-economic and political change, and that a specific case study might be used to expose – much as a prism refracts a beam of light into its constituent colours – the effects of crime as one phenomenon mediating between structured inequality and the form of local social relations.

In developing this case study, my interests are both practical and technical. Having spent two years as a resident of the Birmingham study area, I would hope to discuss the issue of crime in terms meaningful to those it affects. In one sense, public experiences and perceptions provide the most authentic definitions available of the crime problem. As such, commonsense understandings of deviance are of interest in their own right. In translating these understandings for planners and policy-makers, my further aim is to seek solutions to a national problem of law and order that are politically and financially viable yet sensitive to local needs.

High inner-city crime rates are accounted for in chapters 3 and 4 in terms of high rates of offender residence, a vulnerable built environment, and other locational disadvantages which exacerbate the risks of victimisation. Chapter 4 focusses specifically on the victims of crime, who, until recently, were relatively neglected in British criminology. Some aspects of victims' lifestyles, and other attributes affecting peoples' vulnerability, are examined. This investigation raises a number of questions about the relationship between crime and the concept of social harm.

Harsh though the realities of high crime rates can be for vulnerable populations, the spectre of inner-city criminality also has a popular public image sustained by the mass media. Through processes discussed in chapter 5, this image, too, is worked into the received wisdom of neighbourhood life. As a consequence of this and a combination of other factors associated with social stress and environmental decay, the fear of crime can gain some independence from the risks of victimisation. In the inner cities at least, such fear can adversely affect the quality of social life.

Chapter 6 considers a variety of policy responses to the social and statistical realities of crime in modern Britain. It examines the processes through which some communities have become alienated from the professional agents of law enforcement, and concludes that, despite much effort and goodwill, there is a rift between the police and the public in a number of urban areas which shows few signs of healing. Some possible routes towards reconciliation are considered, including a strengthening of the bases of police accountability, and a multi-agency approach to the problem of law and order.

Notwithstanding enhanced public confidence in the police, the management of danger in everyday life is often primarily a matter of developing informal crime-prevention strategies. A range of these is discussed in chapter 7 in an argument which moves beyond commonsense perceptions and understandings towards a critical appreciation of the unacknowledged causes and unintended consequences of informal reactions to crime. An attempt is made to integrate theoretically the study of crime and its effects with a broader appreciation of the nature of social organisation and change. The argument of chapters 2 and 3 is pursued to its conclusion, exposing studies of deviance as a medium through which the link between national political economies and the form of local social relations can be traced. This link is implicit in many criminological theories of interest to geographers; to expose and explore it will be to broaden the scope of the geography of crime.

2

On proceeding with the analysis of crime and society

Realism vs. institutionalism: constructive compromise?

It is apparent from chapter 1 that the history of criminological research embodies both a debate amongst interests and a confrontation of philosophical presuppositions. It can be read as a dialogue between those (direct realists) who seek to better specify (and thus more adequately explain) a true figure of crime, and those (interactionists or 'institutionalists') who deny the validity of such an exercise on the grounds that criminality is not a thing in itself but a property attributed to people on the basis of non-legal as well as legal criteria.

Direct realism has been identified as the guiding philosophy of most areal and ecological studies of crime. It encourages a search for the observable correlates of deviance, and demands information on the elusive 'dark figure' of unreported and undetected offences. Together, these facts provide the key to understanding, and the potential to assuage, the problem of crime in society. The institutionalist perspective is informed by humanistic philosophies ranging from existentialism to Marxian humanism, and within this framework crime has no 'objective' reality; it is, rather, the negotiable product of formal responses to deviant actions: 'The hallmarks of the realists are the prevalence of criminals and their acts of crime; more recently victims. The hallmarks of the institutionalists are the prevalence of only such of these as survive institutional validation' (Biderman and Reiss 1967: 9). These very different traditions of criminological research co-exist uneasily, as analysts seek to advance technical, policy-orientated interests on the one hand, and either practical or emancipatory interests on the other. Spatial studies, however, have usually avoided the conflict this implies by affiliating primarily with the spirit (if not the precise detail) of direct realism.

Realist and institutionalist approaches to the analysis of crime are commonly treated as mutually exclusive, and in so far as their philosophical presuppositions express different beliefs about the nature of reality, this is justified. Yet analysts need not be constrained to assume that knowledge yielded by one perspective is any less authentic than that of the other. Hindelang (1978), for instance, prefers to differentiate between realism and institutionalism in terms of a continuum of explanations for deviance rather than in terms of a sharp dichotomy. Such explanations would adopt theoretical positions ranging from those which define criminality as a property of an act or event, to those which define it as a product of differential processing in the criminal justice system. Theories explaining the incidence of crime in terms of the defensibility of space or the lifestyles of victims would stand at one end of the spectrum; labelling theories invoking the notion of 'secondary' deviance (offences committed to fulfil the behavioural expectations implied in a criminal label) would stand at the other. Most theories would fall somewhere between these two extremes and the appropriateness of those explanations occupying one position rather than another on the continuum could be assessed through empirical research (acknowledging that such explanations might be time, place and culture specific).

It would be wrong, then, to deny any scope for rapprochement between the ostensibly conflicting traditions of realism and institutionalism. In fact, in recent years, the continued refinement of both positions has produced remarkably similar trends in so far as the practicalities of research are concerned. This is true regarding both the scale and thematic content of analysis, as sketched below for each tradition in turn.

Direct realism and the geography of crime

Realists rarely quibble with the authenticity of official crime statistics, but they do not doubt that such figures give only a partial view of crime in society. To exploit the full potential of the realist perspective, therefore, it has seemed appropriate to begin to bring the dark figure of unreported and undetected offences into statistical light. Such a task is obviously important, for while a dark figure remains some offenders will go unnoticed, police resources may be misallocated, and the plight of victims will tend to be underestimated: 'errors in our knowledge of the volume and distribution of criminal incidents may considerably disguise human misery and limit our ability to understand even the most basic facts about society' (Skogan 1977: 43).

One means of supplementing police statistics is to collect data from other agencies, who collate certain types of criminal incidents for their own administrative purposes. The procedure can be illustrated with reference to the areal data collected as part of my own research in Birmingham. Here, seven alternative indicators of crime were available, as listed in table 2.1. A visual comparison of the distribution of selected official and unofficial crime rates is given in figure 1.

The official picture is one in which city-centre wards emerge as the highest rate areas for personal crimes (per person), burglaries (per dwelling) and the areal concentration of offences (crimes per unit area). A band of high personal crime rates runs from the south-east central to north-west central wards, while the areas most prone to burglary spread further to the north-east, and extend across the affluent south-west sector of the city. The most intense areal concentrations of crime are, by contrast, confined to a central wedge running from the south-east to the north-west.

A composite index of telephone crimes (combining, within exchange areas, rates of telephone-box vandalism and of malicious false alarms), mirrors the official pattern of high rates extending through north central Birmingham. It departs from the official picture in terms of the relatively under-represented central city zones (partly due to the introduction of specially strengthened cash boxes in these exchange areas), and in the high rates found in the east and south. The map of assaults on bus drivers also shows a tendency for crime to cluster in north central and north-west central neighbourhoods. Although no diagram is offered for the distribution of parks vandalism (whose locations depend on the distribution of parks, so that no meaningful base rate could be devised by ward), the pattern of inner-city concentration is reinforced by the knowledge that the five inner-area parks, which form 7.5 per cent of the total listed (66) account for over a quarter (27.7 per cent) of the criminal incidents collated by the city's Amenities and Recreation Department.

The pattern of doubtful fires and damage to 'road furniture' owned by the public transport authorities both offer a slightly different view. Central wards (especially to the north and west) are still over-represented, but so are a number of suburban wards. Perhaps there are more opportunities for damaging road furniture

Table 2.1 *Sources of 'unofficial' crime statistics in Birmingham, 1978 and 1979*

Crime type	Source	Time period (months)	Areal units	Total incidents	Rate (where applicable)
Telephone box vandalism	Post Office engineers' returns	18	Individual call boxes; exchange areas	7934	4.3 per box, 441 per month, in city area
Malicious false alarms	West Midlands Fire Service,[1] operators' sheets for emergency calls	14	Exchange areas	2351	1.3 per call-box, 168 per month
Doubtful[2] fires	West Midlands Fire Service, 'reports of fires' by chief officer at incident	22	Fire location	512	23.3 per month
Wilful damage to parks	Amenities and recreation department of the city council	18	Park location	419	23.3 per month, 6.4 per park/ recreation ground
Damage to road furniture	WMPTE[3] damage records	20	Location of damaged item	753	31.4 per month
Criminal incidents on buses	WMPTE divisional operations managers' reports	24	Bus routes	896	37.3 per month
Assaults on bus drivers	WMPTE incident reports	24	Location of incident	99	4 per month, 2 per 100 employees

[1] False alarms are divided into those due to faulty apparatus, those made with good intent, and those thought to be malicious. The last of these is recorded above.

[2] Doubtful fires cannot be shown to have begun accidentally, but neither is there conclusive proof of arson.

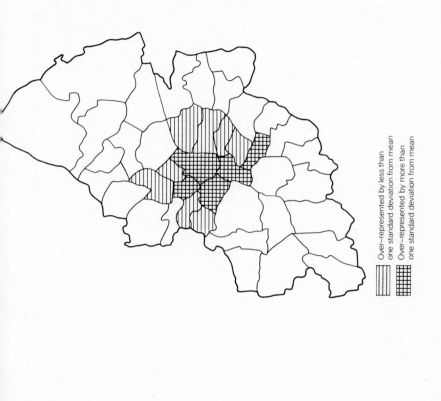

Personal
crime rate

☐ Over-represented by less than
   one standard deviation from mean

☐ Over-represented by more than
   one standard deviation from mean

Burglary rate

☐ Over-represented by less than
   one standard deviation from mean

☐ Over-represented by more than
   one standard deviation from mean

(1) Over-representation of personal crime rates and
    burglary rates, by ward.

☐ Over-represented by less than
   one standard deviation from mean

☐ Over-represented by more than
   one standard deviation from mean

(2) Over-representation of the areal concentration
    of crime, by ward.

Fig. 1. Spatial distribution of official and unofficial crime rates in
Birmingham

31

(4) Assaults on bus drivers employed by the West Midlands Passenger Transport Executive 1978–9.

——— Birmingham City boundary

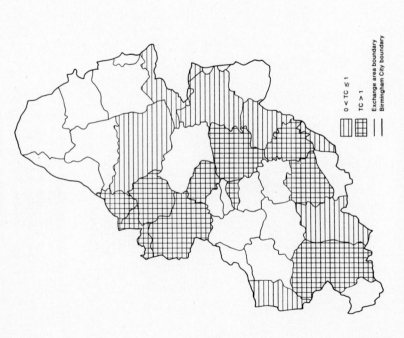

(3) Over-representation (standard deviations from mean) of telephone crime (TC), by exchange area.

0 < TC ≤ 1

TC > 1

——— Exchange area boundary

——— Birmingham City boundary

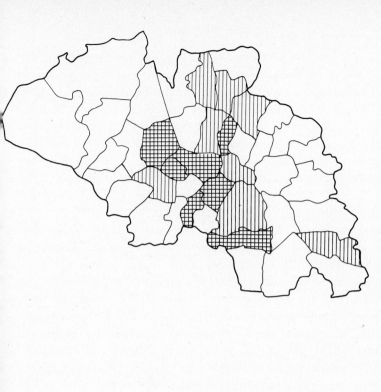

(5) Over-representation (per hectare) of doubtful fires, by ward.

(6) Over-representation of damaged road furniture
(per head of population), by ward.

Fig. 1 (cont.). Spacial distribution of official and unofficial crime rates in
Birmingham

33

in the suburbs, where shelters are less intensely used (and therefore less defended by potential witnesses). Perhaps, too, fire officers do not expect deviance in many suburbs, and prefer to save embarrassment by initially using the flexible term 'doubtful' to describe suspicious fires in these areas, rather than applying the decisive label 'arson'. But this can only be speculation, and in terms of the consistently high rates observed in the inner city (and to some extent in the north central sector as a whole), the patterns of official and 'unofficial' crime do not seem that incongruous. Mawby (1978, 1979b) drew similar conclusions in Sheffield.

Probably the major value of these alternative crime data is the novel perspective they present on the nature and extent of deviant acts. They certainly offer a sobering view of the consequences of such actions. The total cost of repairing vandalised telephone boxes in 1978 and 1979, for instance, came to £31 755.47, more than half of which was labour costs. Similarly, in 1978, the Amenities and Recreation Department spent £15 466 on repairing the targets of wilful damage. The harm to life and property caused by the absence of fire crews unnecessarily responding to false alarms is unquantifiable, but has potentially grave consequences.

Yet, only a few such sources of supplementary data will ever be available to fulfil the realist ideal. It is hard, too, to imagine that the effort and expense of systematically collating such data over long time periods will justify the limited additions made to the official picture. The total number of unofficial incidents documented in the Birmingham study (12 964) adds a mere 4.3 per cent to the officially recorded total. This is hardly a sufficient basis from which to question findings based on crimes known to the police. Moreover, it can be argued that by relying on the routine administration of these other agencies to define crime, any bias introduced by one bureaucratic organisation (the police) is merely replaced by that of another, yielding figures just as far removed from the social context in which they are generated.

Some of these criticisms have been avoided by a second popular means of supplementing official crime statistics, which involves surveys of potential offender and victim populations. Initially, such research compared the crime rates of self-admitted delinquents with those of convicted criminals. Later (during the 1960s) the emphasis gradually shifted towards random household surveys (crime surveys) designed to elicit a measure of the incidence of crime based on the experience of victims, whether or not such experiences were reported to, or recorded by, the police. This approach, much more than recourse to the informal statistics of other agencies, seems likely to enhance our understanding of the incidence and effects of crime, and subsequent chapters draw freely from information provided by national and local crime surveys in Britain.

Crime surveys, however, seem as unlikely to yield a 'true' figure of crime as do the reports of non-police public authorities.* Indeed, the more research that takes place, the less attainable in practice seems the theoretical ideal of the realists. What survey techniques do offer, however, and what is not provided by other statistical sources, is a fuller appreciation of the behavioural precursors and social effects of victimisation. This is a step nearer to fulfilling realism's criteria for explanation, which demand a move beyond surface appearances to explore the underlying mechanisms which link the incidence of crime with the environment it arises from. The advent of the crime survey might therefore be taken as an acknowledgement that if areal analysts are truly to work in the spirit of direct realism, it will be necessary to shift the focus of empirical research away from descriptive mapping and towards an explanatory understanding of the variable processes from which mappable statistics arise.

The move towards smaller-scale, in-depth study is also demanded if a second string to the realists' bow – ecological analysis – is to be brought into tune. Chapter 1 identified three persistent themes emerging from the multivariate studies of the 1960s (studies which, but for such consistency, might have been condemned to the archives of analytical dead ends). Brief consideration of these three enduring foci is sufficient to indicate that progress in the spatial analysis of crime requires both a change of scale and a shift of thematic emphasis.

The first and most contentious theme concerns the notion of 'social disorganisation'. One of the most powerful predictors (statistically) of urban crime rates has been a factor or principal component whose constituent variables remind analysts of the nature of deviance in early twentieth-century Chicago, and so invite the label 'social disorganisation'. The measures such a label summarises usually include some indicator of the presence of immigrant groups or racial minorities, together with indices of overcrowding, mobility

---

* They rarely detect corporate or victimless offences, and they are subject to the human errors of forgetfulness and forward telescoping which are so unpredictable as to defy all attempts to accommodate them in weighting algorithms (see Levine 1976, Schneider and Sumi 1981).

and poor housing. Too often, unfortunately, the term refers to complex multivariate factors whose interpretation otherwise defies analysts' imaginations. It can be an inappropriate and insensitive descriptor of minority groups and the underprivileged, and Whyte (1961) suggests its use indicates only that observers have failed to understand their subject matter. If 'social disorganisation' has any significance in relation to crime rates, this is no longer apparent from summary spatial statistics. Its salience can, however, be appreciated with recourse to the insights of those who first identified the condition which merited this unfortunate but curiously enduring term.

For W. I. Thomas, social disorganisation was not a set of abstract empirical measures. Rather, it denoted a condition (which these measures might roughly describe in space) arising out of various combinations of subtly negotiated attitudes and values. Wirth (1910, 1939), too, envisaged social disorganisation as a product of the tensions generated by shifts of allegiance between contradictory systems of norms. Such tensions might occur in societies undergoing rapid change through processes such as migration, or in societies where more than one independent system of norms prevails.

A key point to be gleaned from examining the comments of these early theorists is that social disorganisation was essentially conceived of as a complex set of interpersonal relationships which helped explain broad spatial regularities between urban structures and social phenomena, including crime rates. If it merits attention as a descriptor of crime rates in urban areas, it cannot stand apart from a more detailed evaluation of the quality, quantity and consequences of the processes of social interaction which construct larger-scale crime patterns. 'Social disorganisation' is a complex concept encapsulating the subtle nuances of exchange amongst culturally diverse populations. The origins of what has today been reduced to a convenient (and, as such, discredited) label, reflects an early appreciation of the need to understand broad ecological analyses in terms of a more enigmatic structure of social relations underlying them.

A second theme running through the multivariate ecological analyses of the 1960s and early 1970s is reflected in a fierce but inconclusive debate questioning the relevance of crowding and density as predictors of crime (cf. Choldin 1975). A review by Freedman (1975) illuminates well the inconsistencies in the literature on this theme (see also Kirmeyer 1978). While both population density (people per unit area) and crowding (persons per occupied room) have been included in ecological studies, it is usually the latter that is most strongly associated with crime (e.g. Roncek 1975; Harries 1980). There is no consensus on the relevance of this, however, and Verbrugge and Taylor (1980) have suggested that the pathological significance of city *size* is more marked than that of density. Other studies, correlating the *inverse* of crowding with crime rates, have lead McCarthy et al. (1975) to explore the criminogenic role of personal isolation in dense urban areas.

Quite what the ecological relations between density and crime mean, and how to explain them, remains contentious. Although both Simmel and Wirth lingered over the social implications of the increasing spatial concentration of populations, neither theorist explicitly associated crowding and density with crime. Most speculation about any such causal link stems rather from more recent controversial claims by ethologists such as Calhoun (1962), Ardrey (1966) and Morris (1969), based on animal experiments. The problem of vindicating or refuting their theses is that ecological studies have always been, and remain, unable to answer questions concerning the effects of dense urban environments on distinctively human social relations. Again, therefore, theoretical speculation prompted by the descriptive links amongst aggregated crime and environmental variables requires, for its substantiation, an evaluation of the form and meaning of individual patterns of social exchange.

A third persistent theme concerns the ecological relationships between class, economy and crime. For many years, and despite earnest sociological interest generated by class-based theories of delinquency, empirical research consistently failed to establish meaningful relationships between the economic characteristics of urban areas and crime rates (cf. Polk 1967). A few exceptions may be found (e.g. Corsi and Harvey's (1975) analysis in Cleveland), but often ecological analysts concerned with the importance of class have turned to a more readily demonstrable link between offender residence rates and housing tenure, so avoiding the controversy over economic class and crime (see Baldwin and Bottoms 1976; Herbert 1979; chapter 3, below).

Recently, however, analyses of the relationship between economic indicators and crime have relied on better specified models than their predecessors (Berger 1980). New findings attest to the strength of those relationships between crime rates and the economy whose empirical vindication once seemed in doubt. The contribution of econometrics has been to revitalise theories linking crime with economic indicators. Realist explanations of deviance, traditionally couched in terms of individual and social pathology, the built environment and the density and heterogeneity of the population must, it seems, now be broadened to include the role of the economy.

Methodologically, then, the realist tradition can progress only when the significance of associations between urban environments and crime rates is appreciated through detailed case studies of the social processes captured in summary statistical indicators (a move urged by Baldwin (1975), Harries (1974) and Herbert (1977)). **Thematically**, the early musings of Quetelet (1842), Clay (1855) and the Chicago ecologists concerning possible relationships between crime and economy are once again becoming topical, and the realist must reconsider the theoretical speculations of these nineteenth-century 'armchair' criminologists whose thoughts have endured for so long while awaiting empirical validation.

The institutionalist perspective

Progress amongst the institutionalists hinges on very similar research directives. This perspective has long preferred to interpret official crime statistics as 'behaviour that is responded to'. To this end, however, analysts have tended to concentrate almost exclusively on the later stages of the processing of suspected or convicted offenders, and on the abstract notion of the law itself. Yet, the discussion below suggests that, at every stage, the findings of the institutionalist tradition direct research towards the general public rather than official lawbrokers as the touchstone of the criminal justice system.

Of course, the definition of crime and criminals must depend ultimately on the criminal law, which is culture-specific and varies over space and in time. Indeed, Lowman (1982) has chastised geographers for failing explicitly to recognise the law as one of the most important components of the social environment of crime. Although the effects of legal difference are relatively easy to explore in the USA, where individual states have a considerable amount of legal autonomy (see Harries and Brunn 1978), Britain has a unified criminal justice system in which disparities in the dispensation of justice must arise not so much from the differential distribution of laws as from the different consequences of violating these laws. Thus, sentencing disparities have been a subject of much interest. It is only since the mid-1970s, however, that concerns have broadened beyond merely monitoring the different attitudes of individual magistrates (see Carlen 1976; Paterson 1974; Wilson 1973). Davidson (1977), for instance, postulates that within a city, sentences will reflect the relationship between courts and the communities they serve. His approach is innovative, although he found no spatial variations in sentencing to correspond with expected differences according to the different housing environments of offenders. Nor did Baldwin and McConville (1977), in their comparison of black and white defendants, find any bias in the post-conviction treatment of offenders. If justice is meted equitably after conviction, it must be at the earlier stages of the law enforcement and judicial process that the source of any discrimination lies. Recognition of this is reflected in the recent surge of interest in the phenomenon of plea bargaining.

In Britain, as in North America, a steady flow of guilty pleas is necessary to prevent serious congestion in the courts. British researchers have only recently begun to suspect that these pleas might not accurately reflect the culpability of offenders (although the theme has become very popular amongst academics in the USA). Perhaps the most comprehensive analysis in this country is concerned with the outcome of contested trials in Birmingham's Crown Court. Baldwin and McConville (1977) were alerted to the bargaining process by the large proportion (over 10 per cent) of guilty pleas which involve a late change of plea from not guilty. Their research suggests that this is not always a function of the defendant's conscience. Rather, late changes of plea reflect pressures exerted by the organisational requirements of a crowded criminal justice system which is forced to allow substantial sentencing discount in order to secure sufficient guilty pleas. The 'bargaining' procedure, which encourages defendants to take advantage of this discount, encompasses not only negotiations of a give-and-take nature, but also 'the use of inducements, pressures of an extreme kind, and, as defendants see it, even moral blackmail' (Baldwin and McConville 1977: 6).

A consequence of the system described above is that individual defendants will often find it more convenient and less traumatic to plead guilty, irrespective of their desire to contest the case. One obvious implication of this is that, given that a proportion of convictions can be so arbitrary, the role of the police in differentially introducing people into the higher echelons of the criminal justice process takes on added significance.

The decision to implement formal or informal proceedings against offenders rests largely with the police, and analysts have been concerned about the criteria upon which such decisions are based. Preliminary studies of cautioning do reveal some social bias in this practice (Farrington and Bennett 1981; Landau 1981; Landau and Nathan 1983; Fisher and Mawby 1982), although Mawby (1979b) found few parallel spatial disparities when comparing the rate of cautioning between high and low offender-rate areas in owner-occupied, private rental and council housing districts (the exception to this was adult males, who were more likely to be cautioned – rather than prosecuted – if they lived in owner-occupied areas, than if they came from council estates).

Variations in police efficiency might also be expected to affect crime detection rates (i.e. the rate at which crimes are solved), and in this respect the police will have some control over the number of offenders in different areas who are arrested or proceeded against. Furthermore differences in police practice, particularly concerning the deployment of officers, are likely to influence the discovery and recording of crime. Although Mawby (1979b) is doubtful that this distorts the incidence of a broad spectrum of crimes, Lowman (1982) points out that for those offences (such as drugs and prostitution) whose discovery depends almost exclusively on police observations, discretionary powers can significantly affect crime rates and distributions.

The key point here, however, is that the proportion of police crime discoveries is very small (less than one crime in seven). This has prompted both Chatterton (1976) and Mawby (1979b) to conclude that many disparities traditionally interpreted as the product of police discretion must actually be attributed to citizen discretion. It is the public who largely control police access to crime-related information, providing the bulk of officials' raw material about the incidence of crime and the characteristics of suspects, and determining whether or not a large proportion of crimes ever come to the notice of the police. Thus, the institutionalist perspective ultimately hinges on an understanding of public behaviour, and with realism, it is forced to take full account of the detailed processes of interpersonal interaction that produce criminal events and known offenders. Institutionalism, too, comes increasingly to stress small-ness of scale and contextual detail as a means of ensuring rigour, coherence and credibility of analysis.

The institutionalist perspective, though forced to acknowledge its roots in an oral-ethnographic understanding of public life, also recognises the salience of economic relations. Although the approach affiliates with a theory of knowledge that is reluctant to admit to the existence of real structural constraints on the form of social relations, the incorporation of interactionism into criminology's institutionalist movement demands of the former explicit recognition of the significance of power relations within the law enforcement and criminal justice systems. As Downes and Rock (1982: 47) point out in support of the institutionalist perspective, 'In complex societies the distribution of deviant phenomena is closely linked to the distribution of power and life chances.' Since so many facets of modern life reflect economically prescribed class differences, it would be surprising if the dispensation of criminal justice did not do likewise. Thus, Engels's nineteenth-century insights concerning the links between crime and economy now merit rediscovery by those concerned with the association between social class and criminality sustained at various levels in the criminal justice system.

In short, realists and institutionalists agree on two key issues: analytically they recognise the importance of detailed studies of the processes of interaction which generate crime and ideas about crime; thematically, both traditions assert the relevance to criminological research of the class structure and political economy. Recently, the first of these mandates has received some attention, as analysts focus increasingly on the incidence and meaning of crime within single cities or neighbourhoods. This has been extremely fruitful. In Britain, for instance, Bottoms and Xanthos (1981) and Baldwin (1974b) have investigated the role of the housing market in the segregation of offenders in Sheffield; Mawby (1977a) and Mayhew (1979, 1981) have focussed on the significance of social and defensible space for local crime prevention; Herbert (1982) and Hyde (1982) have tested the relative efficacy of 'border zone', 'socio-economic heterogeneity' and 'defensible space' hypotheses as an explanation for intra-urban variations in property crime; Evans (1980) has compared social disorganisation, subculture and differential opportunity/status frustration theories in an attempt to account for juvenile delinquency in Cardiff; and I have examined the effects of crime on the quality of interpersonal relationships in Birmingham (Smith 1984a). Similar examples could be drawn from the American literature.

Theoretical achievements notwithstanding, such micro-analytical approaches have rarely, so far, been set in the context of relationships between national crime trends and regional or local socio-economic indicators. Effectively, in furthering the practical recommendations of previous research (concerning scales of analysis), these in-depth studies have glossed over the second, thematic, point of convergence between institutionalism and realism, namely, renewed emphasis on relationships between crime rates and the economy. The chapters which follow begin to redress this imbalance, stressing the importance of approaching local case studies with a theoretical perspective broad enough to place regional crime trends in the context of a national economy, and to interpret national crime trends in terms of the world economy. The aim here is not to invalidate or denegrate intensive small-scale enquiries as studies of importance in their own right. It is, rather, to provide a more coherent framework within which to assess the significance of such research by examining crime as a contingency of social and political-economic organisation. This chapter concludes, therefore, first by assessing the significance of global crime trends, and, finally, by examining the role of crime in modern capitalist democracies, which provide the broad political-economic context of the case studies which follow.

Crime and economy

Recent interest in relationships between crime rates and the economy revives a nineteenth-century insistence, noted in chapter 1, on examining crime rates in terms of their total societal context. The reintroduction of this holistic perspective is perhaps most explicit in the work of Shelley (1981a, 1981b), but it is part of a more general desire to strengthen the theoretical base of criminology.

Bottomley (1979: 70) attributes many theoretical problems of modern criminology to the discipline's neglect of some fundamental issues in the philosophy of the social sciences. A crucial consequence of this is identified by Shelley as the time, space and culture boundedness of the most popular theories of deviance (a limitation affirmed in DeFleur's (1967) cross-cultural ecological analysis of delinquency). In seeking a broader explanatory framework, Shelley makes the following generalisations about most existing theories of deviance:

They apply only to the changes that have accompanied the process of modernization ... [they] ... merely explain the dynamics of crime in the present urban environment. They focus on the dynamics of individual crime commission, the impact of urban decay, and the increased opportunities of city life for the attainment of success. They do not examine the transformation of crime in the rural environment or the dislocation of crime from rural to urban areas, nor do they provide an overall theoretical framework to explain the emergence of new categories of criminal offenders, like juveniles and females, in the period since the advent of the industrial revolution. (Shelley 1981a: 13)

Shelly goes on to suggest that all existing major theories of crime commission may be subsumed within a more general 'modernisation theory', linking crime, society and economic change. On the basis of an extensive cross-cultural literature search, Shelley proposes that crime rates can be interpreted as a barometer of the problems associated with development. Variations in the processes of economic change explain differences in the character of crime between socialist nations, developing nations and modern western societies:

Violent criminality is both a symptom of rural life as well as an indication of the problems associated with the adjustment to urban life. Property crime is a natural consequence of modern urban settlement with its emphasis on material goods unequally distributed to all inhabitants. The crime rate and the relationship between property and violent crime provide indices of a society's transition towards modernization. (Shelley 1981a: 37)

A similar argument was advanced a decade earlier by Wolf (1971), who found a positive relationship between trends in an international set of crime statistics (from Interpol) and indices of development such as industrialisation, urbanisation, mortality, wealth, literacy and technological advance. He concluded that societies' crime rates increase overall with development, although the ratio of the murder rate to property crime declines.

Modern theorists have also used Durkheim's notions of social change to explain some variations in the rates of deviance that seem to accompany industrialisation. Durkheim proposed that, as communities develop, their mode of integration changes from 'mechanical' solidarity (based on normative consensus) to 'organic' solidarity (based on contractual relations). Since this change is accompanied by a flourishing of individual variety which may not be normatively regulated, the possibilities for deviance increase. Analysts have not always found this argument easy to test empirically, however, and while Webb (1972) finds support for the hypothesis that crime rates increase as the division of labour proceeds, Krohn (1978) is unable to express the same confidence in the Durkheimian model.

Authors who take a broader view of the same issue have had more success in relating a worldwide process of urbanisation to increasing crime rates within a theory derived from the writings of Durkheim, Georg Simmel and Max Weber. Their argument is that the ascendency of secular values in the modern period contributes to the erosion of collective sentiments, an increase in stress, and to a greater probability of deviance. This process would account not only for changes in the crime rate through time, but also for its variations in space. Lyerly and Skipper (1981), for instance, argue that social bonds are weakest in cities, such that the residents of rural areas experience higher levels of 'conformity' to well-established norms (as measured by commitment to family, church, school, peers and formal authority). These normative commitments provide a measure of social control sufficient to account for the lower crime rates found amongst rural populations. Arguing in a similar vein, Spector (1975) demonstrates that city size is a good predictor of crime rates in the USA, while Jacobs (1981) attributes the positive relationship between population density and robbery rates to the increase in anonymity that accompanies urbanisation. Crutchfield et al. (1982) suggest that increasing population mobility, a further contingency of urbanisation, also encourages a decline in social integration and an increase in deviance.

Despite the sketchy and sometimes equivocal empirical evidence that is currently available, it will undoubtedly broaden the scope of criminological theory if the crime rates of specific historical periods can be interpreted in terms of a prevailing political economy (i.e. if separate culture-specific theories of deviance can all be lodged within a broader conceptual framework). The value of this approach is convincingly expounded with reference to Australia by Mukherjee (1982), and by Shelley (1981a) for each of the three types of society examined in her book. Additionally, an approach which relates deviance to patterns of economic development can illuminate the significance of crime – a little-used indicator of the quality of life – as an index of the economic relations *between* societies. Austin (1983), for instance, relates trends in violent crime in the Caribbean island of St Vincent to the process of decolonisation. He interprets intra-group violence as a cathartic release of anger against a colonial power, and documents its steady decrease as colonial rule was dismantled.

These generalisations are undoubtedly thought-provoking, although in an international context they remain necessarily abstract and overly broad in scope. Given international variations in legal and policing processes, crude variations in property and violent crime trends are the most that such sweeping theories can account for; and this offers little guidance to analysts or policy-makers concerned to explain and control detailed patterns of criminality at national and local levels. For practical purposes, a more fruitful approach might be to focus on just one type of society in its specific historical context. The most relevant such example for the purposes of this book, and the one developed below (from a literature dominated by North American research), is that of Western democracies under advanced capitalism.

Crime trends and capitalist democracy

Willem Bonger (1916) was one of the first theorists to argue systematically for a relationship between the development of industrial capitalism and an increasing crime rate. It has been popular to dismiss his contribution as an example of crude economic determinism – a charge which Berger (1980) convincingly refutes. Bonger's basic postulate is that because capitalism requires people to compete for ostensibly scarce resources, self-interest takes precedence over altruism. This encourages people to make illegitimate as well as legitimate efforts to secure access to unequally distributed material rewards. More recently, Gordon (1973) has made the complementary point that capitalism places the burden of economic uncertainty upon individuals. For some people, recourse to crime is one form of insurance against hardship. Gordon argues that many crimes in the USA, particularly organised, 'ghetto' and white-collar crimes, 'represent rational responses to the competitiveness and inequality of life in capitalist societies' (Gordon 1973: 184).

In order to begin to substantiate such claims, evidence is required to demonstrate (i) that crime is, in fact, increasing in Western capitalist democracies; (ii) that changes in the opportunities for crime are contingent primarily upon the development of a capitalist economy; and (iii) that processes within capitalism encourage the increasing exploitation of criminal opportunities by potential offenders.

The first point has been the subject of detailed investigations by Ted Gurr. Over almost a century and a half, Gurr et al. (1977) found remarkable similarities in the crime trends of London, Stockholm and Sydney. Officially recorded crime rates in all three cities plummeted by a factor of eight to one between 1830 and 1930, but have shown a sharp and consistent upward turn since 1950. These trends are not obviously related to changes in the criminal law or in policing, and Gurr (1977) extended the study to compare patterns of criminality since 1945 in eighteen economically developed democracies. His findings (which compare trends not rates, so partially avoiding the difficulties caused by differences in legal procedure and definition) show a fairly universal increase in both property and personal crimes since the 1950s in English-speaking nations, and since the 1960s on the European continent and in Scandinavia. The only Western exception to this is Switzerland, and it seems reasonable to conclude that Western democracies generally *have* experienced an increase in the amount of crimes committed during the post-war period.

Several authors link this upward trend with the steadily increasing number of opportunities for crime offered by the development of capitalist economies; that is, they provide substantiation for the second of the three points listed above. Carr-Hill and Stern (1979) argue that a certain proportion of property transactions will always be illegal, so that, as economies expand and the total volume of property transactions increases, higher levels of crime might *ceteris paribus* be expected. A similar point is made by Zehr (1974, 1976) in his attempt to account for changes in property crime in industrial France and Germany.

Cohen and Felson (1979) also provide evidence that changes in the opportunities for crime are contingent on developments in the political economies of the West. They argue that the separation of workplace from residence, and the increasing participation of women in the work force, leaves property unguarded for longer periods of time. Additionally, increased participation in social and leisure-time activities situated outside the home exposes a greater proportion of the population to the risk of encountering potential offenders. In short, many changes generally recognised to be desirable consequences of economic development also have the less desirable effect of increasing the opportunities for criminal activity.

Two other processes associated with economic development in the democratic West fulfil the third of the criteria listed above, and might so be recognised as the most fundamental explanatory factors responsible for contemporary crime-rate trends. These processes relate to the impact of recession, inflation and unemployment on many advanced economies; and to the polarisation of wealth (socially and spatially) that occurs as economies develop.

The first theme is addressed most explicitly by Wright (1981) and the authors whose opinions are expressed in his edited collection.

The argument running through the volume is that the problems currently faced by Western economies are conducive to a continuing increase in crime rates. It is suggested that inflation, recession, falling productivity and parsimonious government budgets all encourage crime through their various effects on job markets, consumer markets, and on the operations of government agencies. Perhaps the most investigated and debated of these effects concerns unemployment and its relationship with criminality.

It is rarely difficult to demonstrate high unemployment rates amongst cohorts of offenders, but any relationships which might exist between gross unemployment rates and crime rates are far less readily teased out. The United States Congressional Subcommittee on Crime of the Committee of the Judiciary (1978) made a massive nationwide attempt to collate information linking crime rates with unemployment in the USA, and Brenner (1976, 1978) found positive relations between crime rates and unemployment in North America and the UK. Others who have been able to substantiate this relationship statistically include Fleisher (1966), Hoch (1974), Nagel (1978), Phelps (1927), Singell (1968), Thomas (1927) and Wiers (1944). Perhaps one of the most telling recent British studies of crime and unemployment is contained in the 1980 annual report of the Northumbria police (cited by Dean 1982). Not only did both crime and unemployment increase between two six-month study periods in 1978 and 1980 (by 14 per cent and 29 per cent respectively), but crime committed by the employed sector decreased during this time, while the proportion of offences attributed to the unemployed rose.

In addition to analyses correlating crime and unemployment rates, Berger (1980: 88–91) cites a number of self-report studies and studies of convicted offenders that seem to confirm the link between forced exclusion from the labour force and criminality. His generalisations are supported by Jongman (1982), who shows how the long-term unemployed formed an increasingly large proportion of convicted criminals in Groningen between 1961 and 1978. Jongman argues that the threat of deterrence has lost its efficacy against this marginal group, from whom the hardships of recession have stripped both dignity and moral pride.

Sviridoff and Thompson (1983), however, raise a note of caution in a qualitative study that explores the relationships between individuals' employment status and their involvement in criminal activities. The findings reveal the association between crime and unemployment to be more complex than many of the early studies suggest. These authors attribute a variety of biographical patterns to their cohort of released prison interns: some regularly alternate between periods of unemployment and periods of criminal activity; others use crime-related income to supplement a regular wage; a few use their legitimate employment as an economic stake for drug deals or other illegitimate activities.

Obviously, the relationships between unemployment and crime are by no means simple or unequivocal, even though analysts have spent years trying (with varying success) to pin them down. Curiously, amongst the many attempts to elicit a link between crime rates and the economy, little effort has been invested into the study of socio-economic *inequality*: the second theme noted above, and one of the more disturbing consequences of the polarisation of material wealth that has accompanied Western economic development. The neglect is curious, since, not long after the turn of the century, Bonger (1916: 91) pointed out that 'it is not the total amount of wealth but its distribution that bears upon criminality', and Berger (1980: 34) reminds his readers of a central but subsequently neglected insight of North America's influential 'anomie' theorists which claims that it is 'the condition of economic disadvantage in the midst of affluence which is behind the persistence of the crime problem'.

Gould (1968) uses this kind of reasoning to account for changes in the relationship between economic growth and property crime in the pre- and post-depression eras. Before the 1930s, increases in the amount of private property were inversely related to the property crime rate; only as the 1950s progressed did the direction of this relationship change. Gould argues that in the earlier period not only was property scarce and well-guarded, but because it was scarce the majority of the population experienced the same material conditions as their peers; thus their sense of deprivation was less acute than in subsequent, more affluent years when perceived inequality spurred offenders into action. As Toby (1967) puts it: 'poverty is nothing new. It is affluence that is new', and criminality is more likely 'among the relatively deprived of a rich society than among the objectively deprived of a poor society'.

Only in recent years has the speculative wisdom of these theoretical musings been put to empirical test. Analysts have long been interested in the relationships between *absolute* poverty and crime rates and, in an impressive survey of published research, Braithwaite (1979, 1981) argues that there is, on balance, a strong and enduring association between class and crime. His conclusions have been supported in recent self-report studies by Elliot and Huizinga (1983) and by Thornberry and Farnworth (1982). DeFronzo (1983), moreover, has demonstrated that, for thirty-nine North American SMSA's, decreases in the level of public assistance to the poor may be contributing to the rising crime rates of some city areas. Nevertheless, a heated debate continues in which Axenroth (1983), Clelland and Carter (1980), Tittle and Villemez (1977) and Tittle et al. (1978) deny the validity of such evidence, dismiss the assumed relations between class and crime as a myth, and question the adequacy of theories of deviance that contain assumptions regarding the importance of class differences. Some of these studies, however, have in turn been criticised by Hindelang et al. (1979).

The empirical findings of analysts who have focussed on social and economic inequality rather than absolute deprivation are less incompatible. Danziger and Wheeler (1975), examining the relations between various measures of inequality between 1949 and 1970, find that the highest crime rates occur where disparities between rich and poor sectors of the population are most marked. Similarly, Berger (1980), Eberts and Schwirian (1968) and Marlin (1973) all show that relative economic deprivation (as measured by income inequality) is a far more effective predictor of crime rates than is absolute deprivation (as measured by the proportion of a population living below the poverty line). Blau and Blau (1982) argue in the same vein that inequality but not absolute poverty has a significant bearing on murder and assault rates in America's 125 largest SMSAs. Contrary to popular opinion, the effects of southern location, the size of the black population, and poverty are all ineffective predictors of violence, once economic inequality is controlled for. Likewise, Carroll and Jackson (1983) argue that the 'lifestyle-activity' thesis which offers such an appealing rationale for the increased availability of criminal opportunities, merely mediates the effects of income inequality when it comes to explaining actual crime rates: crime depends not only on the existence and availability of opportunities, but also on the strength of factors prompting potential offenders to take up such opportunities.

Stack (1982), however, offers some qualification to studies identifying objective measures of socio-economic inequality as predictors of crime. He shows that, despite the redistribution of wealth secured by the operation of a welfare state, Sweden's crime-rate trends have been no less disturbing than those of the USA in the modern period. Stack's explanation is that *perceived* inequality, as experienced by an expanding youth sector and the newly unemployed, is more important than objectively measured inequality as a predictor of crime rates. In a later paper, Stack (1984) argues that the USA may be rare in supporting a relationship between crime rates and absolute economic inequality. He attributes responsibility for the relationship to a political system which has made no effort to reduce inequality, so that 'it is not surprising that relative deprivation in the American context would lead to highly individualized acts to redistribute income through street crime' (Stack 1984: 251). His contention is that economic inequality is likely to prompt crime only under conditions of 'political alienation'.

Although it can be expected that the inequality thesis will be refined during the next few years, it is already clear that explanations of contemporary crime trends based on the polarisation of wealth which accompanies economic development will be theoretically fruitful. Such explanations tie up neatly with those focussing on unemployment and related problems attendant on the cyclic booms and slumps of capitalism. However, they do not represent the only interpretation of crime trends in modern democracies.

Several authors cite the changing age structure of the population as the prime determinant of crime-rate trends. Gaier (1976), for instance, argues that the maturing of a post-war 'baby boom' accounts for much of the increase in crime in Western democracies. The proportion of the population falling into high offender-rate age groups (sixteen to twenty-four years) increased throughout the 1960s in many countries. This trend allowed Lee (1984) to account for 23 per cent of the increase in Canada's crime rate between 1949 and 1968 in terms of the changing age structure of the population.

The high risks of juvenile involvement in crime may be related to the peculiarities of the adolescent 'stage' as it is experienced by youths in developed economies. Aries (1962) and Glaser (1968) argue that the passage of child labour laws and the expansion of formal education have produced a transitional period for youths characterised by low incomes and long hours of leisure. A feature of this transitional period, according to Matza (1964), is a quest for excitement (or for the means to buy it). High offender rates amongst adolescents might thus express partly the excitement of law-breaking itself, and partly the need for the proceeds of crime to secure access to more formal and expensive forms of recreation.

Recently, however, more emphasis has been placed upon the position of youths in the labour market as an explanation for their high offender rates. Phillips et al. (1972) show that between 1952 and 1967 demographic shifts accounted for no more than 15 per cent of the increase in youth crime rates in the USA. Rather, their econometric analyses reveal that it is the decline in labour-market opportunities that best explains the increase in youth crime rates. A similar argument is advanced by Greenberg (1977), who embraces both the economic and the demographic theses. He explains juvenile delinquency in terms of labour-market conditions under advanced capitalism, wherein little employment is available even to trained teenagers. Property crimes are, he argues, motivated by a desire to participate in social activities when legitimate income is insufficient to finance them.

Attempts to account for the few cases where crime rates have not increased as quickly as economic explanations might suggest are also illuminating, since they draw attention to the interaction between political control and income inequality. Clinard (1978) suggests that low crime rates in Switzerland are secured through the decentralisation of political control, wherein a relatively large proportion of political power is exercised at the level of the individual canton by elected local representatives. Similarly, Mankoff (1976) demonstrates that Western European societies with well-developed working-class political movements, have less crime than equivalent societies which lack this co-ordination. Crime seems best contained when social control is least divorced from the community to which it applies. Moreover, 'political organising around the economic problems of a community might offer disadvantaged populations an alternative to crime which is still supportive of their rebellious instincts' (Berger 1980: 48).

The interaction between politics and economy is clearly significant for any explanation of crime trends in modern society. It has already been argued that progress in the analysis of deviance demands detailed investigations of social relations in particular locales. It is now clear that the contribution of such research to an understanding of crime can fully be appreciated only in terms of the broader political, as well as economic, contexts in which case studies are situated. This argument, recommending both the scale and thematic focus of research, is based on the evidence of practical, if not philosophical, convergence between direct realist and interactionist traditions of criminological enquiry. Building on this convergence, chapter 3 briefly explores the national economic context of crime trends in England and Wales. This provides a framework for the more detailed investigations which follow in an attempt to evaluate the causes and consequences of crime in disadvantaged urban neighbourhoods.

3

Concerning crime in the United Kingdom

The importance of combining large-scale analyses of crime with in-depth contextual studies of offenders, victims and local environments now seems obvious. An argument has been made for the relevance of examining national crime trends in the context of a global economy, and in terms of the politics of particular modes of production. In this chapter, I shall begin to explore the relationships between regional and intra-urban crime trends, and Britain's national economy.

Crime in the regions

To date geographical accounts of large-scale crime patterns have often been descriptive, atheoretic and rather dry. Theoretical observations that have been made often contribute to North America's debate on a southern 'subculture of violence' (e.g. Doerner 1975; Gastil 1971; Harries 1985; Loftin and Hill 1974); they rarely address the possibility of a link between explanations of crime and, for instance, the political economy of regions. Usually, then, empirical analyses of the regional distribution of crime have been in the nature of obligatory and cursorily executed 'ground clearing' for subsequent smaller-scale explorations.

There are two quite logical reasons for this tendency to underplay the significance of regional trends in the distribution of crime. First, since official statistics are so questionable as indicators of the crime rate, analyses at a broad regional scale are thought to be especially suspect. Secondly, as Davidson (1981) points out, most authors feel that regional variations in crime can be explained largely by the relationship between crime and urbanisation (i.e. it is the distribution of large urban areas rather than the character of regions per se that is thought likely to be responsible for national crime patterns).

The first British crime survey (BCS)* contains evidence question-

---

* The first BCS contains information on victimisation, lifestyle, fear and perceptions of crime, crime-prevention practices, police contacts and self-reported delin-

ing these assumptions, in the light of which the significance of regional variations in crime in the UK merits further consideration. After all, geographers have made important contributions to the field of regional science, and they have expressed concern about disparities within and between Britain's regional economies. If crime does bear some relationship to economic performance, this might be expected to manifest itself as clearly *within* a nation as it does in the international context discussed in chapter 2. Although neither the data available nor the scope of this book allow any comprehensive assessment of such an hypothesis, it is impossible to resist including a few tentative explorations in this vein.

In order to investigate the significance of regional differences in crime rates, the constituencies sampled in the British Crime Survey were clustered into larger spatial units corresponding to the nine economic planning regions of England and Wales which were consolidated by the local government reforms of 1 April 1974. According to House (1978), these regions 'correspond broadly to the major provincial or subnational entities which have emerged over the post-war years'. He implies, then, that they have some social meaning as well as a political and economic function. They are 'regions for which economic planning councils and boards have been responsible since the mid-1960s and for which formulation of regional strategies has been actively, if variously, prosecuted . . . there is a sense in which they [the regions] are generating and consolidating their identity, through their continuing use for policy making and its applications' (House 1978: 18). These regions, moreover, have fared differentially in the chilling economic climate of the early 1980s. Based on their experiences in relation to both the economy and to statutory policies in the face of varying economic fortunes, House is able to regroup these nine regions into four: the development regions (the North and Wales), intermediate regions (Yorkshire/Humberside and the North West), regions of mixed trends (the South West and East Anglia), and growth regions (East Midlands, West Midlands and the South East). Inappropriately labelled for today's ailing economy, these distinctions still provide a fair indicator of regions' relative (mis)fortunes.

quency obtained from a complex random sample of 11 000 people in England and Wales and 5 000 in Scotland, interviewed in 1982. Comments in this chapter are based on data relating only to England and Wales. A second BCS (in which Scotland did not participate), completed in 1984, was not available for analysis at the time of writing, though an overview report was published by HMSO in July 1985 entitled: 'Taking account of crime: key findings from the 1984 British Crime Survey' (Home Office Research Study 85).

Both the ninefold division and the four regional types are discussed below. First, however, some words of warning regarding the interpretation of the BCS data are required. The authors of the survey themselves itemise many of the pitfalls likely to mislead inattentive readers (see Hough and Mayhew 1983; Wood 1983). Although the sample size is large (over 11 000 people were interviewed in England and Wales), the number who had been the victim of a crime was, for some offences, very small. Sampling errors thus tend to be large and, because of the configuration of the sample, the error terms are difficult to calculate. The Home Office has constructed a number of 'complex standard errors', taking into account the design effects of a four-stage cluster sample, but these are difficult to generate, and were not available in the form required for the broad analyses discussed below. Thus, it will be hard to say anything about the statistical significance of regional differences in the crime rate. It will be difficult to judge whether observed differences are 'real', or whether they could be subsumed within sampling errors. This difficulty is not peculiar to the present study; it is encountered in the analysis of any survey with a complex design, and this is not the place to become involved in the debate over techniques which might solve these problems. Rather, I will confine myself to comments on the experiences of those people who were interviewed, leaving the larger data sets of the future to confirm or refute the speculations to which this first BCS gives rise.

Throughout the discussion which follows, terms referring to the incidence of crime monitored by the BCS will have specific and consistent meanings. *Victimisation* rates refer to the proportion of surveyed individuals or households who claim to have been the target of one or more crimes of a given type during 1981. *Crime* rates will usually be expressed as the number of offences per 10 000 persons or households experienced during the one-year reference period. The *multiple victim* rate refers to the average number of offences experienced by each victimised individual or household during the reference period. Generally, personal crimes are discussed in terms of individuals' experiences while property crime rates are specific to households.

It was suggested above that the BCS can help allay two reservations associated with official crime statistics that have tended to discourage inter-regional studies of crime in Britain. A brief outline of each of these achievements serves to preface more detailed regional analyses based on the crime survey itself.

First, the survey provides an alternative measure of crime to that contained in official statistics. For some offences, a more complete picture of crime is made available, showing the distribution not only of crimes recorded by the police but also of offences not reported to the police, as well as those reported to the police and for some reason not recorded in the official returns.* (Such crime surveys do, of course, introduce their own problems of definition, recall and so on, which are discussed in detail by Sparks, Genn and Dodd 1977.)

Both Davidson (1981) and Herbert (1982) have described regional patterns of crime in England and Wales, as they vary from police force to police force. It is impossible to gauge from such presentations the extent to which force-to-force differences in the production of official statistics affect corresponding variations in the crime rate. It is also impossible, without special tabulations, to link the administrative areas defined for policing purposes with census data or any other centrally collated socio-economic indicators. Fortunately, the Central Statistical Office's annual publication of regional trends for the United Kingdom contains a regional (rather than force-specific) breakdown of notifiable offences recorded by the police. Comparing these with the findings of the BCS, it is, therefore, possible to examine the extent to which national variations in recorded crime are mirrored by variations in crime as defined by victims' experiences.

To effect the comparison, BCS crime rates, whether for personal or property offences, have to be presented as offences per head of the population (rather than by household, which would have been a more appropriate base for some offences, and which, as stated above, will usually be employed when referring to household offences in the present discussion). When regional variations in the rates of burglary, robbery, theft and handling, and criminal damage, as measured by the BCS and as found in official statistics are compared, the two data sets correspond quite closely ($r_s = 0.83, 0.88, 0.62, 0.68$, respectively). Personal violence is the only exception to this ($r_s = -0.08$), but taking all crime types together the relationship between the two data sets remains fairly strong ($r_s = 0.67$). Accord-

---

* In this chapter, such data refer to all crimes initially identified by victims. Five per cent of these offences were later dropped, either because they proved to be crimes in a category outside the survey coverage, or because further questioning failed to elicit hard evidence that something illegal had happened. I have retained them because my interest is with those who *believe* they have been victimised. Moreover, had the data not been taken from the screening forms, a questionnaire-imposed four-offence-per-victim limit would have led to the loss of 4 per cent of the incidents.

Table 3.1 *Regional crime rates in England and Wales*

Region	Property crimes per 10 000 households	Personal crimes per 10 000 people	Total crimes	
			per 10 000 households	per 10 000 people
Wales	3876	1061	6132	2883
The North	5728	735	7208	3577
North West	4294	1872	8072	3999
Yorkshire/ Humberside	5156	1090	7346	3657
West Midlands	3706	1346	6551	3099
East Midlands	5163	1350	7879	3915
East Anglia	1776	1294	4390	2172
South West	3159	1120	5411	2691
South East	3606	1212	6141	2935
Total (all England and Wales)	4038	1266	6643	3228

Source: First British Crime Survey, data weighted to adjust for over-sampling in inner-city areas, and to be representative of individuals or households, as appropriate.

ing to the BCS (having amalgamated the area of the Greater London Council (GLC) with the rest of the South East, as is necessary when comparing the BCS with published regional statistics), the highest overall crime rates are experienced in the North West (3999 crimes per 10 000 people in 1981) and the East Midlands (3915 crimes per 10 000 people). As table 3.1 shows, the same is true for personal crimes (1872 and 1350 crimes per 10 000 persons), though for property crimes it is the North that experiences the highest rate (5728 crimes per 10 000 households). According to the official statistics it is also the North West that experienced the highest crime rate in 1981 (708 offences per 10 000 people), though it is the East Midlands that dominated for violence against the person (27 per 10 000).

Table 3.2 shows the variations in regional crime rates as they appear in both police and BCS statistics. Those astonished by the apparently higher rates across the board revealed by the BCS should remember two vital qualifications. First, in the words of Hough and Mayhew (1983: 10), 'The survey figures were estimates only and included a high proportion of incidents that were *less serious than those*

Table 3.2 A regional comparison of crime rates: criminal statistics (CS), 1981, and the British Crime Survey (BCS): crime rate per 10 000 people

Region	All crimes		Violence against persons		Burglary		Robbery		Theft/handling		Criminal damage	
	CS	BCS	CS	BCS	CS	BCS	CS	BCS	CS	BCS	CS	BCS
Wales	508	2883	19	428	130	138	1	0	266	1375	71	942
The North	685	3577	23	371	188	216	2	0	363	1751	90	1200
North West	708	3999	22	143	196	227	4	20	363	1573	89	754
Yorkshire/Humberside	616	3657	25	563	163	213	2	38	321	1714	86	1120
West Midlands	584	3099	23	606	158	230	3	38	303	1575	78	654
East Midlands	583	3915	27	820	134	211	2	13	319	1800	75	1068
East Anglia	454	2172	16	1023	89	38	1	0	277	816	51	296
South West	433	2691	15	609	88	93	1	0	253	1348	51	628
South East	623	2935	18	490	139	228	8	47	346	1383	82	724

Sources: Regional Trends, 1981 (Central Statistical Office); First British Crime Survey, weighted data.

recorded by the police' (my emphasis). Secondly, the confidence limits
around estimates made on the basis of the survey data are very large.
Some of them are listed by Hough and Mayhew (1983: 8), who show,
for instance, that the estimate for the rate of common assault in
England and Wales, which is 396 per 10 000 persons, could refer to
an actual rate of 396 plus or minus 94. Similarly, the estimated
vandalism rate of 1494 per 10 000 households may actually be as
great as 1676 or as little as 1312. Though it proved impossible to
elicit confidence limits for the estimates of the regional crime rates
given in table 3.1, it is obvious that the apparent differences between
the two sets of figures should be treated very cautiously. Nevertheless, the BCS does indicate that for every crime recorded by the
police, as many as four offences might have been experienced by
victims: twice as many burglaries took place as were recorded by the
police, five times as many violent crimes, twelve times as much theft
from the person and thirteen times as much vandalism.

A second factor that has tended to undermine regional studies of
crime in Britain is the assumption that urbanisation (rather than
broader aspects of regional political economy) accounts for subnational spatial variations in the crime rate. However, although the
BCS confirms that there is an important relationship between crime
rates and urbanisation, it also indicates that this relationship does
not fully account for the regional patterns of crime observed in
England and Wales.

Concerned about the criminogenic role of urbanisation, the first
report on the BCS stresses the vulnerability of inner-city areas,
where rates of robbery, burglary, theft from the person and
vandalism are all at their highest (Hough and Mayhew 1983).
Nevertheless, there are five offence types which exhibit apparently
significant regional variations (vandalism, burglary, theft from the
person, wounding and robbery) and when the effects of the inner
cities* are removed, these regional patterns of crime and victimisation rates remain very similar. Moreover, when overall victimisation rates are compared across ten regions (for the moment
dividing the South East into the area of the Greater London Council
and the Other South East), with victimisation rates calculated to
exclude the effects of the inner cities (i.e. again controlling for an
important aspect of urbanisation), rank correlation coefficients
range (according to crime type) from $r_s = 0.86$ to $r_s = 0.98$.

---

* Inner-city areas were identified in the BCS on the basis of the classification of
parliamentary constituencies developed by the planning and applications group of
the Centre for Environmental Studies, as discussed by Webber (1978).

Irrespective of the effects of the inner cities, therefore, East Anglia has the lowest victimisation rates for vandalism and burglary (overall, 0.8 per cent of households were burgled at least once, and 4.8 per cent suffered at least one act of vandalism, in contrast to the highest rate area, that covered by the GLC, where 6.4 per cent and 12.6 per cent of households, respectively, fell victim to the same offences). The South West has the lowest victimisation rate for theft from the person; residents in Wales and the South East (excluding the area of the GLC) have least experience of wounding; and no respondent from Wales, the North, East Anglia or the South West was the victim of a robbery during 1981. These regions experience the lowest victimisation rates for the offences mentioned above, whether the contribution of the inner cities to these rates is taken into account or not. Moreover, only minor changes in the ranks of the highest rate areas occur when the effects of the inner cities are controlled for. The area of the GLC, for instance, which has the highest overall victimisation rates for a number of crime types, is displaced from its prominence with respect to victimisation rates for vandalism and burglary by the East Midlands and the North West (which tie for second place in the overall rankings) and is matched in its robbery rates by Yorkshire and Humberside (which ranks only third when the inner-city neighbourhoods are included).

In general, then, it seems likely that regional differences in the crime rate do exist which are neither an artifact of official statistics nor a simple reflection of different degrees of urbanisation. This is of considerable interest in its own right, and it provides an appealing starting point for an examination of the relationships between crime, economy and environment in the British context. Notwithstanding the similarities between regional trends in official and BCS crime statistics (and reluctantly passing over some intriguing differences), what follows focusses only on the findings of the survey, exploring the relationships between crimes experienced by the public in England and Wales and some regional indicators of economic well-being. The potential for such kinds of analyses seems enormous, given the rapid development of regional science and the important spatial emphasis this brings to economics. The practical implications of such studies might also be far-reaching, despite House's (1978: 499) concern that 'public recognition of the importance of a spatial perspective in national affairs has been both tardy and grudging'. His charge is as true for the issues of crime control and law enforcement as it is for that of economic investment. However, if the two aspects of public policy are linked in some way, then an appreciation of the significance of regional variations of crime in England and Wales will be essential.

It seems logical to begin such a study at the broadest scale, focussing intitially on House's fourfold grouping of Britain's economic planning regions. Tables 3.3 and 3.4 list various crime rates specific to these regional types. The highest incidence of property crime was reported by respondents living in development and intermediate regions. Development regions are characterised by relatively high and persistent unemployment and a narrow industrial base with an excess of declining industries. Their populations survive on median incomes well below the national average, and they experience generally poor living environments, especially in the inner cities. Intermediate regions evince similar problems, but generally of somewhat lesser intensity. They are not as peripheral in spatial or economic terms as the development regions, though their industrial sector retains an over-representation of slow growth industries, and townscapes dating from the industrial revolution exhibit serious dereliction.

The low rate of property crime in regions of mixed trends is very striking, particularly for the offences of vandalism, burglary and household theft. Such regions have least territorial coherence and lowest population densities. The competing interests of rural and urban residents are thought to create a certain amount of tension. In these regions, the victimisation rates for vandalism are particularly low (5.3 per cent of households were the target of at least one incident, whereas for the other regional types, the proportion of households victimised ranges between 9.5 per cent and 9.9 per cent). However, while the crime rate for vandalism is low (1057 per 10 000 households in the mixed trend regions as compared with 1746 per 10 000 in the other three regional types combined), the rate of multiple victimisation is somewhat higher than elsewhere (respondents experienced an average of two incidents per household in regions of mixed trends as compared with an average of 1.8 incidents each elsewhere).

This tendency towards low property crime and victimisation rates in regions of mixed trends holds for burglaries (which were experienced by only 1.5 per cent of households in these regions, in contrast to growth and intermediate regions where 3.6 and 4.1 per cent of interviewed households were burgled in 1981), for other household theft and, to a lesser degree, for thefts from motor vehicles (for this offence, highest rates are experienced in development regions which contain 12 per cent of the surveyed population

Table 3.3 *Property crime rates for regional types in England and Wales per 10 000 households*

Type of region	Vandalism	Theft from motor vehicle	Burglary	Theft of motor vehicle	Bicycle theft	Theft in dwelling	Other household theft	All property crime
Development	2188.8	904.1	356.6	60.6	75.4	27.2	1093.6	4706.2
Intermediate	1861.7	800.7	444.7	175.5	69.7	86.3	1259.4	4696.3
Mixed trends	1057.2	667.3	153.1	66.9	81.2	121.7	585.2	2732.3
Growth	1593.6	637.2	462.7	191.6	157.4	147.6	682.4	2872.5
Total	1667.0	711.4	410.1	158.0	118.0	115.7	858.3	4038.3

Note: The table is based on 2185 property crimes and 5413 surveyed households. All data are weighted to adjust for over-sampling in inner-city areas, and to be representative of households rather than individuals.
Source: First British Crime Survey.

Table 3.4 *Personal crime rates for regional types in England and Wales per 10 000 people*

Type of region	Common assault	Wounding	Theft from persons and robbery	Other personal theft	All personal crimes
Development	308.2	94.9	87.3	410.9	918.7
Intermediate	893.0	130.9	143.0	336.4	1507.8
Mixed trends	630.3	106.6	46.5	380.9	1173.6
Growth	468.8	91.8	221.4	466.9	1256.0
Total	567.3	103.0	167.4	420.0	1265.6

Note: The table is based on 1410 personal crimes and 11 139 individuals. All data are weighted to adjust for over-sampling in inner-city areas, and to be representative of individuals rather than households.
Source: First British Crime Survey.

but 15 per cent of victimised households). Two exceptions to this pattern are theft in a dwelling, and bicycle thefts, 70 per cent of whose victims cluster within the growth regions (the remaining 30 per cent are distributed between regions in proportion to the population).

Respondents living in the intermediate regions record by far the highest rate of personal crimes. Table 3.4 shows that this is accounted for in particular by the high rate of common assault, as well as by the above average incidence of wounding. It is interesting that the *victimisation* rate for common assault varies little between regional types (i.e. victims, but not the crimes they experience, are distributed amongst the regions in approximately the same proportions as the general population). The high crime rate in intermediate regions must therefore be accounted for by a high rate of multiple victimisation. In fact, the victims in these regions each experienced an average of 4.28 assaults in contrast to a rate of 1.43 assaults per victim in development regions, 2.32 in regions of mixed trends and 2.01 in growth regions. The only other personal crime for which *victimisation* rates vary markedly by region is robbery. Although the numbers are small, it is still striking that the growth regions, which contain 53 per cent of the surveyed population, house 80 per cent of the victims of robbery.

One important theme to emerge from analyses of regional economic problems in recent years is, as Randall (1979) observes, a growing awareness of the distinctive problems peculiar to specific regions. It may be at this locationally specific level that the large-scale analysis of crime can make its most significant contribution. For some initial explorations into the link between crime rates and economic indicators across the nine economic planning regions of England and Wales, the following regional indicators were selected: Gross Domestic Product per person in 1981 (measured in terms of an index set in 1979); redundancy rates per 1000 employees between 1980 and 1982; the average domestic rateable value for 1981; the proportion of the economically active population who were unemployed in 1981. Areal variations in these four are easily compared with the patterns of three crime rates: the overall crime rate (the rank ordering of regions is the same whether this is calculated as offences per 10 000 persons, or per 10 000 households), the property crime rate (per 10 000 households) and the personal crime rate (per 10 000 people). The more marked of the relationships (where $r_s > 0.6$) seem worth commenting upon.

Most noticeably, there is a relationship between property crime rates and both redundancy rates ($r_s = 0.6$) and unemployment ($r_s = 0.63$). The lowest redundancy and unemployment rates are found in East Anglia, the South West and the South East. Here, too, are the lowest property crime rates (1776, 3159 and 3606 crimes per 10 000 households, respectively). With redundancy rates at 12.4, 17.8 and 11.9 per 1000 employees respectively, these regions seem considerably better off than the remainder, whose redundancy rates average 30.1 per 1000 employees and whose property crimes average 4154 per 10 000 households, with a maximum of 5728 per 10 000 households in the North. Similarly, the unemployment rates for East Anglia, the South West and the South East were 9.9 per cent, 10.8 per cent and 9.1 per cent, whereas the average for the other regions was 14.5 per cent, rising to 15.8 per cent in 1982.

The South West and East Anglia are both regions of mixed trends. In both areas, a relatively large proportion of population growth can be attributed to an influx of retired persons so that, to some extent, low crime rates can be explained demographically (in that it is the younger section of the population that usually perpetrates most crime). Nevertheless, manufacturing industries are poorly developed in these regions, where the labour force possesses a restricted range of skills and experiences below average standards of housing, education and wealth. In fact, average incomes in East Anglia are the lowest in England and Wales, and it is pertinent to ask why there is not more property crime in the locale. Speculative answers would make recourse to the low availability of property in absolutely poor areas, the absence of steep socio-economic gradients (which tend to emphasise inequalities in the distribution of wealth and may tempt criminal activity amongst those who perceive themselves as unjustly deprived), and the low population densities (which suggest that the opportunities for crime are more widely distributed, and therefore less accessible, than elsewhere). It will, unfortunately, require a much more sensitive and detailed study to confirm or refute these suspicions.

The highest property crime rates are experienced in the North – a region where unemployment seems endemic and has persisted at over one and a half times the national average since the war. Even acknowledging that any link between crime rates and unemployment is tenuous and contentious it is hard to ignore the implications of the region's critical problem of industrial restructuring and its inability to attract a buoyant service industry. Similarly, poor housing stock and inadequate recreational facilities must take their toll in terms of crime and delinquency. The economic plight of the North seems inseparable from a high crime rate, both in engendering a pool of potential offenders – unoccupied, bored and often in desperate financial difficulty; and by providing opportunities for crime in the form of structurally unsound building stock and in decaying environments that cry out a welcome to vandals and pilferers.

Another finding that at first generates some excitement is a relationship between property crime rates and average domestic rateable values ($r_s = -0.65$). Highest rateable values occur in the South East, the West Midlands, East Anglia and the South West – the four areas with the lowest property crime rates. This brings to mind all kinds of explanations concerning the ability of the wealthy to protect property and the tendency for those who can least bear the economic costs of crime to be most at risk. However, the correlation is not sustained for burglary rates alone, and is probably accounted for more by the numbers of people available to commit petty crimes of vandalism (e.g under- or unemployed citizens, bored and disillusioned youths) than by the quality of domestic property (although on a smaller scale, some relationship between burglary rates and unsound/insecurable property might well be expected).

A more interesting relationship is that between personal crime rates and Gross Domestic Product ($r_s = 0.65$). This correspondence is not always very marked. The South East, for instance, with the highest GDP, ranks fifth according to personal crime rates.

However, other rankings *are* more similar; the East Midlands ranks second, and the West Midlands third in terms of both personal crime rates and GDP. What is intriguing is that the relationship is considerably strengthened when GDP is compared with just one component of the personal crime rate, namely robbery rates ($r_s = 0.83$). The highest robbery rates occur in the South East (47 per 10 000 people), where GDP per head was 113.4 in 1981 (measured against an index of 100 for the United Kingdom in 1979); lowest robbery rates are found in East Anglia, the North, the South West and Wales, where no survey respondent reported an attack. In these regions, GDP was 94.7, 94.3, 93.2 and 90.0.

It is interesting, in the light of previous discussions of the relationship between crime and inequality, to note that the North West, whose residents experience the highest personal and overall crime rates, is characterised by House (1978) above all by its inequalities. Randall (1979) emphasises, too, a serious problem of obsolescence in much of the region's infrastructure and environment. Primarily, however, it is the locational mismatch between population growth and economic potential that House highlights as especially crippling in times of economic recession: 'nowhere in Britain has there been such a slow growth momentum, in population, or employment, in relation to the scale of problems to be faced . . .' (House 1978: 69).

Again, no firm conclusions can be drawn about the relationship between personal crime and the frustrations engendered by a region's economic fortunes. Some may feel such speculations are confirmed by an appeal to commonsense; others will reject such a brief overview as potentially misleading. Therefore, while tempting, it would be unwise to pursue these arguments further. At the moment, the data available and the lack of time series can justify little more in the way of analysis than informed speculation. If, however, by engaging in this diversion, a few readers turn their attention towards the notion of crime as an externality of regional economic growth (cf. Hemley and McPheters 1974), or as an index of the selective impact of recession, then I believe that the contribution of geographers to the study of crime will be significantly enhanced.

Crime rates and the inner cities

While it has been argued that regional differences in the experience of crime cannot be accounted for simply by organisational variations

Table 3.5 *Crime and the inner cities: proportion of households/persons victimised by property/personal crimes (%)*

Crime type	Inner city[1]	Elsewhere	Proportion of victims resident in inner city[2]
(a) Property crimes			
Vandalism	10.2	9.2	7.6
Theft from motor vehicles	7.3	5.4	9.0
Burglary	8.4	3.1	16.9
Theft of motor vehicles	2.7	1.3	13.2
Bicycle theft	1.5	1.1	9.3
Theft in dwelling	0.6	0.5	7.8
Other household theft	7.1	5.5	8.7
(b) Personal crimes			
Common assault	2.5	2.3	7.3
Theft from persons	3.1	0.9	20.6
Wounding	1.1	0.7	10.2
Robbery	1.9	0.2	44.2
Sexual offences	0.3	0.1	27.3
Other personal theft	5.2	3.1	10.5

[1] As defined by a classification of parliamentary constituencies given in Webber (1978).
[2] Overall 6.8 per cent of respondents (victims and non-victims together) live in inner-city locations.
Source: First British Crime Survey, weighted data.

in policing or by uneven patterns of urbanisation, the British Crime Survey does draw attention to the very high vulnerability of inner-city residents in all regions. Table 3.5 shows that crimes of every type are associated with higher victimisation rates in the inner cities than elsewhere; and for every offence group, more inner-city respondents have been victims than their numbers in the population would suggest (only 6.8 per cent of survey respondents come from inner-city areas, yet the proportion of victims living in the inner city exceeds this for every crime type).

For a number of offences, including vandalism, bicycle theft, theft from dwellings, common assault, sexual offences and wounding, the differences in crime rates between inner-city constituencies and others are not great. In contrast, burglary, theft of motor vehicles, other household theft, theft from the person, robbery and other personal theft are quite noticeably over-represented in the inner cities. Moreover, Gottfredson (1984) shows that when inner-city residence combines with other factors associated with the risks of victimisation, vulnerability is especially high. He points out, for instance, that the risk of personal victimisation for someone aged between sixteen and twenty-four who lives in the inner city is approximately ten times greater than that for someone aged over forty-five and living in a rural area.

Although I shall concentrate on trying to account for the incidence of crime in the inner cities in the remainder of this chapter, it is worth emphasising that inner-city neighbourhoods by no means generate the bulk of known crime in England and Wales. For most offences, well under 20 per cent of victims live in the inner city and, for those personal crimes where this figure appears higher, the small numbers and large error terms involved should warn against sensationalism. The inner cities do contain more than their fair share of crime, but this does not constitute the majority of crime in England and Wales.

These observations notwithstanding, I use the example of the inner cities to explore the role of crime in society in most of the chapters which follow. This emphasis on a general type of urban area rather than on one specific region seems appropriate for two reasons. First, as Townsend (1981) demonstrates in his study of major job losses in the UK, by the beginning of this decade all regions had been affected by the 'deepening and spreading' effects of recession, so that even the most affluent areas now contain pockets of distress and unemployment. To the extent that this has any bearing on the crime rate (through the vulnerability of poorly maintained environments, or due to the tendency for economically disadvantaged people to engage more frequently in heavily censured crimes), it might best be explored in terms of the high risks of victimisation which characterise the inner cities irrespective of their regional location. Detailed analyses within such areas will give an insight into the nature of the crime problem in a particular sector of the country's economic space, where the effects of crime hit hardest, and where people have relatively limited social, political and economic resources with which to protect themselves.

Secondly, the BCS has confirmed that high inner-city crime rates are not merely a product of the processes involved in the generation of official statistics. Irrespective of any bias that creeps into police recording and arrest procedures (and selectivity here is demonstrable), the disproportionate incidence of crime in the inner city does reflect the experience of victims. This might be an appropriate setting, therefore, in which to examine crime rates as indicators of the quality of life, viewing crime as one of a number of forms of disadvantage that beset the residents of the inner city.

It is important to stress that neither crime nor other forms of disadvantage are exclusive to the inner city. Sim (1984) has recently demonstrated not only that inner-city deprivation persists into the 1980s, but also that the social and economic disadvantages of other urban areas, especially outer-city local authority housing estates, are increasingly acute. Kinsey (1984) has made a similar point, drawing attention to the effects of crime in some peripheral estates. My aim, therefore, is not to treat the inner city as a discrete container for the ills of the British economy. Rather specific inner-city neighbourhoods are examined as a microcosm of the working-class experience of crime. Such examples are intended to have more than local interest in that some general implications hold for a broader cross-section of urban Britain. The examples, then, are always to be viewed in their widest economic context, as a locational manifestation of uneven development within a national economic system. As Harrison points out (1983: 24) 'It is important not to view the inner cities as unusual or isolated phenomena . . . The inner cities simply suffer from the problems in a denser and therefore more visible form.' Nevertheless, as he goes on to argue in a later chapter: 'The level of crime is one of the key features that distinguishes the inner city from other kinds of area. It casts a shadow over life, and the poorer the family and the neighbourhood, the deeper is that shadow' (Harrison 1983: 324). It will not, therefore, be inappropriate to take such areas as foci for in-depth studies of the social reality of deviance. In so far as the inner city encapsulates some areas of concern in British social policy, a balanced analysis of the origins and effects of crime in such areas seems timely.

I shall not be concerned to elucidate the nature and origin of inner-city problems across a broad front. Those unfamiliar with the issues might turn to Paul Harrison's incisive, journalistic study *Inside the inner city* (1983). Less graphic but better referenced accounts are given in Evans and Eversley (1980), Hall (1981) and Lawless (1981). An interesting critique of the ideology surrounding the term 'inner city' is offered by Forrest et al. (1978), while Schwartz (1981) sets the British dilemma in an international context.

It should be acknowledged at the outset that the term 'inner city' is not unambiguous. It has a statutory definition for the sake of the

Urban Programme, and for the convenience of local planners. It has symbolic import at all points on the political spectrum: soaked in the vivid imagery of the mass media, the inner city might signify anything from moral disintegration to the crumbling of capitalism. From all this, Rex (1984) has managed to distil a working definition of the inner city which I adopt in this book. There is, he claims, 'a special type of area which we should think of as the "inner city's inner city". This is the area of poor housing and high immigrant [or British born black] density. Such areas may not be geographically in the inner ring at all, but rather in the surrounding area which has not benefited from urban redevelopment' (Rex 1984: 192–3). The general well-being of people living in such areas is adversely affected by at least four interrelated sets of problems: environmental decay; problems of unemployment stemming from (a) industrial dispersal and (b) economic recession and restructuring; the problem of developing adequate social services; racial segregation, discrimination and racism. These broad underlying conditions of the inner cities cannot be the primary focus in what follows, but they are themes which recur time and again in connection with the issues of victimisation, crime control and law enforcement which *are* the foci of this volume.

Subsequent chapters often draw from a series of case studies, completed in 1978–9, in various parts of north central Birmingham spanning the four inner-city wards of All Saints, Aston, Handsworth and Soho. The studied neighbourhoods fall within the inner core of Birmingham's Inner City Partnership area, belonging to a zone with 'the most acute problems, where housing and social conditions are generally worst, and which contains the main area of old and declining manufacturing industry' (Birmingham Inner City Partnership 1978: 6). Within this zone, the study areas form one of three pockets characterised by the most severe social problems in the city. This 'pocket' is part of an arc of late Victorian and Edwardian housing which surrounds the city's redeveloped inner core (of high-rise council properties, whose construction began in the early post-war years). The arc is itself encircled by a band of post-1920 suburbs containing both public and privately owned properties. Thus, while 'north central Birmingham', as referred to in this book, is not the literal inner city, it does form part of a secondary inner ring which now contains the worst housing and environmental conditions. This ring is marked out by a patchwork of Housing Action Areas (HAAs) and General Improvement Areas (GIAs) designated during the 1970s in an attempt to alleviate the conditions of 'twilight zone' residents. Yet, although the obsolescence within these districts was accelerated during a period of lodging-house development in the 1960s, the decay continues. For Rex (1981), at least, it quickly became apparent that the GIAs and HAAs in Birmingham 'were to include houses so poor and squalid that, however strong the intention to improve them, they would still be the most squalid in the city (Rex 1981: 29).

Despite an overall decrease in recorded crime in Birmingham between 1978 and 1979, all the police beats of the study area experienced an increase in some, if not all, crime types. Police statistics, at least, show that north central Birmingham experienced a disproportionate share of woundings, burglaries (especially from dwellings) and robberies in the two years of the research. However, as chapters 5 and 7 will demonstrate, the aspect of crime in north central Birmingham that receives the widest documentation is its popular association with race. Justifiably or not, the two themes have become inseparable, and are now as much a feature of the 'crime-prone' environment of the study area as the defensibility or otherwise of urban space. Before considering this, however, some more general factors associated with the incidence of crime in Birmingham's inner city, and in areas like it, demand attention.

In attempting to account for the high crime rates of the inner cities, three facets of offending need to be considered: the extent to which it is a consequence of high local offender residence rates; the extent to which high crime rates reflect the abundance of opportunities for crime in an inner-city environment; and the contribution made by victims' attributes and behaviours to their likelihood of experiencing crime. While these three elements are obviously interrelated, it is helpful conceptually and analytically to treat them separately. The remainder of this chapter will consider offenders and the environments in which they operate. The role of the victim, which, until the present decade was relatively neglected in the British literature, will be considered in chapter 4.

Offenders in the inner city

Since Shaw and McKay first documented the decline in offender residence rates from a peak in the inner-city transition zone along a gentle gradient to the suburbs of Chicago, analysts have been preoccupied with the criminals of the inner city. In recent years, however, the segregation of offenders within peripheral council-housing estates has received attention as a distinctive aspect of the ecology of crime in British cities (e.g. Baldwin 1974b, 1975). The relevance of this discovery notwithstanding, detailed analyses reveal much higher offender rates in a dwindling but more centralised private rental housing sector (e.g. Baldwin and Bottoms 1976), while recent geographical studies have confirmed the continued prominence of some parts of the inner city as a residential environment for known offenders. Evans, for instance, in a comprehensive analysis of juvenile delinquency in Cardiff, shows that for a range of offender indices, highest rates of residence appear consistently in the inner-city docklands: 'In those areas there does appear to be established a delinquent tradition so strong that it involves such minority groups of offenders as the younger offender and female offenders. These areas also include high rates of offenders committing the more serious crimes' (Evans 1980: 17). Davidson (1981) argues on the basis of his own study in Hull, and Baldwin and Bottoms (1976) support his view, that inner-city slum areas are particularly likely to provide a residential environment for long-term recidivist offenders. In fact, having reviewed a range of spatial studies, Davidson concludes that 'in most British cities one would expect to find a residential concentration of adult male offenders in the older inner areas' (Davidson 1981: 55).

There is sufficient evidence to suggest that the high crime rate of Britain's inner cities is matched by high rates of offender residence. Without denigrating studies of offenders living in middle and outer ring council-housing estates, therefore, it seems timely to restore attention to offenders living in the inner city, with a view to assessing their impact on local crime rates. In order to establish a causal link between offender and offence rates in the inner city, two questions must be answered. First, why are offenders residentially segregated, tending to be over-represented in inner-city neighbourhoods? Secondly, to what extent do offenders commit their crimes locally, and thereby contribute to the high crime rates experienced in their home neighbourhoods? In considering these questions I shall refer to my own study of 543 residents of the study area in north central Birmingham who were charged with a criminal offence in the eighteen-month period from January 1978 to June 1979. The offender rate for the area was 28 per 1000 (over 18 months) which is somewhat lower than the worst rates monitored by Baldwin and Bottoms (1976), but comparable with Lambert's (1970) findings during his research in south central Birmingham.

Criminal areas and subcultural delinquency

In the post-war era, a number of analysts, rarely geographers, were enthusiastic about the notion of criminal areas (e.g. Mays 1963; Morris 1957). It is an idea indebted to the imagery and language of the Chicago School, and, as Herbert (1982) points out, a vision of urban areas with high offender rates and high degrees of social tolerance of criminal activity has raised more questions than it has answered. Moreover, when such a concept is received into the world of commonsense and policy-making, the consequences can be damaging:

The fake stereotype of the criminal area – of the wild beasts that live at the margins of the social order – has a whole series of real effects for the community concerned. For example, it demoralizes the inhabitants unduly, it causes exodus from the area at an undue level and leads to over-enthusiastic reaction from authorities. (Lea and Young 1984: 41)

Nevertheless, acknowledging that 'criminal areas' do not exist in the form of neighbourhoods where most people are regular offenders, both Evans (1980) and Herbert (1982) provide evidence that variations in public attitudes underpin spatial variations in delinquency rates. They interpret this in subcultural terms, viewing delinquency as 'the product of a social tradition or organisation which condones and encourages delinquent behaviour'. In fact, Evans (1980) favours subcultural explanations of delinquency above all other common theoretical interpretations.

Tacit agreement amongst criminologists and sociologists would define delinquent subcultures as systems of deviant values and behaviours tending to be localised within certain areas of the city. As Matza puts it:

Deviance typically is not an individual or group innovation, rather, it has a long history in particular locales. Thus, according to the sociological view, the deviant is linked to society in minimal form through companies of deviants and through local traditions – when these minimal links appear, we speak of a deviant subculture. (Matza 1964: 63)

It is this notion of territoriality that has proved so attractive to geographers, prompting Herbert (1977: 213) to argue that 'subcultural theories can be extended from gangs and their turfs to more loosely defined collectivities with locality or neighbourhood as the relevant spatial context'. According to this reasoning, it might be possible to explain high offender-rate inner cities in cultural terms: they are areas where delinquent value systems are most fully developed. My own preference, however, is to consider any localisation of delinquent 'subcultures' only in relation to any clustering of potential offenders that is first prompted by structural factors. More specifically, I favour an explanation of the clustering of offenders in the inner city that is couched first in terms of those disadvantages which derive from the unequal distribution of material wealth and life chances within cities. Only then can the 'cultural' expression of this inequality be seen as part of a process sustaining 'deviant' traditions in some inner-city neighbourhoods.

Three structural factors appear in the literature as particularly relevant in explaining the localisation of offenders within the inner city. They reflect employment status, housing opportunities and social class. I consider in turn the possible contribution of each of these to high inner-city offender rates and to subcultural delinquency.

In that part of the Birmingham study area for which offender data were available, the offender rate amongst unemployed residents (40.9 per 1000 over eighteen months) was almost three times that amongst the employed (14.9 per 1000). Moreover, in February 1979, the local unemployment rate ran at 10.9 per cent as compared with 6 per cent for Birmingham as a whole, 5.7 per cent for the West Midlands county and 5.9 per cent nationally. The young were hit especially hard (cf. Birmingham Education Department Careers Service 1979), and by the end of the year the number of young workers registered at employment centres serving the study area accounted for more than half the total for the city as a whole.

It is hard to ignore the link between offender rates and unemployment, given this kind of evidence, and that mentioned in chapter 2. The acknowledgement of such a relationship does not necessarily imply that unemployed people need be singled out as especially criminal. Only a small proportion of any population is represented in official crime statistics; and as Braithwaite (1979) argues, economically disadvantaged offenders are more likely to engage in the most frequently sanctioned crimes. The point is that unemployment is areally selective even within cities, and in so far as the offences of the unemployed contribute disproportionately to the kinds of offences noticed by the police and gathered in victimisation surveys, this selectivity helps account for the high offender rates of the inner city.

An aspect of employment status to be considered alongside unemployment is the role of the school as a catalyst for delinquency. One third of the surveyed offender population of north central Birmingham is of school age, and the offender rate for the area's school-aged teenagers reached 60.9 per 1000 over eighteen months. Moreover, group offending (perhaps the most explicit statement of shared delinquent values) is over-represented amongst the young and those at school.

Taking Birmingham as a whole, over a three-year period 44 per cent of school leavers known to have committed an offence during their school careers attended a high offender-rate school (with an offender rate exceeding 40 per 1000 over three years). However, amongst surveyed inner-city offenders and their accomplices whose schools are known (n=211), 69 per cent attend a high-rate school. If schools in some areas can act as an incubator or catalyst for criminal behaviour (as Hartnagel and Tanner (1982) believe they can), it seems that the inner city might be particularly vulnerable to these effects.

Cicourel and Kitsuse (1963) interpret schools as offender-rate-producing agencies, variously protecting their pupils from, or exposing them to, the labelling mechanisms of the criminal justice system. It may be that schools in the inner city are more likely to begin proceedings against pupils than are schools located else-where. But whether the statistics represent real crime or the differential operation of bureaucratic procedures, the evidence does suggest that the sociology of education has some bearing on an understanding of high juvenile offender rates in the inner cities.

Employment status – as reflected in the intra-urban selectivity of unemployment and of subcultural delinquency in schools – is just one factor contributing to the segregation of offenders. A second key factor concerns housing opportunities and the residential environment. As mentioned in chapter 2, the possible impact of the housing market on the distribution of offenders was first examined in the Sheffield Study on Urban Social Structure and Crime. This research exposes the very high rates of offender residence on some council estates, and accounts for them in terms of estates' variable reputations (Baldwin and Bottoms 1976). Bad reputations are not, according to Baldwin (1974b), initially acquired because the local authority 'dump' problem families on the worst estates. Rather, once an area acquires a bad reputation through historical accident, the various statutory agencies help perpetuate the stigma, and the operation of the housing market makes it difficult for individuals to move (see also Bottoms and Xanthos 1981).

Herbert (1977) took up this theme in his study of juvenile offenders in Cardiff for the years 1966 and 1971. His results draw attention to the high offender rates in (centrally located) enumeration districts

Table 3.6 *Offender rates by housing tenure and dwelling type*

	Total dwellings in housing sector		Offender[1] dwellings		Total offenders in sector		Sector offender rate[2]
	n	%	n	%	n	%	
(a) Housing tenure							
Owner-occupied	3891	(50.7)	197	(44.3)	228	(42.0)	5.9
Council	1462	(19.1)	82	(18.4)	105	(19.3)	7.2
Private rental	2313	(30.2)	162	(36.4)	206	(37.9)	8.9
Not known	0		4	(0.9)	4	(0.7)	
Total	7666	(100.0)	445	(100.0)	543	(100.0)	7.1
(b) Dwelling type							
Houses	6290	(82.0)	319	(71.7)	383	(70.5)	6.1
Apartment houses	266	(3.5)	49	(11.0)	66	(12.2)	24.8
Flats and maisonettes	1110	(14.5)	56	(12.6)	70	(12.9)	6.3
Not known	0		21	(4.7)	24	(4.4)	
Total	7666	(100.0)	445	(100.0)	543	(100.0)	7.1

[1] Number of dwellings housing one or more offenders.
[2] Offenders per 100 dwellings of stated tenure or type.
Source: Author's surveys.

dominated by private rental dwellings. In tentatively suggesting Rex and Moore's (1967) Weberian housing-class schema as a framework in which to interpret this clustering, he raises a question as to whether housing tenure and the operation of the housing market can help explain the high offender rates of the inner city.

The Birmingham study area is dominated by privately rented and owner-occupied housing. Most of the council property, with the exception of one or two redeveloped pockets, is old stock bought up by compulsory purchase order. The housing tenure and dwelling types for each of the 543 offenders were traced, a count of dwelling units in the study area was made, and a record kept of housing tenure and types in each street. In the absence of detailed population data by household for the same period, offender rates per dwelling unit were calculated (a strategy also used by Mack (1964) and Baldwin and Bottoms (1976)).

Both the under-representation of offenders in owner-occupied dwellings, and the low offender rate of the owner-occupied sector shown in table 3.6, conform to the findings in Sheffield and Cardiff.

In contrast with these studies, however, council properties are not over-represented as offenders' residences, and the offender rate in the public sector is considerably lower than that of private rental accommodation. It is hard to account for this specifically in terms of the housing market, except by observing that the dwindling private rental sector does provide shelter for a number of 'marginal' groups in society who can neither raise the capital or security to buy a home, nor conform to the bureaucratic requirements of the public sector's allocation rules. There are, however, two further ways in which housing opportunities in the inner city may help explain the high rate of sanctioned offenders there.

First, on examining the housing data in more detail, it is apparent that over 25 per cent of offenders in the private rental sector live in streets where the dominant tenure type is owner-occupation. This lends some support to the 'status frustration' theories of delinquency which suggest that relative deprivation, or acutely perceived socio-economic boundaries (which are implicit in the neo-Weberian housing-class thesis) may be at least equal in importance to absolute deprivation as a factor underlying the propensity to offend. It may be the distinctive mix of housing tenures within the inner city, then, that partly accounts for high offender rates.

Secondly, it is clear from table 3.6 that the high offender rates found in privately rented accommodation are not unrelated to the large over-representation of offenders in apartment houses. In turn, the influence of both tenure and house type must be viewed in relation to the variations in offender rates found between Housing Action Areas (HAAs), General Improvement Areas (GIAs) and Non-designated Areas (NDAs) (table 3.7). The three types of planning area are quite different environmentally and they are administered by different sets of housing managers (their victimisation rates are considered in more detail in chapter 4). Housing Action Areas, which display the highest offender rates, also contain a disproportionate share of apartment houses and privately rented dwellings. Thus, offenders' ordered positions in the distributive system might relate to a complex set of factors which interact with tenure type in the dispensation of life chances and opportunities. It seems likely, then, that some wider explanatory framework is required than that provided by the pure housing market model.

One such framework is forwarded by Rex (1981) in a modification of his housing-class schema. He identifies a new 'spatial' class and assigns it to the bottom of the housing ladder. It contains all residents of inner-city improvement and action areas, irrespective of

Table 3.7 *Urban zoning and offender residence rates*

	HAA		GIA		NDA		Total	
	n	%	n	%	n	%	n	%
Total dwellings	4691	(61.2)	2563	(33.4)	412	(5.4)	7666	(100.0)
Total population	11695	(61.4)	6820	(35.8)	544	(2.8)	19059	(100.0)
Total offenders	398	(73.3)	131	(24.1)	14	(2.6)	543	(100.0)
Dwelling[1] specific offender rate	8.5		5.1		3.4		7.1	
Population[2] specific offender rate	34.0		19.2		25.7		28.5	

[1] Offenders per 100 dwellings.
[2] Offenders per 1000 people over eleven years old.
Sources: Birmingham city planning department urban renewal housing ledgers; author's survey of crime reports.

their tenure. If Rex is correct in principle, that is, if conflicts associated with class relations are forced by institutional arrangements to occur between groups who are differentially patterned in urban space, and if crime is part of this wider system of social conflicts (as Murray and Boal (1979) and Boal (1972) believe it is), then this thesis could help explain the distribution and directedness of offending. Certainly, the thesis gains credence from an over-representation of offenders in HAAs – the zones of most acute social and environmental stress. It also wins support in the work of Corden (1983), which suggests that disadvantage in housing markets as well as in employment contributes to the cycle of recidivism followed by persistent petty offenders.

A final structural factor affecting the location of offenders within cities concerns social status. Baldwin and Bottoms (1976:67) have drawn attention to the marked absence of data relating to the social class composition of the known offender population in Britain, though their own study in Sheffield begins to remedy this. Following their example, employed study-area offenders in Birmingham, and their accomplices, were classified into broad groups based on the registrar general's social classes. Of 170 employed offenders, over half (58.2 per cent) fall into social classes four and five (semi-skilled and unskilled manual workers), while a further quarter (26.5 per cent) are skilled manual workers (social class 3). Less than 2 per cent are professionals (class 1) and the remainder (14.1 per cent) are 'intermediate' non-manual workers.

These data reflect the familiar clustering of employed offenders into the lower social classes. Economic theorists from Durkheim (1947, 1951), through Merton (1938) to Cohen (1955) have hypothesised that crime is a consequence of status deprivation stemming from the economic inequalities associated with different class positions. Although vigorous debate surrounds the nature of the empirical evidence required to substantiate this view, two plausible arguments still flourish.

The first hypothesis stresses the criminogenic importance of offenders' absolute positions within the social order. This view was popularised by Miller (1958) as a development of Thrasher's (1927) classical view that lower-class delinquency is a direct but intensified expression of the dominant culture pattern of lower-class communities. This argument implies that exaggerated conformity to lower-class values might inevitably violate the law, since these 'deviant' behaviours are so defined because they clash with middle-class norms. The second, currently more popular theory, is represented by the work of Cohen (1955), Merton (1938) and Cloward and Ohlin (1960), and lays more emphasis on offenders' relative position in the social order. Delinquency is interpreted as the actions of a subordinate class who find their ambitions for improved socio-economic status thwarted. Where legitimate means of achieving aspirations are denied, criminality (the use of illegitimate means to achieve economic advance) is part of an inevitable 'reaction formation' – the wholesale inversion of middle-class values (Cohen 1955).

Both theories interpret crime in terms of a cultural reaction to, or more accurately, expression of, structural disadvantage. This expression is location-specific in so far as high offender rates correspond with the residential clustering of low status populations within the inner city. So far, theories linking crime with employment, housing and social class, to account for the offender rates of deprived neighbourhoods, have often been thwarted by the low proportion of disadvantaged populations (even in 'high' offender-rate areas) who turn to crime. Cultural interpretations of delinquency, as defined earlier, allow for this in acknowledging that involvement in crime, or the tacit condoning of certain illegal practices, is only one of the many ways through which material conditions receive cultural expression. In developing this perspective, geographers might find much of interest in the work of Birmingham University's Centre for Contemporary Cultural Studies (e.g. Hall and Jefferson 1975), and in an illuminating literature review by Brake (1980).

Delinquency and distance

Monitoring and explaining the clustering of offenders within the inner city does not in itself account for the high crime rates of such areas. However, one of the few empirical findings to emerge consistently from criminological studies of offender behaviour is that essentially short distances separate offence locations from offenders' residences. This is particularly true of inner-city areas, which, according to Rengert (1977) are least likely to attract offenders from other locations or to house offenders who habitually travel to suburban areas to commit crimes.

The short distances between the homes of inner-city offenders and the place of their offences have often been documented in Britain. Upon the generality of this observation hinges the relevance of offender residence rates to an explanation of the high rates of crime in the inner city. Lambert (1970) found that most crime in the inner areas of Sparkbrook, south Birmingham, was committed by local residents, in contrast with some high offender-rate/low crime-rate suburbs where offenders seemed much more mobile. Baldwin and Bottoms (1976) found in Sheffield that 60 per cent of property offences were committed within two miles of the offenders' homes. In the north central Birmingham study area, 74 per cent of offences took place within two kilometres (1.88 miles) of the perpetrator's residence, and, as table 3.8 shows, most offences occur within a very narrow spatial range.

White (1932) suggested the generalisation that personal offences are committed nearer to home than property offences – a finding questioned in the present study (in which nearly all crimes were committed near offenders' homes). Baldwin and Bottoms (1976) ranked the following crimes in Sheffield from most to least local: violent/sexual offences, breaking offences, larceny, taking and driving away vehicles and fraud. This ranking differs somewhat from that found in north central Birmingham, where the following ordering was observed: criminal damage/arson, burglary, violent/sexual crimes, taking and driving away, fraud, theft. American evidence suggests that such differences may be accounted for by the different degrees of planning involved in different types of offence. In general, longer 'journeys-to-crime' tend to be made to commit better-planned offences aiming at higher rewards. Capone and Nicholls's (1976) analysis of robbery in Dade City, Florida suggests that the average length of armed trips (which entail at least some degree of planning and professionalism) is longer than that of 'strong arm' trips. Moreover, trip length varies according to the

Table 3.8 *'Journeys-to-crime' in north central Birmingham*

	Mean distance (km)[1]	Standard deviation (km)	Number of journeys[2]
Criminal damage/arson	1.51	1.84	52
Burglary	1.59	2.14	201
Personal violence and sexual crimes	1.79	1.92	175
Taking and driving motor vehicles	2.14	2.64	128
Fraud	2.46	1.63	19
Theft	2.53	2.23	299
Other	1.89	3.17	47
All crimes	2.04	2.22	921

[1] All figures refer to study-area offenders and their accomplices and are based on straight-line distances between offenders' homes and crime locations.
[2] One distance was recorded for each offender for each crime.
Source: Author's survey of crime reports.

quality of the robbed premises, and increases as a function of the value of property stolen. Similarly, Pyle et al. (1974) show that house burglars travel further (an average of over seven miles) to high-income districts than to low-income areas (where the average trip for burglars is less than a mile).

As Lea and Young (1984) point out, most inner-city criminality is ill-conceived, sporadic, opportunistic and rarely organised. Professional criminals are few and far between, and for the most part the targets of crime fall within the offenders' immediate community. In north central Birmingham, neither planning nor the attainment of high rewards characterised the majority of offences. This is apparent from the low value of goods stolen or damaged (over half the property crimes involved sums less than ten pounds) and their subsistence nature (over a third of the goods stolen were described as money, food or clothing).

Short distances travelled to commit offences may reflect the spontaneous and petty nature of much street crime, but this fact does not fully explain the clustering of offences within the inner city: it does not say *why* opportunistic crimes are committed near homes. Two factors which might constrain offenders to a relatively small territory within the inner city deserve consideration at this point.

The first concerns the existence and availability of opportunities for crime in inner-city environments (to be discussed in the last section of this chapter). The second constraint is that imposed on potential offenders' mobility by their images, or mental maps, of the city (a factor examined briefly below).

In the last two decades, considerable interest has been expressed in offenders' perceptions of the existence and availability of opportunities for crime. By matching the areal extent of offenders' perceived activity spaces with the distribution of crimes, a number of authors have tried to flesh out the differences between the images held by criminals and those of non-offenders. Scarr (1973), for instance, has suggested that offenders' tendencies to discriminate spatially between good and bad targets distinguishes their images of the city from those of non-offenders. Carter (1974) also claims in his study of Oklahoma city that spatial patterns of crime are related to criminals' images of the city, that these images differ as between black and white offenders, and that offenders' images differ from those of non-offenders.

Other studies are more realistic in acknowledging the arbitrary dividing line between criminal and non-criminal populations. Thus Carter and Hill (1980) demonstrate that offenders' perceptions of the accessibility of crime locations within the city are related to their social attributes rather than to their distinctively criminal mentalities. Similarly, in two empirical studies of robbers and burglars, Reppetto (1974) relates offenders' spatial behaviour to their age and social characteristics. Young offenders, for instance, are more tied to particular territories than are older criminals; they are more limited to insecure targets (often unsound low-income housing), and usually tend to steal money because of the difficulties of disposing of stolen goods.

In short, it seems most likely that the relationship between crime and distance, in so far as this is contingent upon offenders' urban images, reflects the mobility patterns of the socio-economic and locational subgroups from which offenders are drawn. If restricted images render distant targets unavailable to inner-city offenders, then this may reflect the restrictions on spatial mobility experienced by inner-city populations more generally. Both Lynch (1960) and Horton and Reynolds (1971) found that the processes of acquiring knowledge about urban environments, and the extent of this knowledge, varies between residential (i.e. locational) subgroups. The behavioural characteristics of offenders reflect those of the populations from which they are drawn, and in the inner city this would tend to be reflected in shorter rather than longer journeys-to-crime.

Crime and environment

A second explanation for the relatively short distances inner-city offenders travel to crime, and a key factor underlying the high crime rates of inner-city neighbourhoods, concerns the distribution of local opportunities for crime. If local opportunities are plentiful and available even the most regular of offenders need not go further afield to achieve their ends.

In examining crime as a contingency of available opportunities, we move into the domain of 'environmental criminology' as discussed by Brantingham and Brantingham (1981). The movement gained much of its initial impetus from the pleas of Jeffery (1971), and by 1976 it had appropriated a complete issue of the *American Behavioral Scientist*. More recently the rationale underlying environmental criminology has gained the support of the British Home Office (Clarke and Mayhew 1980; Ramsay 1982), and it now provides the main thrust of crime prevention policy in this country. The appeal of the movement in a practical sense is hard to quibble with. It is surely easier to alter the distribution of environmental opportunities for crime than it is to influence the complex socio-economic factors motivating offenders.

Few would deny that inner-city environments contain an abundance of opportunities for spontaneous, often petty, crime. Insecure window and door fittings in ageing housing stock; entrances exposed by the piecemeal demolition, infill and refurbishing associated with urban renewal; and easy access to homes through vacant lots interspersed with occupied dwellings; these all provide local opportunistic offenders with potential targets. Few commentators on the inner city fail to emphasise the enormous problems of physical decay that daily confront the residents of such areas. Many homes lack the symbolic protection of front gardens, and the distinction between private and public space becomes blurred in areas of subdivided lodging houses, flats and maisonettes.

My own crime survey in north central Birmingham (discussed in more detail in chapter 4) included interviews with forty-seven burglary victims. Thirteen per cent claim the crimes were facilitated by poor building security, 15 per cent blame access through adjacent vacant lots, and 19 per cent note easy (often hidden) access from the rear of their properties. Analyses of official crime statistics for the streets of the study area over a twelve-month period show that one fifth of local burglaries and thefts from dwellings (crimes which account for 36.5 per cent of all crimes known to the police in that area) occur by way of insecure points of entry (primarily unlocked or unlockable doors and windows).

Since the publication of Oscar Newman's very popular, but academically criticised, book on *Defensible space* (1972), observers have been intrigued by the notion that opportunities for crime can be removed or made inaccessible to offenders, both by altering the physical environment and by changing social attitudes towards communal space. To explain the high crime rates of the inner cities in these terms, it is necessary to ask why it is that in the inner city so many potential opportunities are exploited. Why is the environment not better protected? Is there scope for sealing off the opportunities and thereby reducing the crime rate?

While attempting to answer such questions, this is not the place to discuss and evaluate the extensive literature of the 'crime prevention through environmental design' movement. Some of the best critical appraisals are given by Mawby (1977a), Mayhew (1979), Reppetto (1976a) and Taylor et al. (1980). The practical recommendations of most earlier studies, such as that by Brantingham and Brantingham (1975) in Talahasee, Florida usually referred to large-scale programmes for new building projects. But even if the cost of design changes were to be offset by reductions in crime, and even if the physical environment could accurately be described as a trigger or inhibitor of territorial attitudes and behaviour, this type of environmental engineering is not an option available in Britain's inner cities, where planning policies are directed towards upgrading existing buildings rather than towards comprehensive redevelopment.

In fact, the significance of physical cues as indicators of the defensibility of space is in some doubt. Although Wilson (1978) provides convincing evidence that design features can create perceived zones of territorial influence which account for patterns of vandalism on a large sample of inner London estates, many studies (e.g. Dingemans 1978; Mawby 1977b; Merry 1981b) find little relationship between the apparent defensibility of the environment and the incidence of crime. In an attempt to rescue the value of environmentally orientated crime prevention policies, researchers have moved in two directions. First, they have begun to focus on the primacy of social organisation over architectural design as the guarantor of defended space – a possibility highlighted by Reppetto (1974) over a decade ago in the appendix to his volume on *Residential Crime*. Secondly, research has moved towards a 'situational' approach to crime prevention, focussing not on dramatic changes in design, but on manipulating the opportunities for crime at the micro-level. Clarke and Mayhew (1980) have discussed the practicalities of this second option. It requires crime-control measures that can be aimed specifically at particular types of crime, taking due regard for the micro-environments in which each occurs. The aim is to reduce the opportunities for crime as they are perceived by a broad range of potential offenders. In practice this includes target hardening, target removal, removal of the means to commit offences, reducing the payoff, and encouraging public surveillance. In a later publication, Mayhew (1981) expresses some doubt as to the viability of the last strategy, but she does outline the possibilities for at least increasing offenders' fears of being seen.

The question remains, however, as to how effective any measures to enhance social cohesion or manipulate the micro-environments of crime might be in the inner city. In north central Birmingham there is little evidence of any collective protection of space, either formally or informally. The small amount of co-operative activity which does take place is in the form of a 'reactive' victim-support scheme (now common in various parts of many cities in Britain), rather than as a proactive programme of protection and surveillance. But even this involves only a small proportion of the population. Indeed, less than 6 per cent of the survey respondents engaged in *any* form of voluntary activity – a feature not uncommon amongst Britain's inner cities, as confirmed in a report by the London Voluntary Services Committee (Knight and Hayes 1981). Recently, however, British police forces have begun to take the initiative in encouraging public involvement in crime prevention. This is discussed in chapter 6, and although it is too soon to judge the impact of such moves on the incidence and effects of crime in the inner city, some reduction in the opportunities for crime might well be associated with this kind of scheme.

Concerning the role of situational crime prevention, there *is* evidence that some individuals in north central Birmingham take extra precautions to secure their homes and property (a practice also examined in a later chapter). So far, the strategies implemented are piecemeal, individualistic and uncoordinated, and it is hard to predict the effects of more organised approaches to target hardening. However, one important factor which tends to be forgotten in the search for immediately effective crime-control policies concerns the theoretical link between crime and the opportunities upon which it is contingent. If crime is largely an *independent* variable, which the 'defensible space' school prefers to assume it is not, it may not be prevented either by public surveillance or by measures physically sealing off the relevant opportunities. Rather, crime may be displaced in space, in time or by target.

So far, little evidence of displacement in space has been found in a number of North American studies evaluating the success of crime prevention projects (Hakim et al. 1979; Hellman 1981; Mehay 1977). Displacement in time, however, receives some tentative verification in research by Reppetto (1976b) and Smith (1981a), and Gabor (1981) has found evidence of target displacement from residential to business premises, and from marked property to unmarked merchandise. In the UK, some further evidence regarding the importance of target hardening for deterring burglars suggests that displacement does occur (usually in time) and that the offence is most likely to be deferred by signs of occupancy, burglar alarms, dogs and a dearth of cover, rather than by police patrols, passers-by or the presence of locks and bolts (Bennett 1984).

As far as the inner city is concerned, then, offenders are unlikely to be displaced out of the area. Those who engage only in opportunistic crime seem unlikely to be deterred unless current policing schemes have a dramatic effect in the near future. Individuals' expenditure on locks, alarms and other forms of protection will do little to offset the vulnerability created by the poor physical quality of their dwellings, and it seems unlikely that planned improvements have or will alter this to any great degree (cf. Paris and Blackaby 1979). Crime prevention is not a priority in improvement schemes, for the financial impact of petty crime (which bears no relationship to its social and psychological effects) does not warrant substantial investment of public money. The abundance of easily exploited opportunities for 'working-class' crime must therefore go a long way towards explaining the high crime rates of the inner city.

To summarise, having considered the broad regional context of crime in England and Wales, we have moved on to examine intra-urban variations in the crime rate in terms of offenders' residential patterns and behaviours, and in terms of the vulnerability of the environments in which potential offenders live. Both the segregation of offenders and the configuration of environmental opportunities suggest a partial explanation for the high crime rates of the inner cities. Chapter 4 goes on to consider a third, relatively neglected, factor with some bearing on the distribution of crime – the victim.

4

The victims of crime

This chapter emphasises the importance of considering crime in terms of those it affects, and so complements a more traditional geographical focus on where crime happens and who perpetrates it. My concern is not merely with offenders and the built environment, but with the *social* environment of crime and the plight of victims. The discussion begins generally, but soon develops a third perspective on the high crime rates of the inner city to add to those introduced in chapter 3. The central question does not ask why offenders are so active in the inner city, nor why the opportunities for crime are so abundant in inner-city environments. Rather, it asks why and in what way are the residents of the inner city so vulnerable?

Random sample surveys of individuals and households (victim surveys or crime surveys) in Europe and North America consistently find that only a small proportion of crimes experienced by victims are reported to the police. The incidence of victimisation is obviously far greater than official statistics suggest. Although many of the crimes involved seem less serious than those that are reported, this does not necessarily mean that they have any less impact on victims' sense of well-being.

Drawing mainly on the results of published crime surveys, as well as on my own research in north central Birmingham, I now examine some factors contributing to the risk of victimisation.* I shall argue that much of the risk of victimisation is related to lifestyle, and that such risk is inevitable, and acceptable, in so far as it is contingent on generally desirable social processes that work to increase the range

---

* The north central Birmingham crime survey comprises a simple random sample of 10 per cent of households in that part of the study area contained in the wards of Aston and Handsworth (based on electoral registers updated with local-authority rating lists). A response rate of 77 per cent (n = 531) was secured from a target sample of 690. Vacant dwellings, non-contacts and refusals form 9, 3 and 11 per cent respectively of the target sample. The survey is discussed in more detail in Smith (1982a).

Table 4.1 *Observed frequencies of victimisation compared with expected numbers based on a Poisson distribution*

	Number of times victimised in one year[1] (% in brackets)			
	0	1	2	3 or more
Observed	368 (69.3)	110 (20.7)	28 (5.3)	25 (4.7)
Expected	313 (58.9)	166 (31.3)	43 (8.1)	9 (1.7)

$X^2 = 62.23$, 3 d.f., $p<0.0001$

[1] July 1978–June 1979
Source: North central Birmingham crime survey.

and availability of opportunities for social interaction. The risks of victimisation associated with contemporary trends in urban lifestyles will be termed 'absolute' risks, in that they represent a minimum level of risk incurred when people routinely participate in modern society. However, there are also factors which appear to increase the risks of victimisation above the base level set by lifestyle. This added vulnerability (which may be termed 'relative' risk) is also distributed non-randomly, and it augurs less favourably for the quality of life of those it affects. My argument will be that relative risks generally tend to be highest in deprived working-class areas, and that it is relative exposure to risk that crime-prevention policies might realistically seek to reduce. Attempts to achieve an absolute decrease in the crime rate (the aim, for instance, of broad law-and-order campaigns implemented on a national scale) may be less expedient and less socially just.

Victimisation, lifestyle and exposure to risk

It is not uncommon to draw a parallel between being a victim of crime and having an accident, for both are popularly attributed to chance. Yet, just as close inspection reveals systematic variations in accident-proneness, so detailed analyses reveal social and spatial bias in victim-proneness. It is thus in common with numerous other studies (see Biderman 1967; Ennis 1967; Fishman 1979; Sparks et al. 1977) that my own survey in north central Birmingham found more non-victims and more multiple victims than a random model would suggest. Table 4.1 illustrates this, comparing the observed frequencies of victimisation with those expected on the basis of the

Poisson distribution – a formula suggestive of a random generating process when the overall probability of an event occurring is small. There are clearly more non-victims than expected, and a greater proportion than predicted amongst the very susceptible (those experiencing three or more incidents). However, the skew towards multiple victimisation here (where 26 per cent of the sample accounts for 59 per cent of crimes) is not as marked as that reported by Sparks et al. (1977) in London, where 60 per cent of the 582 incidents were directed at 13 per cent of the sample.

Amongst various attempts to explain why the risks of victimisation are not spread randomly, it is the 'lifestyle–exposure-to-risk' model, developed in North America, that has gained most support (exponents of the model include Cohen and Cantor 1980; Cohen and Felson 1979; Cohen et al. 1981; Hindelang et al. 1978). The thesis argues that a certain amount of crime is inevitable wherever behaviour is subject to societal norms and where material rewards and life chances are differentially distributed. The minimum level of crime at any one time depends on the patterns of socialising among potential offenders and potential victims; and on the amount of time property is left unguarded. Both these factors reflect the day-to-day routine of urban living. The risk of victimisation will tend to increase as the options for different types of behaviour increase and as lifestyles improve and are enriched. Thus, rising crime, which, on a national scale, is so often regarded as an aspect of societal breakdown, could in fact index predominantly beneficial processes. Some implications of establishing a positive relationship between crime trends and desirable changes in the quality of life have been discussed by North American authors:

The opportunity for predatory crime appears to be enmeshed in the opportunity for legitimate activities to such an extent that it might be very difficult to root out substantial amounts of crime without modifying much of our way of life. Rather than assuming that predatory crime is simply an indicator of social breakdown, one might take it as a by-product of the freedom and prosperity as they manifest themselves in the routine activities of everyday life. (Cohen and Felson 1979: 605)

In their empirical examination of this lifestyle-activity thesis, Cohen and Cantor (1980) assert the significance of two lifestyle variables as indices of risk: size of household is suggested as a measure of the extent to which guardians are available to protect both persons and property; employment status is taken as a surrogate for major activity, and as such is an indicator of exposure to risk.

Cohen and Cantor argue that single persons are less likely than members of large families to be accompanied out of doors, and less able to ensure that their dwelling is occupied when they themselves are absent. Small households should therefore be most vulnerable to crime. In north central Birmingham, however, differences in the probability of victimisation between one and greater-than-one person households prove negligible, although the British Crime Survey (BCS) indicates that nationally, one-adult households face higher risks than two-adult households. The predictive power of household size increases in Birmingham when the sample is divided into households of one or two, three or four, and more than four persons, but it indicates greater vulnerability amongst larger rather than smaller households. This might be because membership of a large household in the inner city implies not only guardianship, but also the frequent entrance and exit of dwellings by family members and by a large assortment of friends and acquaintances. Thus dwelling security may be *decreased*, and the range of potentially (if only rarely) risky relationships widened.

Employment status, in the sense of a simple distinction between employed and unemployed respondents, also proved important to Cohen and Cantor's thesis, but it has been a poor predictor of victimisation in British studies. Table 4.2 suggests rather the salience of second lifestyle variable – spare-time activities. Theoretically, this would seem even more important than employment status as a risk indicator, because it captures behaviour patterns at times (evenings and weekends) and in situations (the face-to-face contacts made during the course of different social and recreational engagements) when a notable peak of offending occurs. In fact, as many as one-third of the crimes recorded in the Birmingham survey were known to have taken place between six p.m. and midnight. The BCS, too, reveals that 15 per cent of all crimes and 23 per cent of personal crimes occur during the night hours.

Table 4.3 shows that the probability of being a victim in north central Birmingham is least for those whose spare-time activities are least frequent. Only 60 per cent of those active between three and seven days per week remained non-victims, compared with 70 to 90 per cent of those whose activities take place twice a week or less. Variations in susceptibility also seem influenced by the *type* of spare-time socialising which is undertaken. Victims are more likely to engage in all types of activity than non-victims, but a considerably larger proportion of those victimised engage in regular visits to the cinema, theatre, dancing or bingo; and respondents who tend to

Table 4.2 *Variables associated with victimisation*

Variable	X^2	d.f.	p≼	Cramer's V
(a) Discriminating between victims and non-victims				
Spare-time activities	16.66	5	0.01	0.177
Dwelling rateable value	16.262	4	0.01	0.175
Class[1]	10.431	3	0.02	0.14
Dwelling type	6.776	2	0.04	0.113
Age	6.298	3	0.1	0.11
Area type	5.243	2	0.07	0.099
Household size	4.859	2	0.1	0.096
(b) Discriminating between one-time and multiple victims				
Spare-time activities	16.235	4[2]	0.005	0.316
Gender	7.889	1	0.007	0.22
Area type	5.5	2	0.07	0.184

[1] Categories based on the Hope–Goldthorpe occupational scale (see Goldthorpe and Hope 1974)
[2] To calculate X^2 values, two activity categories were amalgamated, reducing d.f. by one.
Source: North central Birmingham crime survey.

meet with friends in pubs or cafés are also twice as likely to have been victims during the reference year as those who do not.

The BCS has established the wider applicability of these findings (Gottfredson 1984). Nationally, the more evenings and weekends individuals claim to spend outside the home, the more vulnerable they are to personal crime. The more evenings per week a home is left unoccupied, the more likely it is to be burgled. Broadly, therefore, the American thesis seems to hold in Britain. Different lifestyles – the characteristic ways in which individuals allocate their time to leisure activities – are differentially related to the probability of being in (or leaving accessible) particular places at particular times, and coming into contact with (or leaving an attractive opportunity for) others, who are potential criminals (Hindelang et al. 1978; Gottfredson 1981). A certain level of victimisation might, then, be expected to accompany particular urban lifestyles. In particular, the hitherto neglected activity variable 'leisure-time

Table 4.3 *Victimisation and spare-time activity rates*

Number of days/evenings per week involved in leisure-time activities (% in brackets)

	7	5 or 6	3 or 4	1 or 2	Less than 1	Less than 1 per month	Total
Non-victims	32 (62.7)	22 (61.1)	72 (60.5)	140 (71.1)	46 (88.5)	56 (73.7)	368 (69.3)
Victims	19 (37.3)	14 (38.9)	47 (39.5)	57 (28.9)	6 (11.5)	20 (26.3)	163 (30.7)
Total	51 (100.0)	36 (100.0)	119 (100.0)	197 (100.0)	52 (100.0)	76 (100.0)	531 (100.0)

$X^2 = 16.66$, 5 d.f., $p < 0.01$

Source: North central Birmingham crime survey.

socialising' appears to be an appropriate indicator of this kind of risk.

The relevance of the lifestyle–exposure-to-risk thesis is indisputable, but it is neither well-developed as a theory of victimisation, nor is it sufficient in itself as an explanation of the incidence of crime in modern society: at least two caveats remain to be stated. First, as Gottfredson (1984) points out, progress in understanding the link between victimisation and lifestyle requires much more detailed analysis of the timing and location of those activities which render participants most vulnerable. Secondly, it is important not to lose sight of the fact that 'absolute' risks of victimisation are given in the lifestyles associated with a specific mode of production and with specific mechanisms of distribution. Lifestyle itself is just one manifestation of more fundamental social and economic processes. The point is well made by Carroll and Jackson (1983), who argue that the lifestyle measures used by Cohen and Felson (1979) are ultimately a reflection of the nature of income inequalities in US society. The implication of this kind of argument is that those seeking to adjust the levels of 'absolute' exposure to risk must concern themselves with the politics of economic development, the distribution of wealth and the broader goals of national government, rather than with more limited analyses of policing and crime prevention. The importance of such visionary approaches cannot be overstated, but my concern with what is currently practicable – indeed desirable – in Britain leads me to emphasise rather the problem of *relative* exposure to risk, and the urgency of finding a just and expedient way to deal with it.

Victimisation, location and multiple deprivation

While few dispute the notion that the risks of victimisation are related to lifestyle, there has been relatively little speculation as to why some individuals and groups seem much more vulnerable than lifestyle alone might dictate. Recently, however, analyses of the BCS have revealed the overwhelming importance of residential location in this respect. Gottfredson (1984) shows that, although victimisation is associated with the lifestyle-related variables of age, marital status, gender, work status and education (irrespective of location), residence in the inner city interacts with these variables to place some groups of people in positions of extremely high risk. For instance, amongst rural residents who tend not to go out at night or at weekends only 4 per cent had been the victim of a personal crime in the previous year. Amongst inner-city residents who do go out at these high risk times, 29 per cent were victims. Additionally, people frequenting pubs in the inner city are more vulnerable than those engaged in the same activity outside the inner city, and people visiting friends in the inner city are more vulnerable than those visiting in other locations.

To date, little has been written about spatial variations in the distributions of victims. Wolf and Hauge (1975) noted some inter-urban differences in Finland, Denmark, Norway and Sweden, where the risk of falling victim to violent crimes is greatest in the capital cities. Within the United States, too, inter-urban variations in the rates of crime against households are quite marked, varying from a high (in 1973) of 131 larceny incidents per 100 households in Los Angeles to a low of 33 per 100 in New York (US Department of Justice 1975). Several victim surveys also confirm the impression conveyed in official statistics of a higher incidence of crime in central urban areas than in suburban or rural zones. Sparks et al. (1977), for instance, provide tentative evidence from Britain (later confirmed by the BCS) that marked discrepancies between the victimisation rates of inner cities and other urban and rural locations exist.

Smaller-scale intra-urban variations have also been noted. Meurer (1979) collated the results of several victim surveys in the United States and discovered that people with the highest probability of victimisation live in the most economically depressed niches of large metropolitan areas. More recently, Sampson and Castellano (1982) have made a similar observation on the basis of National Crime Survey data for 1973–8. They find higher rates of victimisation in low economic-status urban neighbourhoods than in high-status neighbourhoods. It is in those urban neighbourhoods with the highest rates of unemployment that victimisation rates for theft and violence are greatest. In particular these authors stress that 'areal economic status has quite a different impact in central cities [where it is positively related to victimisation] than in rural areas [where it is not consistently related to victimisation] with respect to the production of crime rates' (Sampson and Castellano 1982: 378). Fishman (1979) also finds a marked over-representation of crimes against persons, and of multiple victimisation, amongst the residents of lower-class areas in Haifa, Israel. Block (1979), however, finds crimes of violence most rife in neighbourhoods where the very poor and the middle classes live in close proximity, while Pope (1979a) argues that burglary, larceny and vehicle theft vary with the age and sex structure of urban sub-communities.

Despite the exploratory nature of many of these studies, there does appear to be some agreement that place of residence has a significant effect on individuals' likelihood of victimisation. This suggests that the different levels of risk as between inner city and suburban or rural zones highlighted by the BCS may be only a first-order distinction in a hierarchy of spatial scales at which relative risk is compounded. It therefore seems appropriate to consider further some areal variations in victimisation *within* the inner city which are exposed in the Birmingham study.

Area type (relating to the Housing Action Areas (HAAs), and General Improvement Areas (GIAs) designated as part of the government's environment-orientated urban improvement schemes), was a significant correlate of victimisation in north central Birmingham. As early as 1970, Lambert demonstrated the close association of crime in south Birmingham with different housing environments, and his work suggests the relevance of assessing victimisation in terms of the mosaic of planning zones with which it seems to be associated in north central Birmingham. The rationale for the area-based policies on whose mandate these planning zones were designated is most clearly expressed in the Department of the Environment's *Policy for the inner cities* (1977a). The assumption is that collective deprivation associated with place of residence is distinct from individual deprivation, in that geographical disadvantage denotes a greater degree of deprivation than that represented by the sum of the socio-economic problems which variously beset each household.

The validity of this argument is open to question, and it is debatable whether or not deprived areas have been (or can ever be) isolated accurately for planning purposes. Certainly, areal deprivation cannot be conceived in the final instance in terms of areal causes, since, as Smith (1979) reasons at length, intra-urban locational disadvantage is just one consequence of structural processes acting on a national and international scale. However, given that there are obvious locational variations in well-being at all spatial scales and in diverse political economies, any corresponding variations in victimisation must be worthy of attention. The designated planning zones of the inner city are defined so as to circumscribe differentially deprived areas; and peoples' experiences of crime varies between these same areas. It seems possible, therefore, that victimisation itself can be analysed as an element or

Table 4.4 *Urban zoning and victimisation (% in brackets)*

| | Planning zone | | | |
	Housing Action Area	General Improvement Area	Non-designated area	Total
Non-victims	146 (74.1)	209 (67.4)	13 (54.2)	368 (69.3)
Victims	51 (25.9)	101 (32.6)	11 (45.8)	163 (30.7)
Total	197 (100.0)	310 (100.0)	24 (100.0)	531 (100.0)

$X^2 = 5.243$, 2 d.f., p<0.07

Source: North central Birmingham crime survey.

indicator of inner-city deprivation. Moreover, by examining victimisation as integral to the spatial character of urban disadvantage, new aspects of the problem of deprivation might be explored. This is one response to Norris's (1979) criticism that research on urban deprivation is often constrained by and biased towards the most accessible or measurable surrogates of inequality, evincing an extreme operationalism which, he contends, has resulted in many facets of the problem being ignored. Certainly, the author of Merseyside's crime survey agrees that high crime rates, wherever they occur, 'must be seen as an index of social and environmental deprivation and poverty' (Kinsey 1984: 15).

Table 4.4 details the areal differences in victimisation observed in north central Birmingham. Overall, the highest rates of victimisation were experienced by householders in GIAs and Non-designated Areas (NDAs), but it is in the HAAs that the highest rates of multiple victimisation occur (table 4.5). HAAs contain 31 per cent of all victims but 44 per cent of multiple victims, and while the average victim resident in a GIA experienced 1.5 offences, victims in HAAs average 2.1 each.

GIAs were designated as a consequence of the 1969 Housing Act. They were to consist of basically sound dwellings (though a significant proportion would lack basic amenities), and planning would focus on environmental enhancement. HAAs were a product of the 1974 Housing Act, and were assigned to those more severely

Table 4.5 *Multiple victimisation and area of residence (% in brackets)*

Area type	Total offences in survey	Multiple victims	% multiple victims[1]	Offences per victim	Offences per multiple victim
HAA	106 (38)	22 (44)	43.1	2.1	3.5
GIA	153 (54)	25 (50)	24.8	1.5	3.1
NDA	22 (8)	3 (6)	27.3	2.0	4.7
Total	281	50			

$X^2 = 5.5$, 2 d.f., $p < 0.07$[2]

[1] Multiple victims as a proportion of all victims.
[2] X^2 value represents the difference in the distribution of single and multiple victims between the three types of area.
Source: North central Birmingham crime survey.

deprived pockets, where housing stress combined with social problems in neighbourhoods characterised by low incomes, over-crowding, multi-occupation and a racially mixed population.

Within HAAs (though not within GIAs or NDAs) significant relationships between victimisation and class, age, rateable value of property and housing tenure emerged. These relationships are documented in Smith (1982a). It appears that in those parts of the inner city where people are least likely to be victims, but most likely (having experienced one offence) to be multiple victims, the following groups of people are most vulnerable (in order of statistical explanatory power): those whose dwellings have a rateable value above £164, private renters, the under 25-year-olds, and a group of professional, self-employed, non-manual or skilled manual workers. Least susceptible are the occupants of dwellings with rateable values less than £136, council tenants, the over-60s and the unemployed. Paradoxically, in HAAs – the zones where socio-economic and environmental stress is most acute – it is the least individually disadvantaged rather than the ostensibly most vulnerable who are most prone to victimisation. Those most susceptible are not the old and infirm but the young and mobile. The higher-income groups rather than the unemployed suffer, as do the occupants of higher rather than lower valued property.

Property offences are also most over-represented in HAAs. On the whole, such areas may not be attractive to offenders (hence the lower overall victimisation rates than GIAs and NDAs), but within them, the prime targets are the *relatively* affluent and the *relatively* advantaged. Nevertheless, the incentives offered by insecure and insecurable property may well be an important precursor to the higher rates of multiple victimisation experienced by HAA residents. This is particularly true for private renters, whose landlords are often unable to maintain their property and who are unable to force improvement themselves without entering into complex legal procedures (cf. Paris and Blackaby 1979: 29). It is equally, and almost certainly increasingly, true of low income owner-occupiers, who, as Karn's (1979) analysis confirms, are often unable or unwilling to improve, given uncertain planning legislation and the high capital outlay required.

There is some evidence here that the odds of victimisation are associated with *in situ* deprivation, not merely with personal vulnerability. That the relatively affluent within an absolutely deprived community should be most vulnerable to crime indicates that, even though certain disadvantages may be assessed in terms of the structural position occupied by people living near to each other, multiple deprivation has social consequences which must be appreciated in specifically spatial terms.

The same argument may be extended from the scale of subgroups within HAAs to that of subareas within the inner city as a whole. In GIAs and NDAs, the higher overall victimisation rate may be explained in terms of these areas' noticeably more affluent appearance and by the steep socio-economic gradients that separate them from the HAAs (cf. Winchester 1978). Within the most deprived part of the urban fabric, the inner city, it is the *relatively* affluent subareas that experience the highest rates of victimisation. Paradoxically, in GIAs, protective landscaping, the narrowing of road entrances and exits, and general environmental upgrading seem to have had little impact on the defensibility of space. Within these areas, victimisation is unrelated to socio-economic and demographic characteristics. Susceptibility to crime seems rather to be conditioned by one's neighbourhood of residence.

This 'neighbourhood effect' may be most noticeable in the inner city, where offenders are known to travel short distances and where relative affluence is the most significant indicator of opportunity. There are, moreover, two further aspects of the neighbourhood effect associated with victimisation. First, Gottfredson's (1984) analysis of the BCS shows that those individuals and households most prone to *criminal* victimisation are also prone to other kinds of misfortune. Households and individuals within households where there had been a fire, an accident requiring medical attention, or a motor vehicle accident, were 50 per cent more likely to have experienced criminal victimisation than were other respondents. Criminal victimisation clusters socially and spatially, and the pattern is mirrored by a variety of other problems. The indication is that those factors contributing to the absolute and relative risks of victimisation also contribute to the risk of accidents.

Secondly, the localisation of victimisation questions the received wisdom concerning relationships between victim and offender populations. Society instinctively prefers to draw a sharp line between offenders and victims, isolating criminals morally as well as legally. But empirical research is increasingly gnawing away at the concept of mutually exclusive offender and victim populations, showing it to be a figment of political imagination and a sop to social conscience. Singer (1981) dispels the myth as it stands in the United States, and the BCS reveals a significant relationship between self-reported offending and personal victimisation in Britain (Gottfredson 1984). It seems that the factors most associated with victimisation (and with household accidents) are also most closely associated with offending (see also Gottfredson 1981).

In some instances, therefore, it may be most appropriate to analyse crime as a form of social interaction arising out of specific social contexts in which the distinction between offender and victim is not always conceptually helpful. This is particularly true of direct-contact crimes against persons, and it can be illustrated with the example of personal violence in north central Birmingham.

In the surveyed area, 239 violent crimes were recorded by the police in a twelve-month period. These include 25 sexual offences (10.5 per cent), 62 instances of violence committed for material gain (25.9 per cent) and 152 other violent assaults (63.6 per cent). The most obvious characteristic of their spatial distribution is a tendency to cluster on or near the main thoroughfares which bisect the studied neighbourhoods. In fact, 128 (53.6 per cent) scenes of crime are public highways and 37 (15.5 per cent) are public houses, clubs and other places of entertainment. A substantial proportion of the crimes (16.5 per cent) took place in private residences and a further 3.3 per cent in parks and playgrounds. Five per cent of the incidents occurred in shops, and the remaining 15 (6.3 per cent) are distributed amongst subways, alleys, buses, churchyards and so on.

The impression, then, particularly in an area where street life is still integral to the social order, is that the largest proportion of violent interpersonal offences are perpetrated in primary group settings. Victimologists have often alluded to the importance of these intimate bonds of friendship and kinship which normally *preclude* aggression, but which occasionally break down. In order to examine the social context of violent crimes, the circumstantial details attached to each crime report were used to classify offences as 'focussed', 'unfocussed', or 'primary group' in character.

Unfocussed events were few. In them, the distinction between offender and victim is clear, and the encounter would have given victims little opportunity to retaliate against offenders. Examples include the victim struck on the head by a stranger as he left a public house, and the pedestrian hit by a brick thrown aimlessly by a rowdy group of football supporters. Of course, unfocussed encounters do not require an entirely passive victim. Targets may possess or have created for themselves any of the attributes shown earlier to contribute to victim proneness or susceptibility.

In contrast, focussed events occur when parties have had the potential to engage in some negotiation (whether verbal or symbolic) prior to the commission of the offence itself. Examples include a man lured into a restaurant entrance and then beaten up, a youngster apprehended by a group of other youths who subsequently stole his bicycle, and the drunk robbed by a latter-day 'jack-roller'. Here the distinctions between offenders and victims are less obvious or meaningful. In one instance when a complainant brandished an iron bar at his assailants, the criminal relationship could have been reversed had they retaliated rather than run off. Indeed, it is not uncommon when sifting through violent crime reports to find sequences wherein the complainant for one offence is recorded as the perpetrator of a second, and vice versa.

The 'primary group' crimes are those which take place within a family or circle of close friends, or which obviously arise out of prior socialising within a primary group setting. Examples include the man attacked by a group of 'friends' he had made during an evening in a local public house; the youth invited to a friend's home for a drink and later assaulted; and a youth who seriously injured his father during a domestic dispute.

Only 10.5 per cent of the violent interpersonal crimes listed above can be classed as unfocussed. In contrast, 53.1 per cent were focussed and 36.4 per cent arose directly out of primary group socialising (this includes only 5.4 per cent known to involve immediate relatives – the majority involved friendship rather than kinship links). Thus, in almost 90 per cent of the cases, the offender–

victim relationship must be regarded as negotiable, in the sense that the officially *criminal* incident is merely the culmination of a mutually disagreeable series of exchanges between the parties involved. Block (1981) made a similar observation after finding that the majority of aggravated assaults in Chicago (in 1974) were the outcome of disputes instigated jointly by offenders and victims. Indeed, the so-called father of victimology, Hans Von Hentig, noted that the reality of life 'presents a scale of graduated interactivities between perpetrator and victim which elude the formal boundaries, set up by our statutes and the artificial abstractions of legal science, that should be heeded by a prevention minded social science' (Von Hentig 1940: 309). Forty years later, Singer's observation was in the same vein: 'A key question, then, in explaining personal victimiz-ation as a consequence of the victim's exposure to an offender is the extent to which violence reflects a lifestyle that leads victims to alternate as offenders in the same social environment' (Singer 1981: 780).

This kind of reasoning vindicates Levine's (1978) criticism of overly epidemiological perspectives on victimisation which, he alleges, frequently relegate the social context of victimisation to the status of a mere backcloth against which isolated criminal events take place. In fact, there are facets of interpersonal crime which may be used as subtle and sensitive indicators of the quality and organis-ation of social relations. As such, crime is inseparable from the social context in which it arises.

It seems, therefore, having reviewed the *social* situations conducive to crime (so complementing a more usual emphasis on the built environment), that the relative risks of victimisation attendant on place of residence within the inner city are compounded by exposure to the risks of delinquent involvement (and the higher likelihood of official censure) and to the risks of household or personal accident. Policy responses to this will be discussed in chap-ter 6, but it is worth emphasising here the argument that, for the practical ends of policy-making, the social distribution of victimis-ation must be recognised as possessing two analytically distinct components. Increases in absolute risks reflect the increased oppor-tunities for socialising which are a valued outcome of contemporary economic and political trends. Relative risks reflect less desirable processes underlying the unequal distribution of wealth and life chances that produce socio-economic disadvantage. It may be that an equitable distribution of the risks of victimisation rather than a massive reduction of national crime rates is the most just and realistic goal for crime control strategies in Britain.

Victims, the law and the concept of harm

It has been impossible to explore every facet of victimisation in this short chapter. The constraint of space has denied much discussion of multiple victimisation and precluded any analysis of victims' 'precipitation' or facilitation of crimes. The whole subject of bystander involvement has also had to be sacrificed. As yet none of these intriguing notions is well enough developed to provide insight especially pertinent to victims and potential victims in the inner cities (as distinct from victims generally). It would, however, be inexcusable to leave the topic of victimisation without some examination of crimes which are salient because of what they symbolise or because of the harm they seem to inflict, rather than by virtue of their frequency or severity as indicated by the value of property stolen or by the extent of injuries inflicted.

Because the English criminal justice system is offender-orientated (crimes are regarded as offences against the state rather than against individual victims), the effects of crime on victims is rarely apparent from studies of official statistics. Offences that are most harmful – socially or for individuals – do not often fall neatly into legal categories. Such incidents are therefore more appropriately examined in terms of victims' attributes – a perspective which characterises the remainder of this chapter.

Crimes of symbolic import, judged by qualitative rather than quantitative criteria, include racial attacks, and crimes against the elderly, against women and against juveniles. The symbolism of these offences derives from different sources, though they have in common the facts that (a) none of them has a high known incidence relative to other crime types (interracial violence and child abuse constitute small proportions of all recorded violence, which is in turn a small proportion of all known crime; women and the elderly have lower victimisation rates than men and the younger age groups); (b) each may involve a certain level of harassment to the victim that is morally repugnant even when not technically criminal; and (c) with the possible exception of crimes against the elderly, the offences are probably all disproportionately under-represented in official crime statistics.

Offences against the elderly are of symbolic importance to society because they are an affront to seniority, because the frailty and poverty of the elderly often means that the impact of violent and property crimes is much more severe than for younger, more robust and wealthier sections of the population, and because the mass media often picks up on such offences to express the moral outrage about crime that so many of us feel (some representative studies of victimisation of the elderly include those by Antunes et. al. 1977, Clarke et. al. 1985, Gubrum 1974, Linquist and Duke 1982, and Select Committee on Ageing 1977). The symbolism of offences against women has intensified in recent years as the womens' movement has succeeded in alerting society to the special problems raised by the risk of rape, and because of the overwhelming demands now being made by the victims of domestic violence for accommodation in battered-women's shelters (see E. Wilson (1983) for an accessible discussion of these issues). The abuse of juveniles has only recently begun to receive the publicity it deserves: a whole issue of the *Journal of Clinical Child Psychology* (1983) has recently addressed the topic; the extent of the sexual abuse of children is highlighted in recent publications by Elliot (1985) and West (1985); and other aspects of the victimisation of juveniles are discussed by Mawby (1979a), Feyerherm and Hindelang (1974) and Vesterdal (1983).

Another offence about which the majority of society seems complacent, but which inflicts immeasurable harm (physically, socially and psychologically) on its victims, is racial attacks. The harassment of non-white residents in inner-city neighbourhoods and on council estates throughout Britain has raised the spectre of neo-fascism amongst white British youth, it has impaired the quality of life and sense of well-being amongst members of minority cultural groups, and it has done untold harm to many aspects of race relations, especially those concerning the relationship between the British police and black people. For these reasons, and because the symbolism of the crime and race debate has become so locationally grounded in the inner city, I shall conclude with a brief discussion of racial attacks, making the more general point that the concept of victimisation might have to be extended beyond the confines of criminal law if it is to tap accurately the dimensions of social harm inflicted by delinquent or anti-social actions.

While there has never been any dearth of interest in the relationship between race and crime, analysts' attention has usually centred on the colour and culture of offenders (for some British studies, see Batta et al. 1975, Bottoms 1967, 1973; Bottoms and Wiles 1975; Mawby and Batta 1980; Pope 1979b), or on the bias against black offenders which may be institutionalised within the law enforcement and criminal justice systems of Britain and North America (Brogden 1981; Elion and Magargee 1979; Marx and Morton 1978; Stevens and Willis 1979; Unnever et al. 1980). Although studies have usually revealed that Asians are under-represented as offenders, and that black people of West Indian origin or descent suffer most from unnecessary police stops and arrests, most public attention has been drawn to the over-representation of black offenders in street robberies. (Hall et al. 1978 and Pratt 1980 discuss some of the factors responsible for the 'mugging' panic that swept Britain in the early 1970s.) Bridges argues that over-concern for this minority of offences and offenders has led to a shift in the focus of law and order in Britain 'to a point where the panic over race and crime has become permanent, sustained and orchestrated on a national scale by the police and government itself' (Bridges 1983: 21–2). In contrast, relatively little attention has centred on the differential effects of crime on the majority of the non-white population, who, like the majority of whites, are actual and potential victims rather than criminals (though see Smith 1982b).

In view of the public outrage concerning 'mugging', it is surprising what little moral indignation has been aroused by the problem of racial attacks directed towards the non-white residents of many working-class areas. Such attacks, often believed to be inspired by the extreme right, are not a new phenomenon. They threatened blacks in Britain's port towns as early as 1919; increasing violence against the coloured population preceded the rioting in Nottingham in 1958 (Fryer 1984); 'Paki-bashing' became commonplace in 1970 in London's East End, and in some northern textile towns (see Pearson 1976); and in 1976 further outbreaks of racial harassment coincided with Enoch Powell's anti-immigration speeches. By the mid-1970s concern amongst the Asian population was so intense that the Standing Conference of Pakistani Organisations and the Asian Action Group sent a delegation to the Prime Minister demanding an enquiry into racial violence and the activities of the extreme right (see Gordon 1983 for further discussion of this). However, it is only in the last few years that the government has made any substantial attempt to assess the severity of the problem.

On 5 March 1981, the Home Secretary announced an enquiry into all allegations of attacks by members of one 'racial' group on another within the thirteen police force areas of Bedfordshire, Greater Manchester, Kent, Lancashire, Leicestershire, Merseyside,

South Wales, Sussex, Thames Valley, the Metropolitan Police District, Warwickshire, the West Midlands and West Yorkshire (Hansard, col.408). The first report of the enquiry (Home Office 1981), while not escaping criticism on statistical grounds, does document a disproportionately high level of victimisation against the non-white population as compared with white people, and against Asians as compared with Afro-Caribbeans (the victimisation figures were 1.4 victims per 100 000 white people, 51.2 per 100 000 Afro-Caribbeans and 69.7 per 100 000 people of Asian origin or descent, over three months). The report estimates that about 7000 racially motivated incidents can be expected to be reported in England and Wales per year. This excludes interracial crimes where there is 'insufficient evidence' to decide on a motive, and it excludes offences not reported to the police. More recently, a survey by the Policy Studies Institute with a sixteen- to eighteen-month reference period has confirmed that the Home Office figures are not an overestimate (Brown 1984).

Many localised studies have produced findings to supplement those of the Home Office and the Policy Studies Institute. The Union of Pakistani Organisations claims that racist attacks doubled between 1980 and 1981 from between twenty and twenty-five per week to between fifty and sixty per week (Bridges 1982), Searchlight (1982) details a series of attacks on blacks in London, Liverpool, St Neots (Cambridgeshire), Sandwell, Accrington and Manchester; A. Wilson (1983) provides detailed documentation of the growing level of racist violence in the London borough of Newham, outlining the same upward trend observed by the Ealing Community Relations Council (1981), the Working Party into Community/ Police Relations in Lambeth (1981) and numerous other interest groups. It is significant, too, that information collected by the Metropolitan Police on the 'ethnic appearance' of victims of crimes of assault and 'robbery and other violent theft' for the seven years 1977–83 shows that non-white victims (particularly those of Asian appearance) are consistently over-represented relative to their proportion in the total population (in 1983 the proportions of victims and of the total population constituted by non-white people were 20 per cent and 14 per cent respectively, according to the Home Office (1984)).

The astonishing thing in the light of all this evidence is the indifference with which the majority of British society has greeted it. The national press scarcely acknowledged publication of the Home Office's figures on racial attacks. Just a few weeks later, the Metropolitan Police published a controversial statistical summary of victims' perceptions of the colour of assailants for some types of violent crime. The figures were interpreted by the press as an indictment of black offenders and they made front-page news (see Smith (1982c) for a discussion of this).

The police themselves have, until very recently, seemed reluctant to acknowledge the racial dimension of attacks on the non-white population, and their unenthusiastic response to such events stands in marked contrast to their purge on 'muggings', which are conventionally believed to have white victims. Neither 'mugging' nor 'racial attack' is an official crime category; both are subsumed within the categories of assault, theft, robbery, vandalism and related offences. However, in the case of violence by white people against non-white victims, Kettle and Hodges (1982) claim that the police fail to provide protection for communities at risk, cause unnecessary delays in following up reports of attacks, express indifference when the offence seems criminally minor, and frequently treat victims as aggressors (in particular by questioning their immigration status).

Commenting more generally on the poor response of local services to racial attacks, the Home Office noted that

whereas in predominantly Asian communities the ethnic minorities are perceived to be the victims of racial attacks, in ethnically mixed communities they are regarded as both victims and offenders. We were conscious of a tendency within the police and local authorities to regard the ethnic minorities as a homogeneous group, in which the attacks experienced by the Asian communities were considered in some sense to be offset by the alleged anti-social activities of young West Indians. (Home Office 1981: 15)

The Home Office report, in turn, has been criticised by Layton-Henry for inadequately assessing the role of extremist organisations in encouraging racial harassment. The Home Office enquiry found little evidence that right-wing activity is a direct precursor of racial attacks. Layton-Henry, however, argues that this observation is naive since even when the extreme right condemn specific acts of violence, 'there is no doubt that they foster a climate of violence, approve certain forms of violence and attract members for whom physical action is a major return of participation in the movement' (Layton-Henry 1984: 119).

It is clear from many of the reports cited earlier that the non-white population is subject not only to criminal assault, but to a variety of harassing incidents ranging from intimidation and verbal abuse to petty vandalism, arson and physical attack:

The crime sticks in our mind as the most blatant example of such anti-social behaviour, but it is only the tip of the iceberg. A lot of the more frequent, everyday offences are scarcely criminal – they are 'just' kids fooling around – but they are part and parcel of the same appalling aggression towards defenceless people. (Lea and Young 1984: 57)

In November 1984, a bill was published to outlaw racial harassment against householders and tenants. It was outlined in the House of Commons by the chairman of the Greater London Council's housing committee and it had wide support, including that of the Commission for Racial Equality and London's Housing Aid Centre. It defined racial harassment as 'a deliberate act which interferes with the peace and comfort of an individual, to the detriment of that individual's quality of life, and the act has been committed against that individual because of his racial or ethnic origin' (Race and Immigration no. 175, 1985). The bill proposed to make such harassment illegal and punishable by a fine of £5000 or five years in prison. Currently, however, those subject to the trauma of racial harassment when it stops short of criminal assault or damage have no legal redress. Although a law against 'incitement to racial hatred' was passed in 1977, by the end of March 1984 only forty-four people had been prosecuted under it, and only thirty of these were convicted (Runneymede Trust Bulletin no. 168: 5). Moreover, it seems that the police often refuse to prosecute in cases of common assault, even when a racial motive is detected (Greater London Council 1984). Consequently, individuals feel they must either 'suffer in silence' or go to the expense and inconvenience of bringing a private prosecution.

Probably the majority of racist harassment takes the form of intimidation which is harmful but not criminal. This raises a question as to whether the sociological study of victimisation should move beyond criminal law towards the philosophical question of morality, redefining victimisation in terms of social harm rather than in terms of the law as it is presently constituted (a notion introduced by Schwendinger and Schwendinger 1975, and developed by Kleinig 1978, but curiously neglected in contemporary studies).

The case for reorganising the criminal justice system to respond better to the needs of victims has been argued cogently by a former Chief Constable of Cheshire (Fenn 1984). He draws attention to developments in the United States which have taken account of victims' circumstances, opinions and needs during the processing of offenders. He reasons that the British system would appear more socially just if it, too, took account of the effects of crimes on victims when making decisions relating to bail, sentencing and compensation. Already (since late 1973) probation officers in South Yorkshire have, for minor offences, arranged meetings between victims and offenders to give the latter an opportunity to make amends out of court. More significantly, a government white paper is soon expected to outline a scheme for victim reparations, based on the recommendations of an all-party penal affairs group, whose report, *A new deal for victims*, was published in March 1984. Given these trends in government thinking it seems likely that the advent of national and local crime surveys will play an important part in democratising definitions of victimisation.* This, in turn, may draw just attention to some of the neglected groups of victims mentioned above.

In conclusion, it is worth returning to the central question of this chapter, which asks why inner-city populations are so vulnerable in comparison with their suburban and rural counterparts. Working towards an answer, it has been suggested that, while inner-city residents (like the rest of the population) conform in their victimisation rates to the expectations of the lifestyle–exposure-to-risk thesis, inner-city locations confer an added element of vulnerability over and above this base level. There is a neighbourhood effect associated with victimisation in the inner city which is also reflected in higher household accident rates, and which arises not only from an insecure built environment, but also from a social environment where the sudden and severe erosion of primary group bonds has a tendency (because of the parochial form and public exposure of such relations in working-class areas) to appear in the criminal statistics.

Recognising that many harmful acts are not technically criminal, and that criminal events are just one type of low-quality interaction, the vulnerability of the inner cities to morally repugnant, but sometimes legal, forms of deviance was also considered. The example of racial attacks (ranging from mildly irritating harassment to criminal assault and murder) was selected as one example of such deviance that is locationally and symbolically tied to the inner city. Such attacks deserve particular emphasis since they inflict considerable individual and social harm in an environment where, as the Birmingham victim survey shows, race is not a significant predictor

* The Home Office is encouraging the implementation of local crime surveys by offering to match their costs, pound for pound, with the police authorities. So far, only Merseyside has taken up this offer. It is an important gesture, however, since the only other tangible indication of the government's real commitment to victims is its aid to victim support schemes which amounts to less than £50 000 per year.

of *overall* vulnerability to crime. However, as chapters 5 and 7 indicate, beliefs about, and reactions to, crime *do* have a measurable racial dimension, partly because moral rather than legal definitions of harm make most impression on public sentiment.

While investigating the incidence of racial attacks, Home Office researchers felt that potential victims' fears of harassment also expressed their more general anxieties about life in urban Britain. The evidence of the next chapter suggests this is true for a wider range of offences, and much of the discussion focusses on the major factors underlying public fears about crime. Only having taken into account both the incidence of crime (the subject of this and the preceding chapter) and its effects in terms of public concern, anxiety and fear (the subject of chapter 5) is it appropriate to move on in chapters 6 and 7 to outline and evaluate a range of formal and informal reactions to the problem of crime as it is experienced in deprived urban environments.

5

The effects of crime

Introduction

The effects of crime may be gauged both in terms of their consequences (physical, psychological and economic) for individual victims, and in terms of their impact on the quality of social life in residential communities. Here we are concerned primarily with the latter. This does not reflect complacency regarding the plight of individual victims. Rather, it is an acknowledgement that the effects of crime may extend beyond the population of victims to impinge on more general aspects of public well-being. My aim, therefore, is to examine the fear of crime, its relationship with victimisation, and its association with other elements of the social and built environment.

Fear of crime is described by Maxfield (1984b: 3) as 'an emotional and physical response to a threat'. It is the sense of danger and anxiety that arises from one's perceived likelihood of being harmed. Opinions differ as to the precise character of fear (its subtleties are explored, for instance, by Baumer 1978; Fowler and Mangione 1974; Garofalo 1981a; and Kerner 1978), but it is generally agreed that fear can be distinguished both from concern for crime as a local problem and from a general awareness of crime in the immediate environment (this distinction is demonstrated in relation to Britain by Maxfield (1984b) and Smith (1983)). Whereas *direct* experiences of crime are relatively infrequent for any individual, and take the form of specific discrete events, fear is more widespread, and takes the form of persistent and recurrent or continuous anxiety.

Evidence from the United States is fairly consistent in depicting fear as a serious social problem in urban areas. Clemente and Kleiman (1977) suggest it poses almost as big a threat to society as crime itself, and Katzman (1980) identifies it as contributing to inner-city decline by discouraging inmovers who could inject new life into decaying neighbourhoods. Merry (1981a) shows that fear in the USA can have a detrimental effect on the quality of social relations, particularly on those normally conducted outside a small circle of close family and trusted friends. Yet the potency of fear has been questioned by Canadian examples (Brantingham et al. 1982), and very little is known about the extent to which fear constitutes an important social problem within British cities.

It is known that both in North America and in Britain fear and concern about crime is variously expressed according to people's locations in social and physical space. Boggs (1971), for instance, shows that concern for crime is greater in urban than in rural areas, while Skogan and Maxfield (1981) find that although views of the crime problem vary little between cities, they vary markedly between urban neighbourhoods. Socially, it is often the case that women and the elderly are more fearful than men and the younger age groups.

Preliminary analyses of the first British Crime Survey suggest that while fear is not a problem for this country as a whole, it is severe in its effects amongst inner-city residents and women. Three times more inner-city residents express fears for their personal safety than do people living in rural areas. Over half all inner-city respondents experience some degree of fear in their own neighbourhoods: 41 per cent of women living in such areas feel very unsafe walking alone at night, and more than 60 per cent of all women living in the inner cities feel at least somewhat unsafe – a tendency which increases with age (Maxfield 1984b).

In a local crime survey in Merseyside, Kinsey (1984) found that while 35 per cent of those interviewed view crime as a 'big problem', this opinion is especially strong in the poorer areas (inner-city wards and some council estates). Twice as many inner-city residents as compared with those living in more affluent areas feel unsafe in their own homes, and this fear is particularly noticeable amongst single parents. Fear peaks in the inner city, where one in three residents claim never to go out at night, and a further 15 per cent 'often' do not go out (Kinsey and Young 1985). In one inner-city ward three-quarters of the population believe that women who go out at night face real risks of victimisation, and it is Kinsey's opinion that 'the picture which has emerged is one of the people of the inner city – especially the women – living under curfew' (1984: 23).

There seem strong grounds in the British case, therefore, for focussing on the causes and consequences of fear in the inner cities. Having said that, it should be stressed that Kinsey and Young (1985) have also emphasised the extremely debilitating effects of fear in some of the council estates they studied. Clearly, fear of crime is a problem in working-class areas other than the inner city, and these are no less worthy of investigation. Here, however, I shall continue with my examination of the inner city as a microcosm of working-class society, and of north central Birmingham as a case study wherein beliefs about crime have become entangled with the tenor of race relations.

Before proceeding, there are two aspects of the social environment of north central Birmingham which deserve special comment. The first concerns its socio-economic status, which has been examined by Woods (1975, 1980). Class segregation is quite marked in Birmingham, displaying the usual 'U'-shaped curve, indicating most intense segregation amongst and between the highest and lowest socio-economic groups. Spatially, there has been little change in the class structure of the city since the early 1960s. Immediately prior to that decade, however, changes in the distribution of the social elite had a striking effect on the status of the study area. For the Aston–Handsworth axis was once a prestigious suburb, much sought-after by the well-to-do. During a shift of the high-class sector to the south-west, north central Birmingham rapidly lost its appeal and experienced the familiar process of 'filtering down' – a precipitous decline vividly recalled by a number of the older residents. Unfortunately, the environmental decay contingent on this process was accompanied by the arrival of black immigrants from the New Commonwealth, and many felt, unjustifiably, that the two events were causally related.

The change in the racial composition of the area is a second feature that requires some elaboration. Jones (1979) has summarised the development of racial segregation in Birmingham, revealing the extent to which urban morphology constrained immigrants' initial settlement patterns, and suggesting that, subsequently, the operation of both public and private institutions has worked to sustain the clustering of the black population in the inner ring of unrenewed properties. Although between 1961 and 1971 ward level segregation between black and white residents increased in Birmingham as a whole (the black population's index of segregation intensifying from 50 to 62.4), there was also considerable residential mixing at enumeration district level between Asians and West Indians (particularly in north central Birmingham, whose black population had previously been mainly West Indian). Moreover, the Birmingham Area Health Authority's records of births to non-white parents suggests this pattern of residential mixing within the inner-city wards continued through the 1970s. Within an overall, city-wide, context of racial segregation, then, the micro-level integration of Asians and West Indians, interspersed with earlier Irish immigrants and longer-standing elderly British whites, makes for considerable local social heterogeneity within the study area.

To summarise, prior to 1960 there was a marked and rapid decline in the socio-economic status of north central Birmingham, after which patterns of class-based residential segregation remained fairly stable. In contrast, after 1960 the area became one of Birmingham's main immigrant reception zones and it has experienced increased racial and cultural diversity. It is against this background that any explanation of public attitudes and reaction to crime must be set.

In north central Birmingham, images of deviance and attitudes towards crime vary more strongly with race than with any other social attribute, even though class, lifestyle and location are better predictors of victimisation. Table 5.1 lists the significant associations between race and images of crime. Most noticeably, white residents have the highest probability of believing crime locally to be above average, they more readily believe that the local crime rate (as well as that in Birmingham as a whole, and nationally) is increasing, they are over-represented amongst those able to identify specific trouble spots nearby, and they are the group most likely to feel unsafe in their home neighbourhood.

In addition to perceptions of crime, there are some striking (race related) differences in public images of offenders (table 5.2). A majority of each group perceives the perpetrators of local crime to be drawn from a mixture of races. It is nevertheless striking that over one-third of the white respondents attribute local crime to Afro-Caribbean or 'coloured' offenders, whereas less than 5 per cent of Afro-Caribbean and Asian respondents blame white offenders. Asians are most likely, when labelling another racial group, to have accused Afro-Caribbean offenders – a sentiment again not reciprocated.

The implications of these findings have parallels in other British studies. Knight and Hayes (1981), for instance, interpreted high levels of fear amongst inner-city residents in London as a symptom of a society divided by race. In a much larger survey of 2420 Londoners in 1981 Smith and Gray (1983) found that white people's perceptions of crime are closely related to the presence of black people: white residents in areas of 'high ethnic concentration' are

Table 5.1 *Perceptions of crime by 'racial' appearance of respondents (% in brackets)*

Crime perceptions	Racial category			
	Afro-Caribbean	Asian	White	Total
(a) Personal vulnerability[1] Feel unsafe:				
Always	6 (6.5)	16 (8.8)	29 (11.3)	51 (9.6)
Often	14 (15.2)	37 (20.3)	50 (19.5)	101 (19.0)
Occasionally	16 (17.4)	40 (22.0)	71 (27.6)	127 (23.9)
Never	56 (60.9)	89 (48.9)	107 (41.6)	252 (47.5)
(b) Magnitude of local crime[2]				
None	11 (12.0)	16 (8.8)	10 (3.9)	37 (7.0)
Little	52 (56.5)	63 (34.6)	84 (32.7)	199 (37.5)
Average	22 (23.9)	66 (36.3)	93 (36.2)	181 (34.1)
Above average	7 (7.6)	37 (20.3)	70 (27.2)	114 (21.5)
(c) Distribution of local crime[3]				
Throughout the area	68 (73.9)	159 (87.4)	145 (56.4)	372 (70.1)
Clusters into named places	24 (26.1)	23 (12.6)	112 (43.6)	159 (29.9)
(d) Local crime in last year[4] Trend:				
Increasing	24 (26.1)	74 (40.7)	130 (50.6)	228 (42.9)
Static	52 (56.5)	100 (54.9)	117 (45.5)	269 (50.7)
Decreasing	16 (17.4)	8 (4.4)	10 (3.9)	34 (6.4)
Total respondents	92 (100.0)	182 (100.0)	257 (100.0)	531 (100.0)

[1] $X^2 = 11.486$, 6 d.f., $p < 0.0001$
[2] $X^2 = 34.227$, 6 d.f., $p < 0.0001$
[3] $X^2 = 49.418$, 2 d.f., $p < 0.0001$
[4] $X^2 = 33.451$, 4 d.f., $p < 0.0001$
Source: North central Birmingham crime survey.

Table 5.2 *Public images of the identity of local offenders (% in brackets)*

Perceived identity of local offenders	Appearance of respondent			
	White	Afro-Caribbean	Asian	Total
White	2 (0.8)	3 (3.3)	3 (1.7)	8 (1.5)
Afro-Caribbean	51 (19.8)	6 (6.5)	19 (10.4)	76 (14.3)
'Coloured'	47 (18.3)	2 (2.2)	2 (1.1)	51 (9.6)
Asian	0 (0)	0 (0)	2 (1.1)	2 (0.4)
Irish	2 (0.8)	0 (0)	0 (0)	2 (0.4)
Mixed	130 (50.6)	59 (64.1)	133 (73.1)	322 (60.6)
Not known	25 (9.7)	22 (23.9)	23 (12.6)	70 (13.2)
Total	257 (100.0)	92 (100.0)	182 (100.0)	531 (100.0)

Source: North central Birmingham crime survey.

twice as likely as those in areas of 'low ethnic concentration' to think that local streets would be unsafe for women at night. Similar findings have been published based on experiences in North America. Liska et al. (1982), for instance, show that the racial composition of urban neighbourhoods is related to the level of fear expressed by black and white residents. More recently, Taub et al. (1984) have explored in detail the significance of the association between race and crime as a factor underlying neighbourhood decline in US cities. In view of our scant understanding of how crime, fear and race relations have become so closely associated in the public mind, some further exploration of the British case seems timely.

Victimisation and fear of crime

Early studies of fear centred on its relationship with local crime rates and with people's direct experiences as victims. It came as some surprise to the academic community when crime surveys indicated the weakness of this relationship, and identified other factors to be as powerful as crime or victimisation as predictors of fear. Thus, since the late 1970s, the aspect of fear receiving greatest emphasis has been its *independence* from victimisation – a fact attested to in North American studies by Henig and Maxfield (1978), Klecka and Bishop (1978), Lewis and Maxfield (1980) and Skogan and Maxfield (1981), to name but a few.

In Britain, too, there is evidence that crime may not always be the best predictor of fear. In Merseyside, people under thirty are most likely to be victims, yet anxiety about crime is greatest amongst those over fifty (Kinsey 1984). In north central Birmingham, although only one-third of respondents had been victimised in the reference year, over 70 per cent believe they are vulnerable to personal and/or property offences, one-quarter believe nearby houses are prone to burglary, and 43 per cent think crime increased in the locality in the reference year. In all, more than half the surveyed population consciously feel unsafe in their home neighbourhood from time to time (Smith 1983).

Without doubt, there are factors other than crime itself that fuel people's fears, and these will be examined shortly. However, very recent evidence suggests that analysts may have been premature in underestimating the strength of relationships between victimisation and fear of crime. In terms of its social alignment, fear seems more closely contingent on victimisation once allowance is made for people's exposure to risk and their physical vulnerability. Stafford and Galle (1984), for instance, show that although National Crime Survey data for Chicago appears to reveal that fear and victimisation are inversely related within age, race and gender groupings, in fact fear is positively related to victimisation rates when these rates are adjusted to account for differences in respondents' exposure to risk. Similarly, Maxfield (1984b) argues that the relatively high levels of fear amongst women and the elderly in Britain reflect their greater physical vulnerability, the grave social and psychological conse-quences for women of sexual assault, and the severe injuries to the old and frail likely to be inflicted by physical violence. Finally, Berg and Johnson (1979) suggest that the effects of crime have a disproportionate impact on the elderly because of their relative powerlessness in society to influence crime control and other social policies.

Similar qualifications have been made concerning the spatial association between crime and fear. Hindelang et al. (1978) outline the popular view that people (even those living in high-crime neighbourhoods) tend to see neighbourhoods *other* than their own as most dangerous and crime-prone: geographically, it seems that crime rates and the fear of crime are not directly related. Shotland et al. (1979), however, claim that crime occurring in familiar, regularly used environments elicits higher levels of fear than crime afflicting less well-known neighbourhoods. These authors imply, with Warr (1982), that crime and fear *are* spatially coincident. Maxfield (1984a) has exposed the subtleties of this relationship, showing not only that there are considerable intra-urban variations in levels of fear, but also that people living in high-crime areas tend to be fearful for different reasons from those living in low-crime areas; and while fear in high-crime areas is fairly evenly distributed throughout the population, fear in low-crime areas tends to discriminate between social groups.

Taub et al. (1984) go some way to resolving the paradox of these conflicting findings concerning victimisation and fear by constructing an empirical model of the relationships between fear and neighbourhood conditions in Chicago. These authors conclude that the 'net impact' of crime in any one area depends on the perceived and actual risks of victimisation in that neighbourhood, as compared with perceived levels of danger elsewhere, and seen in relation to the positive rewards of living there. In some places, and at some times, therefore, the risk of victimisation and the incidence of fear may coincide; elsewhere, fear may take on a reality of its own, irrespective of the actual crime rate.

In short, an appreciation of the incidence of victimisation is necessary but not sufficient to explain the distribution of fear, concern and awareness about local crime rates. In recognition of this, Lewis advocated a broadening of victim-orientated studies to include a wider 'social control' perspective on the study of fear. This approach takes into account not only crime but also the selective operation of political and social structures which might play a role in shaping public anxiety. His argument is that high levels of fear can be contingent on the declining capacity of local institutions to control the social disorganisation perceived by residents: 'Fear of crime from the social control perspective is a reaction to the decline of an area. The signs are captured by the general physical and moral disruption of community life' (Lewis 1980: 22).

Communities must vary, therefore, in the extent to which their fears reflect the actual risks of victimisation as distinct from the anxieties generated by other socio-economic processes. In Britain, the BCS and the Merseyside study show that both victimisation and fear of crime are highest in the inner city, where the crime rate also peaks. Yet these and the Birmingham survey suggest that fear is more widespread than victimisation, and can be debilitating in its effects. It is important, therefore, to examine fear in its own right, as a *social* phenomenon and not merely as a facet of individuals' psychology. From this perspective, any comprehensive assessment of the causes and consequences of fear will need to move beyond analyses of crime itself, though it should not lose sight of the fact that victimised populations and fearful populations (which anyway overlap) are structurally bound together by their shared location in social, economic and physical space. Accordingly, in the remainder of this chapter, I first explore the processes by which information about crime is circulated within communities, and then go on to examine the environmental, social, economic and political factors which encourage the translation of mere awareness about crime into fear.

Public fear and moral panic

Several generations of urban ethnographers leave us with little doubt as to the extent of insecurity and uncertainty experienced by inner-city residents (see, for instance, Ley 1974; Hannerz 1969; Smith 1984a; Suttles 1972). According to Garofalo (1981a), two important reactions to uncertainty about the risks of crime are 'information seeking' and 'communicative behaviour'. This tendency for people to turn to the news media and to participate in the local grapevine in order to clarify their images about crime is very noticeable in north central Birmingham. There, over half the population cited the local newspaper, television or radio as their primary source of information about local crime, while a further 36 per cent claimed that hearsay or the experience of friends and neighbours provided their most useful source of knowledge. Although much academic research has focussed on the influence of television on public opinion, in inner Birmingham more people relied on the local newspaper than on television, and this is consistent with Piepe, Crouch and Emerson's (1978) discovery that in Britain the provincial press is a preferred source of *local* news.

In the next few paragraphs, I shall argue briefly, from the evidence in north central Birmingham, that the local press sets a broad agenda for debate about deviance, on the basis of which local crime problems are conceptualised by the public. Within this framework, specific ideas about crime crystallise during the construction and exchange of local gossip. These media are merely the vehicles by which images of crime are formulated and shared. A further argument is necessary to explain how and why general knowledge about crime is translated into fear and concern, and this is introduced later, in the last section of the chapter.

Crime in the news

Crime reporting by the national and provincial press does not reflect the frequency and character of known offences; nor is it intended to. Crime is easy news, and the most serious (and therefore sensational) crimes, which occur least frequently, are most 'newsworthy'. 'Crime waves' are often artifacts of journalistic practices (examples are given by Bell 1962; Fishman 1978; Hall et al. 1978; Medelia and Larsen 1958) and analysts are agreed that total news coverage exaggerates personal violence and robbery at the expense of less newsworthy but more common crimes such as burglary (Humphries 1981; Smith 1985). There is evidence, too, that this bias has some influence on readers' perceptions of crime. Davis (1952) found in Colorado that public estimates of rising crime were associated with increased newspaper coverage rather than with trends in known offences. More recently, Gordon and Heath (1981) found, over a two-year period in Chicago, San Francisco and Philadelphia, that residents whose newspapers allocated most space to crime stories were more fearful than residents of the same cities who read other newspapers. Such trends have their parallel in Britain.

My own seven-month survey of the provincial press in Birmingham shows that while violent personal crimes (including robbery) constitute a little over 5 per cent of crimes known to the police, they feature in over 70 per cent of the total column centimetres devoted to the reporting of crime news. Theft and burglary (over 80 per cent of known crimes) are allocated less than 4 per cent of the space reserved for crime stories. In the north Birmingham study area (where personal violence still constitutes less than 6 per cent of crimes known to the police), respondents who specify the local newspaper as the primary source of their knowledge about crime, and those who claim regular readership of the studied newspaper, are more likely than other residents to believe that local crime is dominated by personal violence or vice, and they tend more often to conceive of crime in general in terms of violent or personal offences (see Smith 1984c for a more detailed account).

While north central Birmingham ranked only third amongst six inner-city areas according to known crime rates in 1978–9, it was the preferred setting for crime-related newspaper articles, receiving a mention in 16.5 per cent of the crime stories (its nearest rival appears in 9.8 per cent of the articles, and none of the other inner-city neighbourhoods is mentioned in more than 4 per cent of the crime-related news reports). Vindicating Walmsley's (1980, 1982) claim for the importance of the newspaper as a source of the public's spatial information, 117 representatives from voluntary and statutory agencies serving Birmingham's inner-city communities identified north central Birmingham – the preferred location for crime-related newspaper reports – as the worst of the city's neighbourhoods (judged in terms of the severity of its crime problem).

The type and locations of crime foremost in the public mind tend to be those accorded most attention by the press, and it seems unlikely that the news is uninfluential in the formation of such images (but see Sacco 1982, for a dissenting voice). That is not to argue that the press *determines* public opinion, but rather to argue that it 'sets the agenda' which frames such opinion. News is a form of communication which helps shape the shared meanings required in public life. Its messages need not be accepted uncritically, but they do create an awareness of particular issues rather than others, so helping to define the boundaries of social reality. The press might not dictate specific fears about crime, but it can indicate what kinds of crimes, in which kinds of (social and spatial) environments, become salient at particular times for the public.

In Birmingham, an important part of the agenda set by the provincial press (with respect to the interpretation of crime) is that which helps stereotype the racial identity of offenders. It has already been suggested that the news media have a significant role in defining white people's images of race relations in Britain (Hartmann and Husband 1971, 1974), and Critcher et al. (1975) show that in the West Midlands Press, when black people appear as individuals, they do so primarily as persons suspected or convicted of crime. In my own study, too, non-white offenders are over-represented in reports of the most sensational crimes, such as sexual offences, robbery and fraud.

For the most part, taking Birmingham as a whole, where location-specific newspaper articles mention black people, the proportion of 'human interest' stories attributed to each named neighbourhood is approximately equal to the proportion of crime-related stories attached to each neighbourhood (though the emphasis tips noticeably towards treating race in terms of human interest for the suburbs and treating race in terms of crime for the inner city). North central Birmingham, however, is named in only 16 per cent of the human interest stories relating to Afro-Caribbean or Asian subjects as compared with an astonishing 31 per cent of the race and crime articles. From more detailed analyses of the headlines and contents of the crime-related articles, journalistic stereotypes emerge, linking people of Afro-Caribbean appearance with violence and robbery, and people of South Asian appearance with petty fraud or intrafamilial and sectarian violence (the process is discussed at greater length in Smith 1984c, 1984d, 1985). At the same time, moreover, the national press, caught up in the government's pre-election law-and-order campaign, was promoting marginalisation, revenge and punishment (as distinct from concern for remedial treatment) as the popular attitude towards offenders (M. Jones 1980). This, too, must have contributed to the distorted vision of the non-white population presented to the public.

The key point here is that the provincial press has characterised inner-city neighbourhoods as high-crime environments in which risks can be assessed in terms of stereotyped images of criminals based on the appearance of non-white cultural minorities. Through routine reporting practices, the press helps define the orthodox view of crime. Journalistic conventions distinguish the universe of things thought and stated from that which is taken for granted. Consequently, the 'common sense' link between race and crime is no longer much disputed: as the next section shows, it has been received into the 'folk' knowledge of local life.

It should be stressed, however, that the public is not a passive audience ready to accept in every detail the wisdom decreed by published news. Information about crime is used selectively by the public when assessing the risks of their immediate environment. In so far as it affects the routine of daily life, crime news is drawn upon pragmatically. It is worked into public opinion through gossip or rumour – a form of collective behaviour through which norms are developed and problems are solved.

Collective behaviour is traditionally divided for analytical purposes into crowd and public behaviour. The former has received most attention, despite the importance attached to the public by Robert Park, who has come to be regarded as one of the founders of social geography. However, at the time of the research in north central Birmingham, crowd behaviour was not a prominent feature of social life. There was little open confrontation either amongst the resident population, or between residents and the police. Neither

did periodic carnivals or street events serve a cathartic function in the sense discussed by Cohen in his research on Notting Hill (Cohen 1980, 1982). Such collective behaviour as could be monitored seemed wholly that of a public generating and resolving inner tensions through the selective circulation of news, which varied in quality, quantity and accuracy. It is this process that underlies the finer details of the spread of information about crime.

Improvised news

The significance of rumour has been the subject of much debate amongst anthropologists. Skogan and Maxfield (1981), however, leave little doubt about its relevance to an understanding of fear. They argue on the basis of their research in the United States that by being linked into local communications networks people are subject to 'vicarious victimisation', since they share the experiences of those who have been the targets of crime. Skogan and Maxfield show, too, that these interpersonal communication channels pay disproportionate attention to personal violence and predatory attacks, and to crimes with atypical 'sympathy arousing' victims (such as women and the elderly). Additionally, there is evidence of a tendency for rumour to be based on the experience of victims who are socially similar to the gossipers themselves. It is under these circumstances that rumour is of greatest importance in affecting people's assessments of risk in their immediate environments (Skogan and Maxfield 1981: 74).

My own research, however, suggests that crime-related rumour is sustained in many contexts, and public risk assessment is only one of them. In north central Birmingham, the received wisdom about race and crime is transmitted euphemistically and it forms the basis of a local orthodoxy – those 'acceptable way of thinking and speaking the natural and social world' (Bordieu 1972: 169). As such, the race and crime issue is integral to the production and reproduction of social differentiation in this part of the inner city. Thus, the account of local rumour which follows is offered only in part as an explanation of how the potential arises for fear of crime to become divorced from the actual risks of victimisation. It is also offered as the first part of an argument (completed in chapter 7) which claims that, although certain structural aspects of social organisation (and my concern is particularly with racism and cultural identification) are pervading features of national political economies or of particular productive/

distributive systems, the social reproduction of these structures is *and must be* a local affair. I shall argue later that the consequences of this are that forms of social relations (such as racism) which are usually (and legitimately) accounted for in terms of general causes (e.g. colonialism, imperialism, the internationalisation of labour systems and so on), actually exhibit a degree of local variability, at a fundamental level, which has so far eluded social theory.

The setting in north central Birmingham provided the opportunity to integrate an essentially geographical study of relations between social distance, spatial proximity and social interaction, with a wide-ranging literature on the organisation of gossip and rumour. The participatory fieldwork involved in this study is described elsewhere in an article on 'News and the dissemination of fear' (Smith 1985); it is based on two years as a resident of the area. The generality of the discussion (and of that in chapter 7) rests on Mitchell's (1983) cogent defence of the case-study method. He argues that the unique can legitimately be used to illuminate the general once it is recognised that ethnographic data, collected within the interpretative, hermeneutic tradition, need not conform to the demands of the empirical-analytical tradition for typicality. Only statistical inference requires a representative random sample; 'logical inference' can produce theoretical (as distinct from empirical) generalisations from the most atypical of observations, since such generalisations are validated not by significance levels and experimental replication, but by consistency and logic of argument. Space for a more detailed discussion of methodology is, regrettably, limited, but for those with particular interests in participatory fieldwork I have amplified this reasoning in discussions of 'Humanistic method in contemporary social geography' (Smith 1981b) and 'Practising humanistic geography' (Smith 1984b).

Table 5.3 shows that perceptions of the local structure of social relations vary between cultural groups in north central Birmingham. The Asian 'community' is diverse and segmented. In that part of the study area selected for analysis, residentially distinct subgroups of Indian Muslims, Sylheti Muslims, East African Hindus and Pakistani Pathans pursue contrasting lifestyles, and their highly integrated social networks are loosely, if at all, interlinked (usually through the English-speaking children).

The Afro-Caribbean community, being largely of Jamaican origin, have quite different patterns of internal organisation. Although traditionally incorporating a busy street life, West Indian community organisation is often thought to be less cohesive than

Table 5.3 *Perceptions of community integration (% in brackets)*

	People know and help one another	People mix within small groups	People keep themselves to themselves	Total
Afro-Caribbean	42 (25.9)	22 (10.9)	28 (16.8)	92 (17.3)
Asian	61 (37.7)	90 (44.6)	31 (18.6)	182 (34.2)
White	59 (36.4)	90 (44.6)	108 (64.7)	257 (48.4)
Total	162 (100.0)	202 (100.0)	167 (100.0)	531 (100.0)

$X^2 = 45.125$, 4 d.f., p 0.0001

Source: North central Birmingham crime survey.

that of the Asian groups. Yet, amongst the youth in particular (many of whom converged on a lively local clubhouse two or three times a week), intimate bonds did spring up, often through the practice of 'reasoning' (Cashmore 1979). This term was originally associated with the Rastafarian movement, but the activity has become more universally adopted by young West Indian and British blacks. It consists of extended but spontaneous discourse, involving lengthy deliberation about virtually any subject. These very fluid exchanges, during which group members come and go, and topics of interest range widely, take place in a variety of settings: homes, shops, cafés, and (most often) in the street itself.

The remaining major subcommunities are the Irish and the elderly English whites. Irish segregation has steadily decreased in Birmingham in the last twenty years. Despite separate schools and churches, some social mixing has accompanied this spatial integration. Yet, many elderly whites remain isolated, tending to converge on only a few select foci. Notable among them are the traditional corner shop retaining its white proprietor, the local pensioners' club, and two local residents' associations.

On balance, the intensity and density of network links amongst the different groups are very much as table 5.3 suggests: white residents are most likely to see their neighbourhood as one in which people tend to keep themselves to themselves; Afro-Caribbean respondents commonly perceive some all-embracing form of community spirit; and the Asians felt that such mixing as does occur takes place within separate and exclusive subgroups. This is the background against which the differential circulation of rumour must be set.

Suttles (1968) observed in Chicago that face-to-face encounters were conditioned by the spatial arrangements of the various social groups; and conversations were heavily restricted to the known world of nearby persons and events. In north central Birmingham, the most obvious alignments of residents' social networks reflected birthplace, linguistic and religious affiliations; and here, as in Merry's (1981a) study of gossip in Dover Square, these culturally bounded social networks apparently channelled the flow of rumour. It soon became clear, however, that rumour also *shaped* local social networks: intensifying or attentuating cultural affiliations; promoting or undermining the identity and legitimacy of local interest groups. As such, rumour is one factor drawing together the effects of crime and the tenor of race relations.

Although rumour generally, and crime-related rumour in particular, is not rife in the study area, that which was encountered has at least two levels of meaning. Only the first of these lies within what Giddens (1982) would call residents' 'discursive consciousness'. At this first level, that which the actors themselves can speak to and give account of, crime-related rumour merely provides information with which gossipers draw up a local map, enabling them to avoid dangerous areas and people during the routine of daily life. In this capacity, rumour is a source of 'folk wisdom' for the management of danger, and the origins of such wisdom are twofold. First, people draw on 'specific' rumour: information about discrete news items or local occurrences from the recent past which can be discussed in some detail. Secondly, they draw on 'diffuse' rumour to reduce the uncertainties left by gaps in the supply of more specific gossip-worthy events. Diffuse rumour has no easily identified origin in local history, but is selected from a vast reservoir of folk knowledge – snippets of information, periodically reworked, reformulated, and recombined for pragmatic ends.

The truth or falsity of the rumours need not concern us at this first level, although Shibutani (1966) identifies as a definitive character of rumour its status as 'improvised news': it comprises inherently questionable information about issues, produced when public demand for news exceeds that made available through formal,

institutionalised channels. The efficacy of such rumours in contributing to workable danger maps depends not on their accuracy but on their plausibility to those who construct and use them. In Birmingham, plausible maps define danger in racial terms.

The remaining levels of meaning contained in crime-related rumour lie outside participants' discursive consciousness. Using Giddens's terminology, these meanings should be explained not in terms of residents' *un*conscious actions but in terms of their *practical* consciousness: 'tacit knowledge that is skillfully employed in the enactment of courses of conduct, but which the actor is not able to formulate discursively' (Giddens 1982: 31). People 'know' they use rumour instrumentally in the sense that they routinely engage in the habits and practices that allow rumour to serve such ends. They would not themselves usually engage in the degree of self-reflection necessary to discuss such processes; but such knowledge is not inherently inaccessible to them. I shall mention three interpretations of rumour relating to residents' practical consciousness.

First, while much rumour is used explicitly to map out a usable area of social and neighbourhood space, it might incidentally be adapted to help manage a tense situation which might otherwise lead to conflict. One rumour (discussed in detail in Smith 1985) concerned an unsolved arson attack on a local teaching centre serving the Bengali population. Amongst one group of Asian and white residents, a common version of the story identified young West Indians as the culprits. At the time, not many streets away, some West Indian car mechanics had been causing disquiet amongst their neighbours, largely because of the congestion caused in the narrow streets by cars being parked, or even serviced, on the roadside. The process by which the West Indians were labelled as criminals, purely on the basis of speculative rumour, served a number of tension-reducing ends: it allayed Asians' fears about the identity of the arsonists ('better the devil that is known . . .' and is therefore easier to avoid); for local whites, it provided 'confirmation' of the shady dealings they believed the car mechanics were involved in; for both groups it allowed frustrations to be expressed in the form of a 'joking relationship' – the execution of judgement through rumour in circumstances where open accusation would lead to conflict and potential danger. In all cases, the rumour was seized on as a means of clarifying and confirming existing suspicions, and as a way to define the extent of social exclusion and spatial avoidance which could justifiably be practised. The truth or falsity of the information was never at issue, since the social context which generated it also rendered it plausible.

Secondly, crime-related gossip has a part to play in the evaluation, construction and transgression of local social rules and norms. Havilan (1977) has argued that gossip constitutes a local 'who's who'; it comprises local biographies which provide a pool of shared knowledge about individuals' reputations. When employed in this way, crime-related rumour in north central Birmingham often took the form of an evaluative assessment of morality, particularly when the participants were elderly white residents. One example concerns the gossip which followed several burglaries at pensioners' homes. The identity of the offenders, though fairly obvious, was scarcely speculated upon. Attention focussed rather on the extent to which victims had 'let their standards slip'; they had not adequately secured their ageing, inherently unsound properties, and must, therefore (so the gossip implied), be contributing to the downhill slide of this once-coveted residential area. By condemning the victims, other pensioners were able to preserve and assert their own status in the neighbourhood – that of the respectable white native. This respectability was sustained by an elaborate system of conventions that Goffman (1981) has termed 'ritual constraints'. There was tacit submission, by many of the elderly, to a set of rules and conventions based on Victorian values of what is right and proper. Conformity to such conventions preserved individuals' claims to good character. Crimes like burglary allowed immorality to threaten this social world, and (unlike personal violence) such offences were considered preventable so long as good standards of housekeeping were maintained. Rumours condemning the victims of burglary were only partly about transmitting information; they were largely an expression and affirmation of norms.

Incidentally, Merry (1981a) raises the question of why judgemental, norm-enforcing gossip fails to provide the degree of informal social control required to prevent local deviance. Her argument is that poor social organisation makes it impossible to translate opinion into effective sanction: 'Because the community's social life is broken among discrete, ethnically based networks, only the judgemental gossip of the deviant's own ethnic group and normatively similar subgroup will have any deterrent effect on his behavior' (Merry 1981a: 188). In Birmingham, however, while these conditions may all obtain, the fact is that local social control is only one end towards which crime-related rumour may be turned. Its much broader applications may not always be compatible with its

deployment to the sphere of social control, and in such instances it is the wider concerns which the public prefer to satisfy.

Rumour is not only involved in the consolidation of group boundaries. It also plays a part in the attenuation of social barriers. This is the third element of the public's practical consciousness in which rumour is embedded. The extent to which rumour transgresses or reshapes group boundaries depends on the plausibility of the subject matter. This was evident from a rare conversation between an elderly white resident and her West Indian neighbour, whose dilapidated home had been a source of resentment and discontent for the white spinster (a discontent that had been shared with her small group of friends, many of whom tended to avoid contact with the Afro-Caribbean community as far as possible). The discussion was initiated by the conversants' common surprise at, and common willingness to entertain, a quite implausible rumour about an extensive spate of burglaries supposedly committed by local West Indian youths. The identity of the culprits was an issue over which the two speakers were divided, but the conversation it generated gave both parties a chance to air their grievances and to allay, if not resolve, their mutual exasperations (over badly kept, and therefore vulnerable, houses on the one hand, and over white racism on the other). In discussing a controversial, if implausible, rumour which contained elements of both participants' concerns, some common ground was cleared for conversation without conflict. In Lienhardt's (1975) view, such 'fantastic' rumours are necessary to resolve complexities of public feeling that cannot be articulated at a more thoughtful level. In prompting communication rather than avoidance, such rumours may have positive consequences for the quality of social life.

While the majority of rumour is plausible, if not necessarily true or accurate, there are clearly circumstances in which implausible gossip will be sustained. Shibutani (1966) attributes this to the public's tendency to lose its critical abilities when demand for news greatly exceeds the supply made available through formal channels. In Birmingham, implausible rumour is also likely to be the product of urgent need for negotiation across group boundaries. By its very nature, however, 'fantastic' rumour tends to exaggerate the race and crime issue. Once stated and accepted for circulation, private thoughts and individual experiences, however prejudiced and indefensible, can be swept into the public realm and invested with unexpected, and perhaps undeserved, legitimacy. Ideas, which for individuals began as unformulated and unsystematic speculation, can quickly gain coherence when articulated in terms of a prevailing wisdom linking race and crime; a wisdom which simultaneously authorises and legitimates the tenor of the discourse. Such a process is documented by Bordieu (1972: 189–90), who notes generally how just talking about 'private' experiences lends them an objectivity that was previously unrealised. It is this process, occurring within a framework that takes for granted the nature of deviance, that helps explain why, in the present study, very little could be uttered on the topic of crime, plausible or otherwise, without the gossipers drawing on racial stereotypes of both offenders and victims. Bordieu (1972) claims that this kind of local wisdom will only be challenged when an obvious rift develops between subjective beliefs and the objective conditions of existence. The argument of chapter 7 tries to explain why this rift has not become apparent to the residents of north central Birmingham. The remainder of this chapter considers the relationship between knowledge about crime and fear.

Crime, anxiety and the inner-city environment

Studies of the mass media and of interpersonal communication give some insight into the spread of information about crime. They offer some clues (in the bias of reporting practices and in the structure of local social networks) as to how images of crime come to vary between cultural groups (though why some of these images are sustained by a critical public is not yet fully accounted for). Such studies reveal little, however, about the processes by which mere awareness of crime is translated into fear and concern. Neither can they explain why fear is sometimes and in some places debilitating, while at others it represents simply a healthy awareness of the risks of victimisation. The existing literature suggests that the answer to both these outstanding questions is contained in the character of the urban environment (built and social) within which fear is experienced.

American commentators generally agree that fear in individuals is related to dissatisfaction with their residential settings and to anxiety about the quality of neighbourhood life as a whole. Fear is greatest amongst people who perceive their communities to be in decline when they are powerless to intervene. In Britain, this is often the case in working-class areas, where investment in housing and infrastructure is low and where welfare services are understaffed and must spread resources thinly amongst a population with high demands. Drawing together the threads of a growing American literature, I have used the findings of the north central Birmingham crime survey to assess their relevance to an understanding of fear in a British inner city. The full analysis appears in Smith (1983); here, I shall mention three aspects of the social and built environment that most obviously contribute to peoples' fears, relatively independently of their experiences as victims. They do so as part of a process whereby anxieties associated with the rigours of an inner-city life-style are translated into anxiety specifically about crime. My argument is that the *effects* of crime (as distinct from its known incidence) can become a problem for communities as a direct consequence of residents' marginality in economic, social, political and locational terms.

First, it appears that environmental 'incivility' – the presence of abandoned buildings, vandalism and other signs of physical decay and neglect – influences people's perceptions of crime. Fear is generated when an environment *looks* as if it might attract vandals or shelter undesirables. In Birmingham, a measure of incivility was based on whether or not the main problems experienced locally by respondents were indicative of a decaying physical environment. Where this perception obtains it proves much more closely associated with people's images of deviance than with their direct experiences of crime. Similar observations have been made in North America by Garofalo (1981a), Lewis and Maxfield (1980) and Skogan and Maxfield (1981). The potency of incivility is also well illustrated in Merry's (1981a) study of inner-city Philadelphia. There residents identified dangerous places not on the basis of crime incidence but on the basis of architectural design, the social identity of people habitually using the area, and their own familiarity with the environment.

A second factor often influencing attitudes towards crime has been termed 'community affect'. This may be measured in terms of (i) residential satisfaction (whether people like, dislike, or are indifferent to living in their home neighbourhood), and (ii) social satisfaction (the extent to which residents experience a comforting sense of 'community spirit' in the locality). The latter proved especially important in Birmingham, in that those with little sense of community spirit are most fearful, most likely to think local crime is above average and increasing, and they are twice as likely as those with a strong sense of community spirit to define crime as a problem. Merry also found fear closely related to the form of local networks and the quality of social interaction: 'Insults, mockery, racial slurs, harassment, and flirtatious sexual comments that assault a person's sense of order, propriety and self-respect awaken feelings of danger even when they contain no threat of actual physical violence' (Merry 1981a: 143). In a related vein, 'displacement' of anxiety is particularly likely to occur when people perceive themselves beset by a range of problems for which there is no easily accessible solution. Such problems ranged in north central Birmingham from housing stress to racial harassment, and where people felt there was no organisation to turn to for advice they experienced higher levels of fear and anxiety about crime.

There has been some suggestion, following the reasoning of classical theorists such as Durkheim, Mead and Simmel, that fear, even when individually disturbing, can be socially positive. The logic of these theorists implies that a well-developed sense of community spirit can be expected to accompany high levels of fear. Shared fears can promote group solidarity and prompt collective action against criminals, who, according to this argument, are identified as a minority of 'outsiders'. Such fear helps preserve and promote the identity of the fearful. It instils a healthy degree of caution into individuals, and mobilises them to act against those who violate institutionalised norms.

This argument may well have some plausibility for a whole nation, where a morally indignant elite have the power to formulate and dispense a range of crime-control policies. In a single working-class neighbourhood, however, where residents have relatively little control over the implementation of legislation which affects them, there is every evidence that fear is socially detrimental. In north central Birmingham, fear appears to impinge on processes of socialisation, fostering withdrawal and isolation. High levels of fear are not accompanied by a widespread sense of community spirit. Conditions in the study area offer more support for Conklin (1975) than for the classical theorists: as a consequence of the suspicion and mistrust generated by fear, crime is instrumental in undermining social cohesion.

A third source of anxiety, frequently displaced onto anxiety about crime, reflects people's concerns about the changing racial composition of local populations. This process has attracted much attention in the United States but has only recently been documented in Britain. At one level, such displacement might be accounted for in terms of the images linking race and crime that are nurtured by the mass media and sustained by local gossip. It might also be accounted for in terms of the shared experiences of local cultural groups (with respect to economic opportunities, police practices etc.). American commentators, however, argue for a more fundamental explanation.

Following the race riots of the 1960s, Ohlin (1971: 32) argued that in American cities 'Fear of crime serves as an easily justified camouflage for a more pervasive fear of racial integration, which is much harder to debate publicly'. A decade later, Merry found that much the same argument applied in Philadelphia. She extended the generalisation by finding historic parallels in fears about the Irish in Boston, Italians in Chicago, the Chinese in New York, and English oil-workers in the Shetlands, and concluded: 'In the light of this pattern, the recent American pre-occupation with crime could be a reaction to rapid social change and demands for social justice by minority populations as much as to increases in the rate of crime itself' (Merry 1981a: 212–13). The conflation of race-related and crime-related issues, and their expression in public fear may thus be seen not only as a consequence of the economic and social factors which underlie incivility and community affect, but also as a contingency of political factors relating to the position of racial and cultural minority groups in the national and local power structure. Fear of crime might be related to victimisation at one level, but more fundamentally it reflects the differential distribution of power in all its forms: economic, political and ideological.

Conclusion

The evidence available to date suggests that fear is a problem in Britain, at least in working-class (and especially inner-city) areas. It is a problem in high-crime areas, but its effects are more pervasive than individuals' experiences of victimisation might suggest. Moreover, there are facets of inner-city life – the risks and uncertainty it nurtures, the struggle to cope with an ageing environment, the inaccessibility of information and services – that are sufficient in themselves to exacerbate public fears and concern about crime.

Fear is a *social* phenomenon, related to crime in so far as vulnerable and fearful populations overlap, but mediating many other facets of community life. Interpreted broadly, fear is a manifestation of: (i) the economic marginality of the inner city, with its ageing infrastructure and widespread 'incivility'; (ii) the social marginality of inner-city residents, where kinship networks have been disrupted, where high population mobility can diminish community affect, and where isolation encourages the debilitating effects of fear to eat away at the quality of social (especially race) relations; (iii) the political marginality of inner-city institutions which denies residents a say in defending the local moral order in the face of social and economic change (cf. Lewis 1980). In short, fear as a social phenomenon is bound up with the differential distribution of power within society as a whole, and within the inner city itself. The implications of this for the structure of social relations will be considered in chapter 7, where an analysis of informal reactions to crime examines how structural marginality is interpreted by and incorporated into the routinised practices of daily life.

To conclude that fear is a problem in its own right is not to detract from the problem of crime which also faces the residents of working-class neighbourhoods. It is rather to anticipate chapter 6 and speculate as to whether the crime-control policies implemented to allay national (i.e. politically voiced) fears are likely to impinge significantly on the factors which underlie the most acute manifestations of fear in the inner city. Fear at its most debilitating is very much a problem of the working classes, who are most likely to be victims of crime and who have least power to influence public policy. Nationally, the tendency has been to respond to public fears through centralised law-and-order campaigns. The temptation has been to distinguish clearly between the respectably fearful and the criminal classes; and Pearson shows how 'respectable fears' have affected policies towards, successively, 'rookeries', 'slums', and 'inner cities'. His concern is that too often respectable fears reacting to panic over mounting disorder have conveniently detracted from wider social issues associated with political and economic change. The consequence is that: 'matters of vital importance – jobs, homes, schools – are swallowed up in the maw of "law-and-order" discourse, and publicly addressed as if the only important consideration was whether these social deficiencies might lead to crime, vandalism and hooliganism' (Pearson 1983: 239). On the basis of her cross-cultural and historical survey of fear, Merry (1981a: 220) too concludes that 'the fear of crime serves as a way of rationalizing and legitimizing increased control of the subordinate populations who are labelled as dangerous'. Respectable fears provide popular support for stringent crime-control policies, but these are not the fears that the evidence of this chapter identifies as most acute. The kind of fear that affects the quality of life in the inner cities has causes quite apart from the moral indignation that fuels national politics. The question of whether national law-and-order campaigns or more comprehensive, locally sensitive schemes best help the relatively powerless populations amongst whom fear is most harmful is addressed in the next chapter.

6

Crime and public policy

I now consider the achievements and problems of formal responses to crime effected by the statutory services, offering suggestions, where appropriate, as to how these responses might become more sensitive to the diverse needs of the public. It seems logical to begin with the police response, since this organisation spearheads the government's law and order programme. I shall argue that the police have a vital role to play in the well-being of British society. There are, however, important ways in which the effectiveness of the police in dealing with crime is limited; and there are areas of concern for crime in which the police should be prepared and able to relinquish their responsibilities.

In some areas of policy, police effectiveness is limited by the incompatibility of the organisational demands of, on the one hand, national law-and-order campaigns, and, on the other hand, the management of crime at a local level (which in turn reflects the present constitution of formal relations between the police and the public). Some problems associated with this incompatibility are discussed below. In other areas of policy, police effectiveness is impaired because the causes and consequences of crime are rooted outside the sphere of policing itself and within the jurisdiction of other agencies. The role of other agencies and their relationship to the police is considered in the second part of this chapter.

The policing response

Since the war, the number of offences (indictable, serious and notifiable) recorded in England and Wales has increased by a factor of five, to give an annual total by 1984 in the order of three and a half million (6000 crimes per 100 000 people). This trend, together with renewed concern for public order following the urban riots of 1980–2 and accompanying the miners' strike of 1984, has been sufficient to justify continued investment into crime prevention, law and order.

Thus, between 1971 and 1981, the police force increased in size by 50 per cent. By 1983, forces were operating at full strength with just over 121 000 officers employed in England and Wales. Whereas in 1961 there was one police officer for every 602 people in the country, in 1982 the ratio was 1:394. Additionally, there has been a large increase in the employment of civilians by police forces. The salary of police constables (of the lowest rank) has increased dramatically from a maximum of £3918 in 1977 to a maximum of £9798 in 1982. By 1983, the total cost of the police service was running at £2.5 billion per year, and expenditure on law and order generally has more than doubled since the Conservative government took office in 1979.

In Britain, as in most other Western democracies, massive public investment into policing has had little demonstrable impact on crime-rate trends (Heal (1983) discusses this difficulty of national law-and-order campaigns in some detail). There is little evidence to suggest that larger, better-equipped police forces are more efficient in detecting crime (Carr-Hill and Stern (1979) find no relationship between police efficiency in Britain and either the size of forces or their workload); or that greater police presence acts as a deterrent to potential offenders (some authors, such as Huff and Stahura (1980) and Jacob and Rich (1980), even argue that more intense policing can, as a consequence of the labelling process, lead to an *increase* in recorded crime).

The 'clear-up' rate (a common measure of police efficiency in solving crimes) remains low, generally. The proportion of crimes solved fell from 69 per cent in 1977 to 41 per cent in 1979. By 1984, the clear-up rate varied from a low of 28 per cent for burglary, 22 per cent for robbery and 23 per cent for criminal damage (crimes which together account for 35 per cent of all recorded offences) to a high of 74 per cent for violence against the person and 72 per cent for sexual crimes (which constitute only 5 per cent of crimes known to the police), in England and Wales.

Nationally, then, the impact on crime of increased public investment into policing has not been particularly marked. This is not surprising if, as suggested in chapter 4, increases in the crime rate are contingent on some of the most prized developments in the nation's political economy. My concern, therefore, in examining the police response to crime, centres not on success or failure in controlling gross crime rates, but on the effect on local communities of the organisational changes in policing that have accompanied recent increases in the establishment and budgets of the police service.

The legislative basis of the dramatic changes in policing which have occurred in England and Wales over the last two decades is the 1964 Police Act. This act extended the jurisdiction of individual constables from their own and neighbouring forces to the whole of England and Wales; it authorised Chief Constables to make collaborative arrangements between force areas; and it considerably strengthened the powers of the Home Office to influence the organisation of policing (Critchley 1967 gives a more detailed account of the implications of the 1964 Act). Most significantly, the Home Secretary was given a new duty and power to promote the efficiency of the police. An integral part of this mandate proved to be the removal of small forces, and in May 1966 Roy Jenkins launched a nation-wide programme of amalgamations which was to reduce the number of forces in England and Wales from 150 to 41 (plus the Metropolitan and City of London Police).

Currently, one-third of the British population is policed by only five forces. Consolidation has been accompanied by increased emphasis on an authoritative model of professionalism, and by increased bureaucracy. Policing has shifted from being locally based and loosely co-ordinated to become 'a tightly integrated, national network of highly professionalized, autonomous police bureaucracies' (Baldwin and Kinsey 1982: 104). The increased size of forces has distanced the majority of policy decisions in policing from large sections of the public. The potential for police accountability to local communities seems diminished, while the powers of Chief Constables are consolidated and concentrated.

This process of centralisation and consolidation might itself have been sufficient to generate tensions between the public and the police in some areas. Any such tendency must, however, have been exacerbated by two key shifts in policing strategy during the late 1960s and early 1970s. These are analysed at length by Baldwin and Kinsey (1982: 26–103). First, unit beat policing became the standard method of servicing residential areas. This began as an ideal combination of foot and car patrols, aiming to marry rapid response with community involvement. However, shortage of officers, together with a powerful occupational culture that devalued the role of area constable (or 'beat bobby'), soon produced the reactionary 'fire brigade' model of policing that currently elicits so much criticism.

Secondly, the collection of local intelligence, which was traditionally undertaken by local plain clothes officers, familiar with their patch and involved in a range of CID duties, has now become the domain of special intelligence squads. Information that was once gathered using discretion and judgement conferred through contextual understanding is now collected indiscriminately by specialists: 'the job description itself demands that these officers mix with only those sectors of the population that are considered, in advance, to be suspect or potentially criminal. The result is that suspicion is institutionalized as contact between the police and public is diminished' (Baldwin and Kinsey 1982: 42). Police–public encounters are decreasingly characterised by mutual optimism at the prospect of local community involvement in the law-enforcement process.

Whatever the reasons, the problems caused by organisational changes in policing during the 1960s and 1970s proved more pressing for some sections of the population than for others. This is clear from Lea and Young's account of how differences in the extent of urban decay have allowed cities to be divided for policing purposes into 'respectable' and 'non-respectable' parts: 'Around this polarization grow two types of policing; one in the inner city based on force and coercion, the other in the suburbs and the smart part of town based on consensus'. (Lea and Young 1984: 65). They argue, too, that it is likely to be the areas and social groups which are most heavily policed which are least able, in practice, to hold the police accountable for their actions. Centralisation, consolidation and organisational change have distanced the police from local communities, but the gap seems widest in the inner cities and amongst racial and cultural minorities.

While it is true that the police in inner-city areas have some of the country's highest crime rates to contend with, the methods of responding to these have, in the eyes of many inner-city residents, made mockery of the concepts of an impartial and independent police force, and of the notion of equality before the law. Smith and Visher (1981) found in the United States that, in addition to taking into account the seriousness of offences and the preferences of victims, police officers are most likely to arrest people in positions of social disadvantage, such as blacks. Much the same charges have been levelled in Britain. The Select Committee on Home Affairs (1980) found, in common with a number of other studies, that Section 4 of the 1824 Vagrancy Act (the 'sus' law, repealed in 1981) was not applied consistently in different parts of cities, nor evenly against different sections of the community. Arrests were heavily concentrated in London, and within London they clustered in Westminster and Lambeth. In 1977, 1978 and 1979, over 70 per cent of those arrested in Lambeth were black.

Smith and Gray (1983), in a comprehensive study of *Police and people in London*, confirm that black people are disproportionately likely to be stopped by the police, and they add that the police are often reluctant to act energetically where the victims of crime are Asian. These authors also note that police behaviour towards black people was amongst the worst they encountered during their research. It is hardly surprising then that some of the most critical views of the police revealed by the British Crime Survey are held by ethnic minorities and inner-city residents as well as by the young, the unemployed and those stopped by the police (Southgate and Eckblom 1984). Few would extrapolate to Britain Jackson and Carroll's (1981) contention that police resources in the United States are drawn upon when minority groups seem threatening, but Anning and Ballard (1981) have already criticised the police for ignoring the motives behind attacks on black and radical bookshops, and the British police are finding it increasingly difficult to sustain a non-partisan image.

The apparent rift between the police and some sections of Britain's inner-city communities seems to be a consequence of what Lea and Young (1984) describe as the undermining of 'consensus' policing and a drift towards 'military' policing. They suggest that, as a result of apparently unjust law-enforcement practices, communities can become increasingly closed to the police. People become unwilling or afraid to co-operate with enquiries, and gradually block the flow of informal information on which the detection of crime has traditionally depended. Lacking reliable links with the community, the police must begin to compile 'local intelligence' records, which may contain information unrelated to crime, on the assumption that they might prove useful to subsequent investigations (Baldwin and Kinsey 1982: 59–103); the police must operate increasingly with stereotypes of 'likely criminals' (GLC Police Committee Support Unit 1983a: 115–23); and they will begin to replace detailed analyses of known offences with less reasoned targetting of likely criminals as the main principle of detecting crimes: ' "Do not do anything in case you are stopped by the police at a road block or in some sudden and random street search" becomes the form of deterrence replacing the "do not do anything because you are sure to be caught eventually" of consensus policing' (Lea and Young 1984: 174). All this, in turn, must further compound the crisis of confidence in the police experienced in a number of urban areas with a working-class character or a concentration of minority cultural groups.

In an attempt to break into this vicious circle (and, in some cases, to stop it forming), the police have begun to implement various community based crime-prevention exercises, while police authorities have begun to set up local consultative committees to identify the needs of the public. I shall discuss these initiatives briefly in turn.

The police and the public

Police forces throughout the country have begun to shift the emphasis of their policies away from a reactive 'fire brigade' model (all that remains of the unit beat ideal) and towards a preventative community based model. The importance of re-establishing such a principle was a bitter lesson to the now-defunct Law Enforcement Assistance Administration in the United States: 'The crime issue had been nationalised in presidential elections, but when it got down to actually deciding what to do, policy makers kept rediscovering that crime remained a distinctly local matter' (Cronin et al. 1981: 135). Policing methods introduced to deal with this local matter in Britain range widely, from simple community involvement/liaison (where perhaps 2 per cent of uniformed officers are assigned a public relations role) to full-blown 'community policing', which demands a radical renegotiation of the social contract between police and public.

The move towards community liaison, while an important gesture, has remained within the traditional reactive/pre-emptive policing style. It operates through separate community relations departments (which are often viewed as having low status vis-à-vis other departments such as traffic and CID) within organisations more committed to deterrence than prevention as a means of controlling crime. The community liaison model works in an environment which favours an extension of police powers on the assumption that increased discretion will not be misused.

John Alderson's concept of community policing turns the simple liaison model on its head. Alderson implemented his initiative when he was Chief Constable of Devon and Cornwall in the 1970s (see Moore and Brown 1981 for an account of this scheme). His fundamental argument that policing styles must be flexible to local needs was taken up by Butler (1982), who calls for a revision of police management structures in order to adopt this principle. Alderson's philosophy, however, demands more than local sensitivity (see, for instance, Alderson 1982). It requires the entire force (not merely a community relations branch) to take on the responsibility of community involvement. It encourages self-policing and informal social control, placing the emphasis in crime control on prevention rather than deterrence. Most radically, it demands that policing should abandon its untenable apolitical image, acknowledge the politics of decision-making, and agree to a more circumscribed range of powers, whose use is increasingly accountable to the public.

Alderson's community policing package did not, as a whole, prove amenable to the Association of Chief Police Officers. Nevertheless, some elements of the model have been retained, and recently some styles of community policing have been brought to the inner city. (Details of the various styles of community policing are given by Kuykendall 1974; Bradley 1984; Brown and Iles 1985.) One of the earliest such initiatives, and closest to the Alderson model, was the Lozells project implemented in 1978 in Birmingham. It was based on pro-active policing, aiming to strengthen informal social control and harness local resources for crime prevention. The scheme was aided by a grant of £50 000 p.a., which the police shared in a ratio of 1:3 with the Birmingham Inner City Partnership (a more detailed account of the project is given by Brown (1982)). More recently, in 1982, the Metropolitan Police introduced neighbourhood policing to Notting Hill and Hackney, establishing 'a geographical community-based focus for policing, rather than the more conventional temporal or shift-based approach' (Newman 1984: 42). The scheme was extended to Brixton and Kilburn in 1983. Additionally, the police are taking initiatives in establishing neighbourhood watch and victim-support schemes, in an attempt to forge a crime-prevention partnership with the public.

The rationale for this shift in emphasis in policing is outlined by Heal (1983). He points out that the deterrence model of policing breaks down at a fairly low threshold. The existence of a police service reduces crime, but a point is quickly reached where further increases in police activity have no effect on the crime rate. A prevention model that develops and involves community resources seems more likely to keep crime under control than do further increases in police establishment. Moreover, as Mawby (1981) points out, this is probably the only way that the police will gain access to the large numbers of crimes that occur in private places.

Unfortunately, police-led community crime-prevention schemes have not always generated high levels of public support, particularly in working-class neighbourhoods. Heal (1983) identifies part of the problem as being that many people find the cost of living with crime to be less than the cost of crime prevention. He suggests that public response could be improved through financial incentives, professional assistance, persuasion through publicity, and regulation through the law. In some areas, however, seeming apathy towards community policing has more fundamental roots. Some sections of the public greet the advent of community policing with suspicion rather than enthusiasm because they interpret it as a potential threat to civil liberties. The most extreme views on this are expressed by Bridges, who condemns community based policing as merely a means by which chief officers have 'set about reorganising their forces the better to penetrate and spy on the community and to suppress social and political unrest' (Bridges 1983b: 32). Short (1982: 78), too, is concerned that the development might become a way of undermining political pressure groups. The GLC Police Committee Support Unit (1983b) fear community policing might supplement rather than replace reactive policing. They believe that police involvement in community activities could become a form of surveillance, perhaps leading to pre-emptive action against potential (and not necessarily *actual*) criminals. Moreover, apparent co-operation with other agencies might extend the powers of the police into other spheres of social control, which Reiner (1984) suggests could be interpreted as one element of a drift towards a police state.

Far-fetched though some of these fears may sound, the fact remains that for many people the ideal of community policing encroaches too far into matters of civil society and local government, given the limited powers of the public to challenge police motives and actions in the pursuit of law enforcement (but see Savage 1984). It will be remembered, however, that Alderson's *ideal* of community policing was based on consultation and accountability as well as on police acknowledgement of and participation in the politics of decision-making. Moves towards increased consultation are considered immediately below, but it is the thorny question of police accountability, addressed in the following section, on which the effectiveness of community based policing ultimately rests.

The public and the police

It may be that the ethical question mark over community policing
will be removed, and the benefits of the movement reaped, once
adequate consultation between the public and the police is secured.
Scarman (1981) points out that such consultation rarely occurs
spontaneously, and recommends the establishment of statutory
liaison committees to guarantee adequate communication between
the police and the public. Although the new Police and Criminal
Evidence Act does not go so far as to make consultative committees
a statutory requirement, it does require police authorities to make
appropriate arrangements for 'obtaining the views of the people'
about the policing of their areas. Following Scarman, and in anticipation of the Police and Criminal Evidence Act, Home Office
circular 54/1982 was issued, containing guidelines for the establishment of consultative arrangements.

Several hundred consultative committees had been established by
1984, and these were surveyed by Morgan and Maggs (1984). Only
six (from a total of forty-one) police authorities had made no
changes in their consultative processes, and twenty-four had
installed consultative committees for the entire force area (the
remainder had various pilot schemes underway). There seems to
have been a preference to base the committees' jurisdictions on
police subdivisional boundaries (covering fifty to eighty thousand
people) rather than on local authority administrative boundaries.
Morgan and Maggs (1984: 25) suggest that this choice 'may be
infused with more political significance than external observers
appreciate', since it implies that police practicalities rather than
elected representatives' interests will best be served by the proceedings. In a subsequent publication, in fact, they argue that police
priorities generally are the ones accepted by consultative committees (Morgan and Maggs 1985).

The committees usually consist of police representatives, county,
district and parish councillors, employees of the statutory services,
and advocates from various interest groups and voluntary organisations. Their main activities seem to be to collect public opinion
regarding local policing problems, and to promote the role of joint
crime-prevention panels. For the most part, the Home Office's
terms of reference have been accepted: there is no discussion of
individual complaints against police officers, nor of other individual
cases under investigation, and there is no dialogue regarding the

method and timing of police operations or the deployment of police officers.

The Commissioner of Police, Kenneth Newman (1984) has outlined similar consultative arrangements implemented in the Metropolitan Police District. Nineteen of the thirty-two London boroughs have consultative committees, though Bradley (1984) notes that some conservative councils have rejected the idea on the grounds that they believe their relationships with the local police to be sufficiently constructive as it is. Newman describes London's consultative committees as 'the corporate expression of individuals' responsibility, shared with that of the police, for the maintenance of law and order'. Additionally, he notes that twelve crime-prevention panels were active by the end of 1983.

The shift towards a community based focus for policing, together with the establishment of a network of consultative committees, suggests that increased expenditure on the police should be beneficial at a local level, even if its impact on national crime trends appears negligible. That many observers do not find this so reflects the fact that increased consultation with the public does not imply that the police have become more *accountable* to local communities. The public have no real power and few opportunities to challenge operational and organisational decisions within their police forces. Chief Constables maintain a doctrine of 'operational independence', despite the arguments of Clayton and Tomlinson (1984) which expose the concept's flimsy foundations to be based on 'bad history and dubious law'.

Margaret Simey's (1984: 136) concern as chair of the Merseyside Police Authority is that 'The political dimension of policing as a public service has been taken over by the professionals and with it has gone all possibility of effective democratic scrutiny. So long as this basic imbalance of power between police and policed continues, it must constitute a source of grave danger to the very concept of policing by consent.' Clare Short's (1982) objection to the present form of community policing in Birmingham is similar. She argues that the police have acted as a channel for resources, and have influenced the allocation of services and the development of policies across a broad front, without submitting to the same degree of accountability to the local authority that would be required of other agencies acting in the same capacity.

Lea and Young (1984: 14) find the crisis of accountability at its most acute in the inner cities, and it is their opinion that the riots of

1981 reflect 'the fact that the growing frustrations of inner-city communities have not been effectively channelled into the institutional patterns of political compromise which characterise modern capitalist democracy'. Harman (1982) is more direct in pinpointing the lack of democratic accountability of the police as a key factor in the breakdown of relations between the police and black people in London.

Public and political opinion is currently polarised over the issue of police accountability. Left-wing politicians argue for increased local democratic participation in operational policing; the political right claim such a move would undermine the independent non-partisan character of police forces and may allow pressure groups to gain control over, and perhaps misuse, the service. Obviously, a police force must be subject to some form of regulation. Obviously, no service should be allowed to fall into the hands of extremist minorities. Yet, the accountability debate must be explored if the trend towards community policing and local consultation is to benefit all sections of the public. In examining the issues, below, I shall suggest that geographers' concerns with the relationship between local and national state politics, and with the nature of local state autonomy, can usefully inform the accountability debate, and provide a solution consistent with the stated demands of both sides.

Police accountability and local democracy

The present arrangements for police accountability were established under the 1964 Police Act and, with the exception of some changes in the complaints procedure and extra provision for local consultation, this system is left intact by the new (1984) Police and Criminal Evidence Act. Technically, the police are formally accountable to national government (via the Home Secretary), local government (via the police authorities), individual citizens (by virtue of the police complaints system) and the law.

The power of the Home Secretary to influence Chief Constables has increased since 1964, and some of the consequences were discussed above. The police authorities are committees of local councils (although their decisions need not be ratified by the councils), and their powers are more limited. Two-thirds of their members are councillors, the remainder being (non-elected) magistrates (the Metropolitan Police does not have a police authority, and is answerable only to the Home Secretary). The authorities are charged, under section 4(1) of the 1964 Police Act, with a general duty to 'secure the maintenance of an adequate and efficient police force'. Although they have no power to formulate or control operational policing policy, the authorities are expected to approve budgets and agree on the size of the force, to appoint senior officers and deal with complaints against them, to provide buildings and equipment, and to call for reports from the Chief Constable. Their efficacy, however, seems to have diminished in the two decades since they were established. Rhind (1981) attributes this to the fact that little can now be achieved in the realms of policing without Home Office consent, to the tradition of the operational independence of Chief Constables, and to the fact that local government itself has become more structured, casting police authorities into a more rigid framework of decision-making.

If concern is with general policing practice, as distinct from specific individual complaints and disciplinary matters, the main statutory form of influence on local policing is exerted through the police authorities. The exception to this is in Greater London, where local politicians and pressure groups continue to argue their case for such an authority to be constituted (see Boateng 1982; Greater London Council Police Committee 1983b). It is worth noting, however, that more of the burden than is necessary rests on the police authorities as a consequence of the apparent failure of the complaints system. Complaints against the police in England and Wales average about 30 000 per year. Despite the introduction of a Police Complaints Board in 1976 as an external check on police-led investigations, disciplinary action against police officers was recommended in less than 1 per cent of complaints filed in 1980 (see Baldwin and Kinsey 1982). This may change with the advent of the Police and Criminal Evidence Act, which introduces a new Police Complaints Authority. Procedures for dealing with the most and least serious complaints have been reformed, but Merricks (1985) doubts whether there will be much improvement in dealing with the majority of grievances.

The power of the police authorities to challenge the decisions of Chief Constables seems small in comparison with that of the Home Secretary. Demands for greater accountability have led police authorities into conflict with their Chief Constables throughout the country, but most notably in Merseyside, Greater Manchester, South Yorkshire and Derbyshire. Margaret Simey (1982) has written an illuminating account of the difficulties of maximising the constructive role of the police authority in Merseyside while continuing to fight for a meaningful system of accountability. Some of the issues she raises are further discussed by Scraton (1984). Bitter disputes over the role of the police authority in Greater Manchester reached a climax in 1984 which prompted the Chief Constable to appeal to the Home Office to clarify the extent of his powers. During the miners' strike of 1984, councillors in labour-controlled metropolitan areas in particular began to express their opinion that only by ensuring the greater accountability of the police to the elected representatives of the public could policy-makers restore the quality of police–community relations.

The crux of the accountability argument is over whether the interests of central government, mediated by Chief Constables (who are primarily accountable to the Home Secretary), or local public interests, are expressed in local policing policies and practice. Can and should local democracies exert an influence on Chief Constables to balance that of national government? Is there any sense in which policing can be regarded as a local resource subject to local control?

Phrased as such, the controversy concerning police accountability impinges on a debate amongst geographers about the conflicts of interest between local and national governments. So far, there have been few British studies that focus explicitly on the spatial organisation of policing, and those that do are basically empirical analyses of policing practice (see, for example, Mawby 1979b) rather than theoretical considerations of the relationships between police and society. In tackling this second, very fundamental issue, there is considerable scope for recent thinking amongst political geographers to make an important contribution.

Dear (1981) has argued that there is both a distinction and a tension between national and local 'states' in advanced capitalist economies, and Duncan and Goodwin (1982) discuss some British examples where the resolve of local councillors has triumphed over the policies of national government regarding the management of local affairs. Today, one of the most prominent sources of such tension concerns the exercise of police powers, and it is over the question of accountability that national and local government conceptions of police powers are most at odds.

The argument against local democratic participation in policing is based on a claim that it is incompatible with maintaining a non-partisan police force that is fundamentally accountable to the law. Accountability to the law is reckoned to ensure the independence of the police and the impartiality of their actions. Citizens are equal before the law, and since laws are constituted democratically, accountability to the law is, by definition, a source of the democratic accountability of the police (Jefferson and Grimshaw (1981, 1984a, 1984b) give a detailed critique of this reasoning, while Baldwin and Kinsey (1982: 104–45) outline the history of police accountability in Britain).

Yet, absolute accountability to the law is a practical impossibility, in so far as it would demand the consistent application of unambiguous rules to define a wide range of human behaviours. Accountability to the law requires that sanctions be applied equitably against all illegal acts wherever and whenever they occur. However, as the GLC Police Committee Support Unit (1983b) point out, the law must, given the limited resources, information and time available to the police, be *selectively* enforced. It is the accumulating evidence that this selectivity is not impartial, that discretion in enforcing the law is not compatible with the notion of equality before the law, that a non-partisan police force cannot exist (because decisions must be made about which laws to enforce, when, where, and against whom) and probably should not exist (a point forcefully argued by Simey 1985), that has encouraged current demands for local democratic participation in the policing process.

The concept of accountability is an anathema to many senior police officers, who perceive it as an attempt by local pressure groups to gain control over policing, possibly intending to misuse the service. On close examination, such fears (which, in principle, are well founded in the demands of a minority of political extremists) appear to stem from a lack of clarity about what degree of local autonomy is demanded, and what kinds of democratic accountability are possible.

Clark (1984) has recently attempted to clarify the different meanings of local autonomy that are commonly used but often conflated. He identifies the key factors contributing to local autonomy as (a) the initiative allowed to local governments to regulate and legislate in their own interests, and (b) the immunity of local governments' decisions from the veto of higher tiers of the state. Combining these, he arrives at a fourfold classification of local autonomy, characterised as follows: (i) initiative and immunity, (ii) initiative and no immunity, (iii) no initiative and immunity, (iv) no initiative and no immunity.

Police accountability as currently in place, through the operation of the police authorities, lies between types (iii) and (iv). The police authorities can only endorse operational decisions made by Chief Constables; they can only assent to directives issued from the Home Office. Any 'immunity' (claimed in model (iii)) from the veto of central government refers merely to a degree of local variability in the implementation of policy decisions which reflects the traditional independence of Chief Constables. Essentially, the present system of accountability tends towards a model in which the local state functions as a bureaucratic executor of decisions shaped primarily by central government. For the most part, police authorities administer rather than initiate police policy and organisational decisions.

Those who see danger in changing this appear to assume that the institution of local democratic accountability must follow the model of type (i), which accords all power to the local state. In this case, however, local political influence on policing would itself be unaccountable. This is obviously undesirable, but since Clark likens type (i) arrangements to those practised in governing 'the walled cities of feudal times', it is hardly likely to be a model appropriate to the highly integrated urban systems of an advanced industrial democracy.

The arrangement for police accountability that I would favour is close to type (ii). In this model, the actions of local democracy can be constrained by reference to a higher principle (such as the law) imposed by central government, but within this fundamental framework police policy and operations would be based on local initiatives and subject to local control. The model demands that 'legitimacy resides with the local government: its actions can only be constrained, and in this manner legitimacy flows from the "bottom up" ' (Clark 1984: 201). I conclude this section by discussing some proposals for police accountability that seem consistent with this model.

I begin with the premiss that all policing must take place within the law, but that accountability directly and only to the law is a theoretical ideal which cannot be achieved in practice in a system where discretion and selectivity in law-enforcement is necessary (and probably desirable). I also assume that accountability within the law to a local public must be secured in democratic terms. To this end, Baldwin and Kinsey's (1982) suggestions regarding the representation of local public interests in the policing process seem appropriate. They call for police authorities to consist entirely of people elected to local councils (thus excluding non-elected magistrates), and to be given the power to lay down 'policy guidelines' for Chief Constables. In formulating such guidelines, the authorities should consider the views of local community police councils which would be set up by statute at force divisional and subdivisional levels. These too would consist wholly of elected members, with whom the police would have a statutory obligation to consult. Baldwin and Kinsey stop short, however, of according any real power to the electorate, clearly distinguishing their concept of accountability after the event from active participation in police decision-making:

accountability is liability to account for a decision after it has been taken; control, on the other hand, exists where influence is exerted in making a decision. To demand control over Chief Constables is, therefore, to ask for a say in making policing decisions; to propose that Chief Constables be accountable is to emphasize their freedom to decide operational matters but to impose on them an obligation to justify those decisions afterwards. (Baldwin and Kinsey 1982: 106)

This definition of accountability, however, because it denies the police authorities any direct participation in Chief Constables' decision-making processes, neutralises much of the value of mandatory consultation between the police and democratically elected members of local communities. I believe the distinction that Baldwin and Kinsey draw between accountability and control is unnecessary when the type (ii) model of local autonomy proposed by Clark (1984) is adopted. *Within* the law policing can exhibit great variability. If there is true commitment to the notion of locally sensitive policing it is at this stage, i.e. at the level of police operations within the law, that the public should have a say in the formulation and execution of local policing policy.

Jefferson and Grimshaw (1981) explore this idea by formulating a socialist solution to the problem of accountability. They argue that the gap between the theory and practice of legal accountability should be filled by accountability to another principle – that of social justice. They argue that it is social equality rather than equality before the law which is the key to civil equality, on which their conception of democracy rests.

Thus, unlike at present where Chief Constables can 'within the law' pursue virtually any public policy consonant with the duty to enforce 'a range of laws', or under the proposed changes where the same would be true though subject to Police Authority guidance and veto, the system that we are proposing would require that law enforcement policy decisions be justified, and challengeable, according to their contribution to social justice. This would not mean, of course, that prioritising social justice dispenses with legal justice. On the contrary, that would remain the limiting factor: all police work would still have to be legal, but it would *also* have to measure up to the criteria of social justice to escape challenge and censure. A 'socially just' policy would necessarily be legal: but legal policies of law enforcement are not necessarily socially just. (Jefferson and Grimshaw 1981: 24)

Relating this to the model of accountability suggested by Clark's type (ii) version of local autonomy, the law would be the source of 'no immunity' from the veto of national government, whereas 'initiative' would be introduced through the democratic formulation of locally relevant conceptions of social justice. Such initiative could only be constrained if it impinged on the law. Conceived in this way, the concept of accountability could not be compatible with the activities of extremist groups seeking to control the police or undermine the law. It would, however, ensure that local policing policy and practice responds to the needs of the public it serves.

I have argued so far that changes in the organisation of policing in the last two decades, contingent on growing enthusiasm for a national law-and-order campaign, have not guaranteed the effectiveness of policing at a local level, especially amongst the more disadvantaged segments of the population. Increased investment into policing has not achieved an overall reduction in the crime rate; relations between the police and the public have continued to deteriorate in the inner city, to an extent that often undermines the benefits of community-based policing initiatives.

A solution to the present dilemma in policing appears to depend in part on securing the greater accountability of police forces to local democracies. This is a process which might be seen as politically acceptable once it is acknowledged that local accountability does not require the police to be stripped of their powers under the law. At its most appealing, the notion strives for a sharing of powers to secure effective crime-control policies *within* the law. To conclude this chapter, I shall consider the possibilities for further 'democratisation' of the management of crime by exploring areas of public policy and social service outside policing where there is scope for involvement in crime prevention and the alleviation of fear.

The role of other agencies

Nationally, the main thrust of the government's response to rising crime rates has taken the form of investment into policing and the criminal justice system. This is part of an attempt to arrest an upward trend in the rates of recorded crime. However, I have already discussed the evidence that such an increase is inevitable, given the preferred lifestyles and political/economic systems of the West in the twentieth century. It is worth considering, therefore, whether public money allocated for crime prevention and control might not more beneficially be invested into the work of other welfare agencies, who, in consultation with the police, could be better placed to implement locally effective schemes to reduce both the risks of victimisation where these are disproportionately high, and the fear of crime where this is unnecessarily debilitating.

Present British initiatives in neighbourhood policing are not of an explicitly multi-agency nature, and in tackling the problem of crime they do not directly confront the adverse effects of fear on people's quality of life and sense of well-being. Where the police co-operate with other services at the moment, the model is one of 'inter-agency' co-operation, initiated, directed and controlled by the police, rather than a fully integrated multi-agency endeavour where power and initiative are shared on a pluralist model.

In so far as the inter-agency model is adopted, current British policing schemes are similar to those implemented in the United States in the early 1970s. They emphasise the education of victims and the reduction of opportunities for crime, but they leave little scope for the public to define their own problems or develop their own solutions, and they are organisationally unprepared to deal with factors other than crime which may exacerbate fear, but which fall outside the conventional boundaries of policing. As Boostrom and Henderson (1984: 375) observe of the American experience, 'police usually have an instrumental view of citizen participation in which citizens are expected to help out as a means to an end as defined by the "experts" '. British schemes are similarly subject to the criticism made by Cronin et al. (1981) of the programme of the USA's Law Enforcement Assistance Administration: they are 'policemen's programmes' and suffer from the limited role accorded to other agencies.

My argument, then, is premissed on the belief that without a multi-agency approach it will be difficult to deal with local variations in the crime rate, or with the effects of crime (especially the problem of fear in the inner city). With a multi-agency model, on the other hand, it may be possible to develop local initiatives that are success-ful in both reducing the unnecessary risks of victimisation and containing the more debilitating consequences of fear.

In chapter 4 I suggested that conceptually and analytically it is possible to distinguish two components to the odds of victimisation. The distinction between 'absolute' odds (contingent on lifestyle) and 'relative' risk (most obviously related to location) brings to mind two facets of social disadvantage which, as Kirby (1981) acknowledges, are too often conflated. These are deprivation in the market place and deprivation *in situ*: 'people poverty' and 'place poverty'. In terms of crime, these refer respectively to the set odds of victimisation which people differentially encounter (by virtue of the lifestyle options made available to them) and to the attributes of individuals and groups, including their residential location, which independently increase their probability of becoming victims.

It seems doubtful whether the absolute risk of victimisation could substantially be reduced without also curbing some of the more desirable social trends in our society. For an absolute decrease in vulnerability would have to be accompanied by less social mixing, restrictions in geographical mobility and limitations on activities outside the home. This would be unacceptable to most people, causing distress sufficient to offset any increase in the quality of life brought about by a fall in the crime rate. Depressed activity rates are themselves indicators of social malaise: they contribute disproportionately to mounting levels of fear and to the social isolation which may now characterise many communities (cf. Knight and Hayes 1981). The opportunity to participate in leisure activities, in contrast, has a positive effect on the quality of life, both socially and psychologically.

On the other hand, 'relative' risks of victimisation, as examined in the context of the inner city, can be interpreted as as aspect (and a surprisingly neglected one) of locational or *in situ* disadvantage. Any reduction in this kind of vulnerability can only enhance the social well-being of the country's more deprived communities. My argument, therefore, is that it is relative rather than absolute risk that realistic and egalitarian crime-prevention policies will seek to reduce, and that the relative risks of victimisation can be tackled as part of a broader planning strategy to ameliorate the 'multiple deprivation' of some working-class areas.

Hamnett (1979) and Kirby (1981) are at odds regarding the general principles underlying such a strategy, and their arguments are representative of those which continue to fuel a debate on the efficacy of area-based planning policies. Hamnett argues that the spatial character of deprivation reflects inequalities in the allocative sphere which can only be reformed by challenging the organisation of the productive process itself. Kirby, however, argues that some elements of disadvantage are problems of consumption; they are locally rooted and will respond only to area-based solutions. Since the scope for large-scale structural change in Britain is politically limited, spatial inequalities in the overall risks of crime engendered by the prevailing political economy are unlikely to be eradicated by policies implemented at this level. In fact, national policies seem, by aiming indiscriminately to reduce the absolute risks of victimisation, to exacerbate locational inequalities in the distribution of relative risks. There must, however, be scope at the local level to remove some of the more obvious precursors to vulnerability, especially those associated with a decaying physical environment: insecurable dwellings; vacant buildings and broken fences which make access easy for the opportunistic offender; and an under-supply of garage space which necessitates 'on-street' parking, exposing vehicles to the risk of vandalism and theft. Moves implemented at this level may be short-term palliatives, but they could substantially enhance the quality of life amongst the disproportionately victim-prone. To this end victimisation in the inner city can appropriately be examined and dealt with within an area-based planning framework along the lines discussed by Jones (1980), Kirby (1981) and Rex (1981) and epitomised in the inner-city partnership programme.

One advantage of dispersing some of the responsibility for crime prevention away from the police is that the resulting policies may be more compatible with the need to manage the fear of crime. Police campaigns encouraging the public to protect their persons or property often use frightening posters and television advertisements. Their message is obviously important, and as Warr (1982) argues, one condition for the reduction of levels of fear is the reduction of crime itself. But this is not a sufficient condition, and it is possible that in some locales the impersonal messages of the mass media may cost more in terms of people's psychological well-being than is gained in terms of crime reduction. Much greater scope to gauge the potential impact of crime-control initiatives could be secured by ensuring that such initiatives are locally based and have an input from a range of organisations in touch with a local community. If this approach is adopted (and police forces' increasing initiatives in neighbourhood based crime-prevention schemes, together with the public's growing demand for consultation and accountability, suggest it will be), it should be possible to integrate crime prevention and control policies with policies needed to alleviate the consequences of excessive fear.

At one level it seems likely that fear could be alleviated by simple environmental management policies similar to those involved in reducing the relative risks of victimisation. I suggested in chapter 5 that physical decay in the residential environment exacerbates people's awareness of and concern about crime in their neighbourhood. Simple, well-coordinated and rapidly implemented strategies of environmental improvement might therefore alleviate anxiety about the risks of victimisation quite independently of reducing the crime rate. Moreover, if such strategies are not implemented, it could equally be argued that reductions in the crime rate will have little or no impact on levels of fear in a community. It may, therefore, be necessary to question the general utility of policies directed towards crime control alone (such as campaigns for the installation of locks, bolts and alarms) and to re-evaluate the orientation and phasing of environmental planning.

It is, however, at the level of social policy that the greatest strides are likely to be made in terms of a multi-agency approach to both crime control and the management of fear. My own analysis in north central Birmingham implies that the detrimental effects of fear could be alleviated (i) by increasing people's satisfaction with their social environment, and (ii) by encouraging higher levels of primary group interaction and communication within communities. Merry (1981a), in her study of fear in Philadelphia, reached similar conclusions.

To achieve an increase in social satisfaction with a vew to allaying fear, it will be necessary to remove a broader set of anxieties which, on the evidence of chapter 5, tend to be translated into concern for crime. One significant source of worry stems from those problems of inner-city life which appear (to those experiencing them) to have no means of control or solution. Those residents of north central Birmingham who identified no such problem were most likely to perceive crime as below average or decreasing; they were least likely to express any fear of crime, or to adjust their behaviour to avoid victimisation. Most people, however, did experience at least one major problem, and over a third of these felt there was no-one to turn to for advice. This group were much more likely to fear crime, and tended to alter their behaviour accordingly.

If any one agency currently bears the brunt of problems causing the public anxiety it is the police, and Southgate and Eckblom (1984) acknowledge that they perform an important service in this respect. Yet, the police have neither the resources nor the expertise to deal with the majority of non-criminal grievances, and Kinsey's (1984:48) evidence in Merseyside suggests that the public do not want them to. Respondents were clear in their demands for the police to concentrate on crime and criminal investigation, and if necessary 'the survey would indicate that this could be done at the expense of "service" provision and other police work of an "indirect", pre-emptive nature'. Similarly, where the police seem most effective in allaying fear is in uniform on the streets (Balkin and Houlden 1983), and in being seen to be involved in crime-specific activities (Smith 1982a). Fear seems to increase where the agents of crime control are perceived to be ineffective or preoccupied in activities unrelated to crime. Certainly, it can be argued that police effectiveness in controlling crime is limited by the sheer volume of non-crime services which they currently provide (Elliott 1983). The eradication of displaceable anxiety likely to cause fear lies not in assigning a broad service role to the police, but in developing co-operation between the police and other agencies to allow the co-ordination of workloads, thus promoting the wider availability of caring and advisory services, and ensuring that people feel their most pressing problems can be shared.

This kind of approach is compatible with the encouragement of a second trend likely to reduce fear, namely increased social cohesion, communication and mutual support amongst the public. A number of studies have shown that it is voluntary rather than statutory agencies that are perceived as most available and useful by inner-city residents (Gladstone 1979; Knight and Hayes 1981). Voluntary organisations both increase the social cohesion amongst partici-pants and provide the necessary outlet for anxieties which might otherwise manifest themselves as fear of crime. Indeed, reduced levels of fear might well be added to the benefits of switching resources away from state agencies to voluntary organisations which were itemised by Gladstone (1979).

This is certainly the implication of Northwestern University's extensive 'reactions to crime' project, focussing on urban neighbourhoods in Philadelphia, Chicago and San Francisco. Podolefsky (1979), reporting on the study's analysis of collective reactions to crime, points out that the public are not likely to respond positively to the problem of crime merely because they are informed of its magnitude and severity in their local area. Such publicity is more likely to increase fear, encourage social isolation, and reduce informal surveillance. The most effective collective anti-crime activities are carried out by multi-issue groups and 'attempts to increase involvement in neighbourhood groups *for whatever reason* are likely to be effective, indirectly, in increasing participation [in collective responses to crime]' (Podolefsky 1979; 55, my emphasis). The implications of this study are that moves *generally* to increase mutual support and local social cohesion in a neighbourhood (moves which seem likely to reduce the more debilitating effects of fear) will also encourage public involvement in local crime-prevention schemes, whether or not these are initiated by the police.

In advocating the inclusion of the police in a multi-agency approach to the management of crime and fear, I should reiterate that the desired ends are unlikely to be achieved if the police are regarded as the prime movers and principal authority for such undertakings. McPherson and Silloway (1981) have already shown that many neighbourhood-level statutory crime-control schemes in the United States failed to improve residents' quality of life substantially because they were police dominated and unable to capitalise on local initiatives. According to Lewis and Salem (1981), such failure reflects residents' perceptions of their limited capacity to control the changes occurring in their lives and environment. Communities' political and social resources may be important factors affecting the relationship between perceptions of crime, other neighbourhood problems and the expression of fear: 'Neighbourhoods with political power, for example, appeared more capable of addressing local problems than did those without it; and this capacity often appeared to contribute to diminishing fear' (Lewis and Salem 1981: 414–15). Similarly, other analysts link decentralised political power with effective local crime control. Clinard (1978) attributes the low crime rates of much of Switzerland partly to the decentralisation of government to cantons and communes, wherein each individual assumes some responsibility for social control. Shelley (1981a) adopts much the same argument in her discussion of Switzerland and Japan.

In short, local democratic control in respect of a variety of governmental issues seems effective in the reduction of fear (by increasing inter-group co-operation and communication) and in the containment of crime (by enhancing informal social control). These effects seem to depend on ensuring that real decision-making power is available at a local level. Other evidence suggests such powers should cover a range of issues, not only those related to crime. For crime itself rarely gives sufficient impetus to sustain the public's interest; it is most effectively managed by groups united around a range of issues, to whose programme any crime-related endeavour might be a relatively late addition (Lewis and Salem 1981). Thus, Lavrakas and Herz (1982) insist that most citizens' anti-crime activities are simply an extension of their general tendency to be involved in community-based voluntary activities. Based on such assumptions, Lea and Young (1984) make the issue of public participation in policing a much wider argument for the extension of local democracy. They point out that community-based policing schemes are implemented to mobilise a latent sense of community spirit. The police aim to be catalysts in the reconstitution of that sense of community lost in the upheavals of urban renewal and economic recession. Where a state of mutual care and loyalty can be restored, informal control should be strong, reducing the potential for offenders to act, increasing the protection of people and property and so reducing the burden on the police. This sequence may fail, however, when the ideal is imposed on residents with no real say in the matter, and who do not themselves bear the responsibility for the projects in which they variously participate. For Lea and Young,

the only way to develop, or rather re-develop, the local community as a political entity is to create the institutions for local democracy. It is no good looking first to see if the local community has properly constituted itself with a degree of political responsibility and only then contemplating the decentralization to the locality of decision-making procedures previously concentrated in the national state. (Lea and Young 1984: 239)

Closely following these recommendations, and encouraging a community-based multi-agency approach to a range of issues, is the 'patch' scheme of the social services. Patch refers to the localisation of social services, with renewed emphasis on community involvement and power sharing. The initiative is discussed in some detail by Croft and Beresford (1984), who describe it as a pluralist approach to welfare, committed to a reduced role for the state with greater emphasis on the voluntary sector. It appears to be a first step in restoring to disadvantaged communities a real sense of control over their lives and futures.

Conclusion

This chapter has examined a range of formal responses to crime in modern Britain. Increased investment of public funds into the police service has neither reduced the crime rate nor increased the likelihood that offenders will be apprehended. Organisational changes in policing effected in the last two decades have sometimes been accompanied by a deterioration of police–community relations, which neither a shift towards pro-active community policing nor the development of more comprehensive consultative procedures has remedied. Rather, unprecedented developments in the centralisation, consolidation and professionalisation of police forces have brought sharply into focus some fundamental weaknesses in the present system of police accountability. Although opinion is bitterly polarised concerning the desirability of a more effective system of local democratic participation in policing, a geographical literature on the nature of local autonomy provides some grounds for rapprochement that are theoretically appealing and politically viable.

If a more acceptable basis for local accountability is a first requirement for the effective implementation of community-based policing schemes, a second requirement must be police participation in a multi-agency approach to law and order. Solutions to the problems of fear of crime, crime control and law-enforcement often fall outside the domain of policing, and, often, narrowly police-based strategies represent a less efficient deployment of resources than do schemes which also attempt to involve other services. Currently, however, a substantial proportion of the population feels there are at least some elements of the crime problem, as they experience it, that cannot or should not be dealt with formally. Chapter 7 considers the implications of this, first by explaining why some people choose not to mobilise the criminal justice system even when the option is available, and then by exploring a range of informal responses to crime used by individuals to supplement the statutory procedures.

7

Social reactions to crime

Introduction

In addition to the variety of policy responses to crime discussed in chapter 6, individuals and groups develop their own strategies to manage those aspects of crime which they perceive as part of the social reality of daily life. Public responses to specific offences may or may not mobilise the criminal justice system; fear and concern for crime may be ignored or reduced through individual and group action. The literature is full of typologies attempting to describe the various reactions to crime which analysts have observed, and some of the most common of these are summarised in table 7.1.

Table 7.1 makes the distinction drawn both by Conklin (1975) and by Schneider and Schneider (1978) between communal and individual tactics. This reflects too the importance that Cohn et al. (1978) attach to behavioural differences between 'private minded'

Table 7.1 *Public responses to crime*

	Type of response		
	Reactive	Protective	Preventive
Individual efforts	report to police or other agency; victim retaliation; bystander intervention	target hardening; guardianship; insurance; avoidance behaviour	join local action group
Collective action	victim support	neighbourhood watch; territoriality; vigilantism	remove perceived causes of crime through broadly based neighbourhood organisation

avoidance strategies and 'public minded' control strategies (these latter being effected through membership of community organisations). Skogan (1981) would add a further category of 'surburban flight' to those of personal precautions, household protection and community involvement which appear in the table. Katzman (1980), however, suggests that crime is instrumental not so much in forcing people out of declining neighbourhoods as in deterring others from moving in.

Table 7.1 also captures a conceptual distinction tacitly made by most authors describing responses to crime, namely the difference between immediate reactions to specific, discrete criminal events (e.g. reporting behaviour) and more enduring, habitual responses to 'vicarious victimisation' – the threat posed by continuous exposure to risk (as experienced through fear or concern about crime and awareness of its import as a local problem). Finally, a distinction is noted between protective behaviour, which aims to reduce specific risks of victimisation, and preventive behaviour which aims to remove the perceived *causes* of crime, largely through the efforts of various community organisations (cf. Podolefsky 1979).

This chapter examines in detail some of the specific behaviours listed in table 7.1. As in previous chapters, however, I shall attempt to integrate the issue of crime with a range of other policy-relevant social concerns. That this is especially important when considering responses to crime is indicated by the comprehensive 'reactions to crime' project conducted in four large US cities by researchers at Northwestern University. This study shows that the general public, unlike welfare bureaucracies, does not tend to isolate crime from a range of other social issues. As a consequence, this survey of public needs suggests that the study of reactions to crime is most appropriately located within specific community-based contexts: 'locality, and more specifically, neighbourhood, is a viable and necessary unit of analysis for understanding the distribution of, and variations in, collective responses to crime (Podolefsky 1979: 363). In view of this, it seems appropriate to develop this chapter around the example of north central Birmingham, which provides a case study useful in assessing the social significance and consequences of reactions to crime in the British context.

Podolefsky (1979) makes a second important point in his account of collective responses to crime in North America. He shows that most collective anti-crime activities are carried out by multi-issue groups, and that individuals' participation in such activities grows out of a more general involvement in local group activity. The value of his analysis is that it conceptualises reactions to crime as part of a broader social process associated with the emergence of community groups in neighbourhood settings. Although, in the Birmingham case study, it is clear that such organised collective responses are rare, I shall argue with Podolefsky for the importance of broadening the reactions to crime literature to include an understanding of the wider structure of social relations from which such reactions arise and to which they contribute.

In my discussion of the British case, I shall make little reference to organised collective responses to crime, which even Podolefsky (1979) found engaged less than 10 per cent of the population. North central Birmingham does contain its share of residents' associations, but in my experience meetings were poorly attended and members rarely discussed anti-crime activities. Vigilante groups, which seem fairly common in the United States (see Ostrowe and DiBiase 1983; Pike 1979), are rarely formed in British cities (though in the light of recent concern about the escalation of racial attacks, the public can hardly be condemned for considering it an option). Thus, I shall be concerned with collective reactions to crime that arise apparently incidentally from individuals' habits and daily routines.

My investigation begins by examining a range of individual responses to crime – reactive, preventive and protective – and then goes on to consider the meaning and implications of any generalisations about group behaviour that can be made on the basis of these ostensibly independent actions. The most obvious such generalisation concerns the importance of race relative to that of other social attributes as a predictor of responses to crime. There are, of course, other emphases that could be made – fear amongst the elderly, the link between crime and gender and the differential effects of crime in the class structure, for instance. However, since the salience of race in public images of deviance was so evident in chapter 5, because the race and crime debate has so often been fuelled by events in the Birmingham study area, and because of the strength of the empirical relations between race and reactions to crime in this case study, much of the discussion which follows aims to account theoretically for the persistent link between the problem of crime and the tenor of race relations in the inner cities. The general form of the argument could, of course, be applied to other aspects of social relations and in different contexts.

Reporting behaviour and the police

It is through the public that the majority of recorded crimes come to the notice of the police. Perhaps as little as 6 per cent of crimes recorded in any one year will have been discovered by the police themselves, and many of these come to light during the questioning of offenders (who often request, or are persuaded, that a number of other offences should be 'taken into consideration') rather than through pro-active patrol observations. Yet, not all crimes experienced by the public are reported to the police. The British Crime Survey (BCS) suggests that in England and Wales as few as one in four crimes known to private (as distinct from corporate) victims are reported. The proportions of offences about which the police are notified ranges from 18 per cent of thefts in a dwelling, to 47 per cent of robberies, 66 per cent of burglaries and 95 per cent of thefts of motor vehicles (Hough and Mayhew 1983: 11). In Scotland (where one in three crimes were notified to the police), the reporting rates are about the same or slightly higher than in England and Wales for all offences except housebreaking and sexual assault (Chambers and Tombs 1984).

Local crime surveys find a similar tendency for crimes to be suppressed by the public: in Merseyside, three and a half times as many crimes of violence and offences involving loss or damage to property occur as are reported to the police (Kinsey 1984); in north central Birmingham, only 111 (39.5 per cent) of the 281 incidents recorded in the survey were reported by victims to the police (although, in a further 7.5 per cent of cases, the police had already discovered the offence or been notified of it by a third party). Reporting rates by crime type in the Birmingham study area are given in table 7.2. These figures corroborate the findings of Sparks et al.'s (1977) London survey, suggesting that, in general, personal violence is less likely to be reported than property crimes, while the reporting rate of fraud and deception is lowest of all.

It is worth noting here that the decision to report is not the only documented method by which public reactions to crime may mobilise the criminal justice system. Merry (1979) has drawn attention to the readiness of people in the United States to file complaints against one another in the criminal courts as a means of handling personal conflicts. Because this procedure costs complainants nothing (i.e. it is as available for use as informal sanctions), Merry believes it could, properly implemented, decrease the incidence of interpersonal violence (which is an alternative means by which victims

Table 7.2 *Rates of reporting for different types of crime (% in brackets)*

Type of crime	Reported to police		Not reported to police		Total crimes experienced	
Theft from dwelling	11	(33.3)	22	(66.7)	33	(100)
Burglary in dwelling	35	(74.5)	12	(25.5)	47	(100)
Damage	18	(23.4)	59	(76.6)	77	(100)
Theft of/from vehicle	30	(58.8)	21	(41.2)	51	(100)
Fraud/deception	3	(9.7)	28	(90.3)	31	(100)
Personal theft	5	(55.6)	4	(44.4)	9	(100)
Personal violence	9	(27.3)	24	(72.7)	33	(100)
Total	111	(39.5)	170	(60.5)	281	(100)

$X^2 = 52.8$, 5 d.f., $p<0.001$ (calculated by amalgamating personal theft and personal violence)

Source: North central Birmingham crime survey.

might retaliate). The public's readiness to use organised means of legal arbitration has led to the establishment of a neighbourhood justice programme in the United States, which provides an alternative to the courts for handling minor criminal and civil grievances. The operation of these schemes depends on the voluntary participation of disputants, and the aim of the programme is to achieve mediation and compromise, which often seems fairer than the 'winner-takes-all' outcome of court cases (see Tomasic and Feeley 1982 for an assessment of this initiative).

In Britain, however, civil action in the courts is expensive, and the police (together with the Director of Public Prosecutions, and, in Scotland, the Procurator Fiscal) are the gatekeepers of criminal prosecution. For the most part, the public's most effective means of mobilising the criminal justice system is the reporting of crimes to the police. In recent years, a large literature has developed recording analysts' attempts to establish why this option is so often rejected. So far, much of the evidence comes from the United States, and it is only recently that an understanding of non-reporting by the British public has begun to receive attention.

The tenor of victims' attitudes towards the police is one factor often examined in connection with the public's reluctance to report crime. This explanation is favoured by Sparks et al. (1977), who, finding no significant differences in reporting behaviour according to the demographic or socio-economic characteristics of victims, devote most of their speculative discussion to the possible effects of citizens' attitudes to the police. In the Birmingham study area, however, the likelihood of victims reporting crimes to the police does not vary significantly according to the following measures of public attitudes: (i) whether victims view the police favourably, unfavourably, or indifferently; (ii) victims' perceptions of the quality of the local police service; (iii) whether victims prefer to call agencies *other* than the police in the event of crime; (iv) when the victim last saw or spoke with a police officer. This seems to be the case in Britain more generally, since the BCS revealed that both in Scotland and in England and Wales less than 6 per cent of the reasons given by victims for failing to report identify fear or dislike of the police as an inhibiting factor (Chambers and Tombs 1984; Hough and Mayhew 1983). A similar conclusion is reached by Skogan (1984) who, in his review of a world-wide collation of crime surveys, draws attention to the consistently limited role of attitudes to the police as a criterion affecting the reporting of offences.

This is not to deny the more general importance of attitudes towards the police for people's quality of life and experiences of fear. Baker et al. (1983) claim that confidence in the police can greatly reduce fear amongst the elderly, and they argue that programmes designed to improve police relations with racial minorities would significantly reduce the anxiety often experienced by such groups. Fortunately, the majority of the British public is generally satisfied with policing. Unfortunately, dissatisfaction appears to be greatest in working-class areas. Although only 6 per cent of respondents in the BCS believe the police do a very poor or fairly poor job (Moxon and Jones 1984), the reputation of the police is at a low ebb amongst minority groups and in the inner cities. A recent study by the Policy Studies Institute (Smith and Gray 1983), based on the experience of black people in London, suggests that between a third and a half of the Afro-Caribbean population have considerable doubts about standards of police conduct. The Merseyside crime survey shows that, although generally twice as many people (25 per cent) are 'really pleased' with the police as are 'really annoyed' with them (14 per cent), in the inner city and on council estates, almost as many express annoyance as pleasure; and the bigger the crime problem is perceived to be, the less inclined are people to believe the police have a good understanding of the local area (Kinsey 1984).

There is evidence that crises of confidence in the police impinge on the quality of social life within both American and British cities, particularly in racially mixed areas. Both Apple and O'Brien (1983) and Smith and Hawkins (1973) show that the racial composition of neighbourhoods affects people's evaluations of police performance in the United States. In Britain, Field (1984) found that the one institution over which the attitudes of black and white respondents in the BCS differ is the police. Thirty per cent of blacks say they have been annoyed with police behaviour during the past five years, whereas less than 15 per cent of whites and Asians express this view. Although two-thirds of white respondents feel the police understand the problems of their neighbourhood, less than half the Asians and only one-third of black respondents share this sentiment. It may be that only a small proportion of the population express negative attitudes to the police, but the social and spatial selectivity of the sentiment must be cause for concern. Moreover, complacency regarding the satisfied majority would be out of place in the opinion of Morris and Heal (1981), who point out that it is hard to tell from surveys whether 'satisfaction' implies acceptance of the legitimacy of the police service as an institution (which few would seriously dispute), or contentment with the actions of a particular local police service (which might be more at issue).

In one sense, this is peripheral to the present discussion of reporting behaviour, since, as I observed earlier, the decision to report seems independent of attitudes to the police. There is, however, some evidence that one *consequence* of people initiating contact with the police (because of having been victimised) can be to lower their opinion of the service. Sparks, Genn and Dodd's (1977) survey in London, my own in Birmingham, and a police-initiated study in Lancaster, Blackburn and Skelmersdale (Lancashire Constabulary 1983) all find that victims are more likely than non-victims to be unfavourably disposed towards the police, or dissatisfied with their services.

In the Lancashire study, 21 per cent of victims say they are not satisfied with the way the police have treated them, either because of officers' attitudes, or because no information was given them regarding the result of investigations. Victims express similar sentiments in Merseyside, where one in four are concerned about officers' attitudes, their inaction or failure to help, and their failure to communicate the outcome of enquiries (Kinsey 1984). Poister and McDavid (1978) suggest it is the failure to keep victims informed about follow-up enquiries that is most detrimental. Using evidence from Harrisburg, Pennsylvania, these authors demonstrate that satisfaction with the police decreases at later stages in the investigation of crime, and that overall satisfaction with police involvement is much more related to the quality of follow-up enquiries than to opinions formed at the time of the crime. Bynum et al. (1982) go on to show that property crimes (the majority of recorded offences) occurring in areas characterised by high economic status receive the most investigative effort; least likely to be followed up are crimes whose victims are poor and non-white. In view of this, it is not difficult to understand why racial minorities and the residents of poorer areas are least satisfied with police practice.

Attitudes towards the police, therefore, seem important in relation to a sense of local social well-being, they are influenced by the quality of public contacts with the police, but they contribute little to our understanding of why people may or may not react to crime by reporting it to the police. A more promising line of enquiry has focussed on the role of incident-specific and situational factors in the decision to report. Fishman (1979), Schwind et al. (1975), Skogan (1976) and Sparks et al. (1977) all provide evidence that the most influential incident-specific factors affecting reporting behaviour is crime seriousness. As Gottfredson and Hindelang (1981: 20) put it: 'victims, like police and judges, are most likely to invoke the criminal law against conduct deemed most harmful'. All the evidence from the BCS seems to support this argument. Most of the offences not reported to the police are less serious than their reported counterparts. According to surveyed victims, over 80 per cent of unreported household offences and over 50 per cent of unreported personal offences seem too trivial to bother the authorities with, do not merit reporting because they entail no loss or damage, or are suppressed in the belief that the police would be unable to deal with them (Hough and Mayhew 1983). In Birmingham, too, surveyed victims judge that almost half the unreported crimes are not serious enough to bother the police with.

Many other situational factors have proved important: time of day, for instance (Greenberg et al. 1982), or the influence of bystanders and friends (Ruback et al. 1984). Today, it is usual to regard crime reporting as an essentially rational and pragmatic act, made on the basis of victims' assessments of the possible rewards and expected costs of notifying the police. Commenting on the findings of crime surveys world-wide, Skogan (1984) confirms the generality of this assertion: the decision to report is rooted in immediate, direct experiences, and reflects the pros and cons, for specific individuals, of contacting the police.

Incident-specific explanations of reporting behaviour are empirically verified and logically plausible. Such explanations do not, however, exhaust the empirical evidence. They provide a necessary but theoretically insufficient account of the rationale for contacting the police. Blum-West (1983), for instance, argues that the decision to report depends less on public expectations of the police than on a personal sense of civic duty. The outcome may still be that the more serious offences are reported, but the intentionality of the actors will be different from that implied by situational explanations; it will reflect commitment to norms rather than calculation of returns. Similar reasoning is invoked by Skogan (1976) to explain why women and the elderly are more likely than men and young people to report crimes. The differences, he claims, reflect differences in the degree of socialisation to legal norms: women and the elderly are more compliant and deferential to legal authority, and therefore more likely to report crimes than to deal with them informally.

Analysts originally began to examine situational and crime-specific factors in the decision to report when the effects of victims' socio-economic and demographic attributes seemed negligible. Subsequently, population-specific factors have often been excluded from empirical testing. However, quite apart from the obvious significance of crime type as an influence on the decision to report (and whether or not this is the strongest predictor of such behaviour), wherever significant differences occur in the proportions of crimes that particular groups of people are able or willing to report to the police, important questions for social theory are raised. Sparks (1981) recognised this when he identified one of his categories of victim-proneness as 'impunity'. This refers to the extra risks of crime that a population faces when potential offenders are aware that the police are unlikely to be mobilised by victimised members of particular social groups (as has sometimes been the case, for instance, in racial attacks). 'Impunity' and its relationship with reporting behaviour is surely more likely to reflect enduring sociological factors than passing, incident-specific qualities.

It is worth drawing a distinction, therefore, between the 'circumstantial' factors which crucially affect the probability of any one crime being reported (generalisations here are made in terms of offence type and severity, and according to situational factors specific to the context in which each crime occurs) and sociological factors (relating to the socio-economic and demographic attributes of different urban subpopulations), which are obviously mediated by the immediate circumstances of an incident, but which contribute to a more enduring trend in the organisation of reporting practices. The second set of factors is also context specific, in that the social alignment of reporting behaviour may only be understood with reference to a wider structure of social relations particular to a neighbourhood, city, region or nation.

It is not surprising, given this conceptual distinction (which is rarely made explicit), that research at different spatial scales or in different cultural milieux produces different evidence as to the precise social alignment of reporting. The challenge here is not in a search for universal correlates of reporting practices, but in explaining theoretically why certain structural or cultural attributes have come to be the axes along which reporting behaviour is aligned in particular contexts. The example of north central Birmingham can be taken as illustrative.

In the Birmingham study area, according to the 1979 survey, variations in the propensity to report crime are not aligned with variations in the probability of victimisation. Whereas the best three predictors of victimisation are spare-time activity rates, dwelling rateable value and class, the only three significant predictors of reporting behaviour (amongst population rather than crime-specific variables) are housing tenure ($X^2 = 11.6$, 2 d.f., $p < 0.006$), race ($X^2 = 14.5$, 2 d.f., $p < 0.001$) and birthplace ($X^2 = 7.9$, 3 d.f., $p < 0.05$). I shall return later to some of the implications of this, which include the possibility that reactions to crime should be interpreted in terms of symbolic (racial or cultural) criteria, prestige or social honour, as well as in terms of economic factors associated with the material conditions of life.

To reiterate, I am not quibbling with the significance of crime seriousness as a predictor of reporting behaviour. It is as obvious a factor in Birmingham as elsewhere. My argument is that the bases for such apparently rational, pragmatic and commonsense decisions vary according to the system of shared meanings within which decision-makers must operate. These meanings are negotiated in relation to structural constraints indexed in part by the different socio-economic and demographic factors which affect people's propensity to report.

Table 7.3 illustrates the reasons for non-reporting according to differences among those variables (housing tenure, race and birthplace) which are significantly related to victims' decisions to report. Owner-occupiers are more likely to respond to crime by reporting it to the police than any other class of occupant. Forty seven per cent of incidents experienced by owner-occupiers were reported, in contrast to 23 per cent of crimes perpetrated against council tenants and 26 per cent of those affecting private renters. Home owners are most likely not to have reported simply because the offence is not deemed serious enough. Private renters, in contrast, have an above average likelihood of feeling that the police would have been unable to help, had they bothered to report the offence. In the case of council tenants, the police were more likely than with other groups to have been informed of the crime by another party. Council tenants are also most likely to have failed to report because they regard the offence as a purely private matter that should not concern the police.

Amongst racial and birthplace groups, Asians and the Asian-born have a higher probability of reporting crime (54 per cent and 52 per cent, respectively) than either the Afro-Caribbean community (who failed to report 79 per cent of the offences committed against them) or white residents (who reported only 35 per cent of the offences they experienced) or any other non-Asian birthplace group. All three racial groups have about the same probability of failing to report because they know the offender and prefer to deal with such crimes privately. The numbers are low, and the findings are consistent with Skogan's (1976) assertion that prior relationships between offenders and victims are not a major factor influencing the dark figure of crime.

From the Birmingham survey, it seems that not only are Asians most likely to report the crimes committed against them, but they are also the group amongst whom non-reported crimes are most likely to come to the notice of the police by other means. Thus crimes against Asians seem least likely overall to be under-represented in official statistics. The notable exception to this concerns racial attacks and harassment, which could not adequately be measured in the survey discussed here, but whose import was discussed in chapter 4. Finally, white respondents tend to invest most faith in the police, in that they are least likely to allege that the police would not have been able to help them had a crime been reported. Irish respondents appear to be an exception in this, since they express an above average likelihood of finding the police unhelpful.

Of perhaps greatest concern amongst the findings is the extent to

Table 7.3 *Main reasons for not reporting crimes to the police (% in brackets)*

	Police already knew	Contacted other responsible people	Offence not serious enough	Police would not be able to help	Private matter	Dealt with informally	Other	Total	Proportion of crimes not reported to police (%)
Housing tenure									
Council rental	4 (23.5)	1 (5.9)	4 (23.5)	2 (11.8)	5 (29.4)	1 (5.9)	0	17 (100)	77.3
Private rental	5 (9.4)	1 (1.9)	23 (43.4)	20 (37.7)	2 (3.8)	2 (3.8)	0	53 (100)	73.6
Owner-occupied	12 (12.0)	4 (4.0)	55 (55.0)	25 (25.0)	1 (1.0)	2 (2.0)	1 (1.0)	100 (100)	53.5
Race									
Asian	9 (20.9)	0	20 (46.5)	12 (27.9)	1 (2.3)	1 (2.3)	0	43 (100)	46.2
Afro-Caribbean	2 (6.7)	1 (3.3)	12 (40.0)	14 (46.7)	0	1 (3.3)	0	30 (100)	78.9
White	10 (10.3)	5 (5.2)	50 (51.6)	21 (21.6)	7 (7.2)	3 (3.1)	1 (1.0)	97 (100)	64.7
Birthplace									
UK[1]	6 (7.1)	3 (3.6)	51 (60.7)	14 (16.6)	7 (8.3)	2 (2.4)	1 (1.2)	84 (100)	63.2
Ireland	4 (23.5)	2 (11.8)	5 (29.4)	6 (35.3)	0	0	0	17 (100)	65.4
South Asian	7 (17.9)	0	19 (48.7)	12 (30.8)	1 (2.6)	0	0	39 (100)	48.1
Other New Commonwealth	4 (14.3)	1 (3.6)	6 (21.4)	15 (53.6)	0	2 (7.1)	0	28 (100)	71.8
Other	0	0	1 (50.0)	0	0	1 (50.0)	0	2 (100)	100
Total	21 (12.4)	6 (3.5)	82 (48.2)	47 (27.7)	8 (4.7)	5 (2.9)	1 (0.6)	170 (100)	60.5

[1] Excluding Northern Ireland

Source: North central Birmingham crime survey.

which the Afro-Caribbean population under-reports. A mere one-fifth of crimes committed against this group in the twelve-month reference period were notified to the police. This may not be surprising given the deterioration of relationships between black people and the police in recent years. The consequence, however, is that an important public service – policing – is less available to them than to any other racial or birthplace group. The numbers are small, but Afro-Caribbean respondents are greatly over-represented amongst those claiming not to report crimes because they believe that the police would be unable to help, and they are under-represented amongst those who do not report merely because the matter seems too slight.

This questions Skogan's (1984) generalisation that the principal effect of non-reporting is to divert the attention of the criminal justice system away from less serious and 'attempted-but-not-completed' incidents (a tendency which increases the efficiency of policing both by screening out crimes with too little evidence to produce or convict an offender, and by reducing paperwork). It is clear from what has been said above that non-reporting also has a social dimension, whose consequences may be less helpful than Skogan's argument allows. Merry (1981a) shows that in inner Philadelphia residents are increasingly aware of the unreliability of formal sanctions (via the police). Those who rely on the police now feel less secure than those who employ violence, threats and other informal sanctions to deal with crime. In the British context, too, where formal arrangements for crime control and law-enforcement are perceived to be inadequate, inefficient or too unreliable to meet people's perceived needs for security, informal responses to crime are effected to compensate. The remainder of this chapter is devoted to an examination of a range of informal responses to crime, invoked either to minimise the specific risks of victimisation, or to allay more general and enduring fears about the causes and consequences of local crime.

Informal responses to crime

Most people consciously, or by virtue of habit, upbringing and tradition, recognise the need to supplement formal arrangements for crime prevention and control. The behavioural consequences of this are wide-ranging: most people routinely lock their doors; only a minority participate in vigilante groups. My interest here is in the various protective and preventive strategies which fall between these extremes. They are considered not in individual, psychological terms, but as part of a broader social process that is reflected in and shaped by informal responses to crime.

Crime surveys commonly bear witness to the fact that people do react to crime on their own initiative. Hindelang et al. (1978), using an eight-city subsample of the USA's National Crime Survey, report that approximately half (46 per cent) of the interviewees have limited or changed their activities in the past few years because of crime. Many more, though not changing *what* they do have adjusted the way they do things to take into account (and avoid) the risks of victimisation. The BCS reveals that amongst people who feel very unsafe (according to a measure of fear for personal safety), 68 per cent avoid going out on foot at night because of crime, 81 per cent never go out alone at night on foot, and 27 per cent claim never to go out *solely* because of their concern about crime. The corresponding proportions of those who feel fairly safe are 9 per cent, 52 per cent and 2 per cent (Maxfield 1984b). In Scotland, too, one respondent in six say that at some time in the past they have avoided going out alone because they fear becoming the victim of a crime (Chambers and Tombs 1984).

In sum, the BCS suggests that fear for personal safety is an important factor limiting both personal mobility and participation in leisure-time activities, and that its behavioural consequences are particularly acute in inner-city areas. This is borne out by the local surveys: one quarter of interviewees in Merseyside said they would often or always avoid going out after dark as a precaution against crime (Kinsey 1984); two-thirds of respondents in Birmingham claim to have made some behavioural response to the risk of personal or property crime (Smith 1983).

Informal responses to crime may be directly or indirectly protective (securing against crime or evading it) or collectively preventive. Below, individuals' protective behaviours are examined with a view to establishing how far those group identities which were reflected in direct reactions to crime (measured in terms of reporting

Table 7.4 *Behavioural responses to crime (% in brackets)*

Any behavioural response?	Afro-Caribbean	Asian	White	Total
Yes	41 (44.6)	129 (70.9)	182 (70.8)	352 (66.3)
No	51 (55.4)	53 (29.1)	75 (29.2)	179 (33.7)
Total	92 (100.0)	182 (100.0)	257 (100.0)	531 (100.0)

$X^2 = 23.538$, 2 d.f., $p < 0.001$

Source: North central Birmingham crime survey.

behaviour), especially those pertaining to racial differences, persist into a wider range of behavioural practices. This prefaces the final theoretical section of the chapter which aims to account for the incorporation of crime-related issues into the reproduction of social relations at a neighbourhood level.

I begin by examining measurable behavioural responses to crime that can be described in terms of a simple distinction between 'target protection' and 'avoidance' tactics. In Birmingham, the best predictor of both these reactions is the fear of personal and/or property crime. Amongst population attributes, however, it is the distinction between racial groups (rather than class, lifestyle or other factors associated with victimisation) that proves most salient in terms of behavioural responses to crime. This is true concerning both the decision to make a response (table 7.4) and the type of strategy effected (table 7.5). This, incidentally, was also the case in Hindelang et al.'s (1978) analysis of reactions to crime in eight United States cities.

The main protective behaviours adopted in north central Birmingham are various forms of target hardening (largely the installation of physical protection – locks, bolts etc. – for the home). Just over one-third of respondents in all three racial groups adopt these tactics of 'defensive withdrawal'. Such actions have been interpreted by Lavrakas (1981) as a response to the threat of violation of personal space and by Skogan (1981) as economically motivated behaviours that are often unrelated to the direct threat of crime. From Skogan's perspective, the small proportion (less than one-quarter) of respondents who claim to spend money on physical

Table 7.5 *Strategies used to reduce the risks of victimisation (% in brackets)*

Behavioural strategy	Afro-Caribbean	Asian	White	Total
Target hardening	19 (35.2)	96 (35.7)	114 (33.9)	229 (34.8)
Stay at home	7 (13.0)	38 (14.1)	70 (20.8)	115 (17.5)
Journey with a group	8 (14.8)	42 (15.6)	49 (14.6)	99 (15.0)
Avoid trouble spots	12 (22.2)	38 (14.1)	41 (12.2)	91 (13.8)
Avoid public transport	0	5 (1.9)	19 (5.7)	24 (3.6)
Ensure home occupied	2 (3.7)	44 (16.4)	9 (2.7)	55 (8.3)
Other	6 (11.1)	6 (2.2)	34 (10.1)	46 (7.0)
Total[1]	54 (100.0)	269 (100.0)	336 (100.0)	659 (100.0)

$X^2 = 55.348$, 10 d.f., $p<0.001$ (calculated by amalgamating the fourth and fifth strategies)

[1] Total reflects the fact that some individuals adopted more than one strategy.
Source: North central Birmingham crime survey.

protection is indicative of the overall disadvantage of the inner city. Either residents cannot afford elaborate security devices, or the necessary outlay (which is often large, given the insecurity of ageing properties) would not justify any potential saving (implying too that there may be little of material value to lose).

When target hardening proves infeasible, insufficient or inappropriate, individuals' behavioural responses to crime must take the form of physical avoidance. Indeed, Lavrakas and Lewis (1980) argue that the majority of urban residents engage in *some* type of avoidance behaviour in an attempt to reduce their likelihood of becoming a victim of personal crime. Of course, protection and avoidance are not mutually exclusive strategies. Where concern for crime is marked, no one protection measure ever seems sufficient, and several strategies are often combined. Asians are especially likely to have adopted more than one strategy in Birmingham. On average, Asians who take any action implement 2.1 measures, compared with a mean of 1.3 for Afro-Caribbean respondents and 1.8 for the remainder. This tendency notwithstanding, Biderman et al. (1967) stress the relative independence of protection and avoidance as behavioural strategies. I shall argue further that these strategies differ not only as forms of intentional action, but also in their unintended social consequences.

Unlike protection, avoidance is fundamentally a social action in that it requires the communication, identification and subjective interpretation of extrinsic cues and symbols. Statistical regularities may obviously be documented: in the Birmingham study area, for instance, Afro-Caribbean respondents, who are least likely to adjust their behaviour in response to crime, are most likely (when they do) to take evasive action and avoid known trouble spots (table 7.5). However, statistical summaries of empirical generalisations concerning avoidance behaviour do not provide an adequate basis upon which to interpret social action. It is possible to demonstrate that behavioural responses to crime take place, without understanding why they take a particular form for specific groups. Yet, as Hannerz (1969: 34) points out, the facts about danger 'are not only statistical, but relational and cultural as well'. They demand interpretative understanding as well as empirical measurement.

Drawing on my experience as a resident participant observer in north central Birmingham between 1977 and 1979, the remainder of this chapter seeks to demonstrate how, and to understand why, the organisation of reactions to crime reflects and reinforces racial and cultural identities. It has already been suggested (particularly in chapter 5) that the political and economic marginality of working-class neighbourhoods allows crime to contribute to the uncertainty and stress of inner-city life. It will further be argued that the informal control of crime in such contexts necessarily impinges on wider processes of racial categorisation which are locally reproduced through practices effected to minimise risk.

Managing danger and handling power

Reactions to crime as discussed above are just one facet of social life, abstracted (legitimately, I believe, but nevertheless artificially) for analytical purposes. Reintegrated, such reactions form part of the routine of daily life in the Birmingham study area. They are not only responses to risk, but also family rituals, regular journeys, and usual friendship patterns. Reactions to crime may be 'discursively redeemable', particularly amongst the most fearful, but more often they are part of the unarticulated 'know-how' of practical reason. In an attempt to explain why the crime problem in north central Birmingham is couched and reacted to in racial terms, I base my argument on three suppositions of the theory of structuration as discussed by Giddens in *A contemporary critique of historical materialism* (1981).

First, I assent to Giddens's view that much of the moral meaning of day-to-day life is excluded from the mechanical routinisation which characterises modern capitalist societies. Because of the disjunction between meaning and action in routine behaviour, the avoidance of dangerous people and the places they occupy, even when danger is defined by racial appearance, need not reflect the shared values of a cultural group. The practice of risk-avoidance may sustain processes of racial categorisation (that are tacitly acknowledged as a fact of life) without imposing any requirement on the actors to exhibit personal racism or to express their own cultural identity.

Secondly, it follows from this that where reactions to crime are routinised, they require little commitment from the actors involved. The need to take precautions is given in folk wisdom; its rationale lies in the realms of Bordieu's (1972) 'doxa' – the universe of the undiscussed and undisputed. Acknowledging that practices are taken for granted, however, does not imply that the outcomes of such practices, if reflected upon by the actors, would be thought desirable or legitimate. Thus, the local structure of social relations whose reproduction is secured partly through reactions to crime does not *necessarily* have the normative support of the actors. People may sustain processes of racial categorisation with or without having commitment to racist doctrines.

Finally, some of the sources and consequences of action (here, the range of reactions to crime) remain unacknowledged and unanticipated by the actors. An appreciation of these is, however, integral to any theoretical understanding of how and why such actions are incorporated into the production and reproduction of local social relations. As Giddens points out, the concept of social reproduction is not itself an explanatory notion; it refers to a process that is historical, contingent and contextual, and which, therefore, in every circumstance *requires* explanation.

I shall argue from the alignment of responses to crime that the unacknowledged sources of such actions in north central

Birmingham lie in the structured inequality of British society, which leaves unchallenged the economic and political marginality of the inner city, and the ideology of racism. These factors are crucial in defining the context of uncertainty in the inner city which lends crime its salience as a spur to social action. The unintended consequences of informal reactions to crime include the reproduction of patterns of dominance, subordination and resistance that are expressed in the national political economy. The form of these relations, however, because of the nature of the resources available to mobilise power in the inner city, reaffirms the salience and legitimacy of race as a principle of social organisation.

With these assumptions and intentions outlined, it is possible to proceed with a discussion of the rationale for, and implications of, reactions to crime in north central Birmingham. Initially, such reactions are examined in terms of the pragmatic logic of daily life. Later, the explanation is completed by relating commonsense risk-avoidance behaviours to the manipulation of power both within the study area and (in so far as it is relevant to the argument) in terms of the location of the study area relative to the power structure of British society as a whole.

Minimising risk in uncertain environments

Social relations are inherently risky because no-one is compelled to obey institutionalised or informal moral norms. The point is well-made by Suttles:

Since deviance is so possible among humans, copresence alone lays people or groups open to victimisation, because one man's deviance is generally a threat to at least one other's welfare or assurance of social order. Social proximity, even of the most adventitious sort, then, is one of those occasions which can arouse fears and requires regulation. (Suttles 1972: 157)

The nature of human interaction – its frequency and unpredictability – must give grounds for wariness. The prospect of danger is woven into the very fabric of urban social relationships. However, the degree of uncertainty varies, and it is constituted more acutely in some locales than in others: where crime rates are believed to be high; where people in close proximity to one another are socially isolated; or where individuals feel powerless to shape the circumstances of their future. These conditions overlap in many working-class areas, including north central Birmingham. It is this uncertainty that Ley (1974) found so characteristic inside the 'outpost' of the black inner city of Philadelphia, and which Knight and Hayes (1981) detect in inner London. Its consequence is a widespread sense of danger, 'rooted in feelings of uncertainty, helplessness and vulnerability triggered by encounters with strangers who belong to unfamiliar, hostile, and potentially harmful groups' (Merry 1981a: 160).

The management of danger requires that individuals gain a certain amount of control over the social relations in which they participate. The process is one that binds and interchanges identity and location. At one extreme, many elderly whites (especially women) retreat into the territorial security of their homes. Chambers and Tombs (1984) note that 13 per cent of elderly women in Scotland never go out at night due to fear, and 20 per cent of women in the inner cities of England and Wales attribute their hermit-like existence to the fear of crime (Hough and Mayhew 1983). Many other studies have noted a similar tendency for fear to restrict the elderly to their homes (Braungart et al. 1979; Greenstein 1977; Lawton et al. 1976; Patterson 1978; Skogan and Maxfield 1981; Sundeen and Mathieu 1976; Wolf 1972). The strategy adopted by the most fearful amongst the aged is one that restricts their range of contacts to a select circle of personal friends amongst whom closeness and continuity of association minimises the risk of rule-breaking (see Jacobson 1971).

Those who engage in a range of activities beyond the home enter into a stream of what Hannerz (1980: 105) terms 'traffic relations'. These are fleeting unfocussed encounters in which participants are barely aware of each other's presence, and feel no obligation to pursue or renew the acquaintance subsequently. In so far as they are a form of interaction, traffic relations represent a passing association that is only tacitly acknowledged by participants who are primarily engaged in other social roles. The only purposive element involves ensuring or defining the appropriate degree of physical proximity to be observed during the encounter.

The danger inherent in traffic relations is handled by the public in one of two ways. First, and accounting for about 15 per cent of the strategies adopted to decrease the risk of victimisation in north central Birmingham, are measures taken to ensure that respondents do not venture out without a companion. The proportion adopting this strategy is about the same for each racial group. The value of securing 'guardians' in this way depends, however, on the effectiveness of cues confirming the association between people involved. Goffman (1971) terms the symbolic gestures defining such relationships 'tie signs'. Surprisingly, in Birmingham these signs rarely refer to shared racial or cultural attributes. Rather they seem representative of a more universal set of cues: the protective arm around the shoulder, sharing a match to light a cigarette, emphasising conversational gestures and so on. This demoting of racial symbols might seem paradoxical, given the theoretical concerns of this section which seeks to establish how crime mediates between location and identity. Tie signs, however, are not amongst those strategies of overt avoidance and territoriality that impinge on the structure of social relations. When these more spatially explicit behaviours are considered, racial and cultural symbols are more readily mobilised. Tie signs, though, preclude the need for overt avoidance. They are emitted to profess solidarity in the face of potentially harmful encounters. As such, they are merely a caution – a neutral indicator of preparation for retaliation rather than a direct affront. Symbols associated with racial identity, in contrast, are much more likely to be interpreted as overt provocation. Where the prospect of danger is only slight, and the aim is to avoid conflict, specifically cultural symbols tend to be played down.

Individuals may also take steps in traffic relations to avoid translating 'unfocussed' copresence into 'focussed' (low quality) interaction. Such evasive action is very subtle – lowering one's eyes, becoming preoccupied with the contents of a shop window, giving strangers a wide berth on the pavement. Such tactics are necessary because the infringement of personal space can easily cause alarm, while more deliberate avoidance strategies make fear obvious (which in itself may attract the attentions of potential offenders).

Merely managing traffic relations, however, is a low-cost strategy, with correspondingly low payoff in terms of reducing objective risks. Physical proximity is played down rather than manipulated, and potential victims remain within easy reach of potential offenders. However, a second element of street wisdom exists, which requires the investment of much greater effort. 'Distancing', as discussed by Suttles (1972) is a strategy in which potentially dangerous social opposites are first unambiguously defined, and then physically avoided. The process 'consists of a wide range of spatial signs, some of which may be exploratory, some invitational, and others discouraging in a sequence of progressively more or progressively less intimate stages' (Suttles 1972: 176). This is the means by which the negotiation of social relations in space interacts with the process of racial categorisation.

During the practice of distancing, control over social relations is achieved by limiting where and with whom a range of non-intimate encounters may take place. It is because of the need for expedience in defining such limits that processes of racial categorisation are sustained through reactions to crime. For cues prompting different degrees of interaction and avoidance must usually be based on easily identifiable extrinsic traits: information of a more personal kind is not available for the majority of urban encounters. Thus, at a pragmatic level, skin colour and other physical attributes, which may have little cultural meaning for their incumbents (but which are defined as salient nationally, through the effects of some legislation and by the mass media) is a convenient means of excluding social opposites (who may be dangerous) in times of stress or in situations requiring a rapid decision. Exclusionary rather than inclusionary criteria are required for the management of danger. Categorical rather than communal relations are at issue when the aim is to minimise risk, and in the inner cities the most convenient stereotype is based on perceptions of racial difference.

Theorists from Simmel and Park to Berger and Luckmann have acknowledged the centrality of stereotyping – the presentation and interpretation of social symbols and behavioural cues – to all social life. Perhaps nowhere is this more crucial for individuals' social and psychological well-being than during the informal management of danger. Thus, in an uncertain environment, racial cues are invested with subjective meaning that proves significant in behavioural terms because such symbols provide the most convenient means of keeping the effects of fear down to tolerable levels. At other times and in other contexts, other social attributes, such as class, might prove equally salient. But in north central Birmingham, class distinctions are not marked enough to provide the overt symbolism required to manage danger effectively. Modern trends in social mobility often make 'objective' class distinctions deriving from the occupational order fluid and intangible (Goldthorpe 1980). Thus, I have suggested elsewhere (Smith 1981a) that the blurred distinctions amongst contemporary socio-economic groups, coupled with the pragmatic requirements of an urban lifestyle, renders race by far the more logical criterion (as far as public perceptions are concerned) upon which to exclude social opposites in order to minimise perceived risks. Furthermore, I shall argue later that because of the nature of social power available to the residents of inner Birmingham, it is *only* through race that such processes can be effected unless participants are put in a position to question the received wisdom incorporated into the 'know-how' of practical consciousness.

It is a short step from the practice of social avoidance to that of territoriality. Conceptually, distancing and territoriality are related, representing the various degrees of spatial sorting required to ensure that 'the possibility of affiliation minimizes the potential of physical harm and negative judgements' (Suttles 1972: 183). Lyman and Scott (1967) regard territoriality as a neglected sociological dimension. Defining it as the attempt to control space, they suggest that territoriality is one of the most fundamental of human activities. More recently, Sack (1983) has itemised ten tendencies associated with territoriality, which he views as a strategy for establishing differential access to things and people.

In the inner city, where location is more a matter of constraint than of choice, there are few opportunities for the public to manipulate residential space – a strategy often thought axiomatic to the practice of territoriality. In inner Birmingham, however, it is the *symbolic* meaning with which space may be invested that is indicative of the process of territoriality. Space and environment have their meanings ascribed by residents, and as such they contain cues that prompt certain forms of behaviour. These meanings are attached to space through a process of cognitive mapping, which Merry (1981a) identifies as an important component of personal reactions to crime. The management of danger is tantamount to identifying and reacting to appropriate social and environmental cues.

There is some evidence from the cognitive maps of study-area residents that the quality 'danger' can be translated between social types and locale or place. The indication in north central Birmingham is that danger is defined in terms of place when dangerous areas can conveniently be excluded from one's necessary locus of activity; danger is defined in terms of types of people or groups when it encroaches on the home locale and cannot be excluded from one's usual action space. This flexible definition gives actors the option of avoiding danger either socially or spatially, or on the basis of various combinations of the two, according to the pragmatic social and spatial requirements of other activities.

Giddens believes that modern geography lacks the concepts which would make space and the control of space integral to social theory. What is missing in his view is some attention to 'aspects and modalities of presence and absence in human social relations' (Giddens 1981: 38). What he appears to demand from this is an appreciation of the translation of power exercised in the control of social relations into social and physical distancing strategies. This would require a conceptual understanding of how such control varies (whether intentionally or not) as between the manipulation of social and physical space. Indeed, it would require a reconceptualisation of social and physical distance as part of a continuum of human interaction rather than as two discrete domains of action. It is in this spirit that I offer as a starting point the above discussion of risk-minimising strategies, which differed in the cultural symbols they mobilised according to the precise degree of spatial distance and social solidarity required to manage a given level of perceived risk.

The management of danger requires the conditions of social interaction to be simplified. Where this cannot be achieved simply by moving outside the sphere of local social relations or by ascribing most danger to another neighbourhood, risk is minimised by creating or assenting to racial stereotyping as a rationale for choosing who to avoid. At one level, such action can plausibly be explained in terms of the pragmatic logic of study-area residents, who require a minimum degree of safety in which to pursue their daily lives. This explanation provides a necessary but nevertheless insufficient account of observed public behaviour. Both Giddens (1984) and Pred (1984) assert that power is an integral constituent of all social relations, but so far the process of racial categorisation in north central Birmingham has been discussed only in terms of the norms and meaning systems of residents. To conclude the chapter, I shall consider the role of power, and argue that it is the form of power relations in north central Birmingham which fundamentally underlies the reproduction of local social relations in their specifically racial form. My discussion refers only to the part played in this general process by public responses to crime.

Power, risk and social reproduction

Analyses by structural Marxists such as Castells (1977, 1978) and Shah (1979) demonstrate that the relationships between social process and spatial form cannot adequately be explained only as the product of 'commonsense' behaviours. Both authors emphasise in addition the importance of power relationships and the social structures through which they are played out. Castells (1977: 180) outlines an hierarchical set of constraints, ultimately rooted in the manipulation of differentially distributed economic power, which determines (and thus, for him, explains) patterns of segregation in capitalist society. Shah (1979: 450) too, argues that segregation as a defensive act is a wholly determined outcome of structured inequality. While these theorists conceptualise power as repressive and coercive, Giddens points out that power is also enabling: 'the origin of all that is liberating and productive in social life as well as all that is repressive and destructive' (Giddens 1981: 51). Power is, moreover, routinely involved in all forms of social relations.

Adopting Giddens's much broader view, it must be accepted that power is integral to the practices involved both in the construction of images of crime described in chapter 5 and in the reactions of crime discussed above (though I should stress that power is not necessarily *purposefully* manipulated in these contexts). I shall argue that any explanation of why these images and reactions so often reflect and affirm racial identities must be rooted in an account of the differential distribution and realisation of social power in the inner city. Only from this perspective is it possible fully to understand how nationally salient conceptions of racial difference are locally reproduced. The reasoning which follows is based on a Weberian understanding of the realisation of power, and on Giddens's conceptualisation of the kinds of resources habitually drawn upon in routine power relations.

Avoidance behaviours and territoriality can readily be appreciated in terms of the manipulation of power. Sack (1983) explicitly links territoriality with power: he defines it as an assertion of control and a means of reifying power. Avoidance, exclusion and territoriality render power visible by marking out social boundaries in physical space. A similar argument is advanced by Boal (1981) on the basis of his studies of segregation and interaction in Northern Ireland.

It is less easy to appreciate how the construction of social images about crime might also be interpreted in terms of power relations. Yet, in so far as such images are shared through human interaction and communication, they must, in terms of the theoretical position adopted here (derived from Weber and Giddens) partly be a realisation of power, albeit a realisation limited to specific groups and locales. As Pred argues, 'power relations are the invisible structural cement holding individual, society and nature together in the time-specific practices by which places continually become' (Pred 1984: 289).

The importance of power as an element in the construction of images about crime is apparent from the work of criminology's 'labelling' or social reaction theorists (Becker 1963; Erikson 1964; Kitsuse 1964; Lemert 1972). Deviance is envisaged not as an act, but as a label, symbolically attached to socially, economically, politically, or locationally marginal groups by those with the power to criminalise. The labelling of crime and criminals is a means of wielding social power, to which both labellers and the labelled respond.

Relevant though this argument has been to our understanding of how the criminal justice system may contribute to the 'amplification of deviance', and though geographers have learnt much from it about the consequences of labelling *areas* (for instance in the work of Armstrong and Wilson 1973; Damer 1974; Gill 1977), the realisation of power through the manipulation of images by groups *other* than formal agents of control (i.e. within the general public) has scarcely been considered. One outstanding exception is Mitchell's (1969) discovery that the urban images held by Africans reflect town-dwellers' social positions. Such images are constructed not merely to provide useful maps but also, and primarily, as a means of accruing, wielding and expressing social power. This, I would argue, is one level at which images of crime in north central Birmingham must also be interpreted.

In chapter 5 it was revealed that a number of images about crime vary more consistently according to race than according to any other social attribute. It was noted, too, that white residents had a disproportionate tendency to label non-white people as the neighbourhood's main criminal offenders. A tendency to lay the blame for a disproportionate amount of crime on the activities of racial minorities, particularly those of (black) West Indian descent has been documented in other studies of north central Birmingham (Brown 1977; Hall et al. 1978; John 1972; Weaver 1980), and in Britain generally (Hall and Jefferson 1975; Miles and Phizacklea 1979). Indeed, Nugent and King go as far as to suggest that 'An image of specifically "alien" or "black" crimes, in particular "mugging", is deliberately propagated [by whites] as evidence of the social dislocation brought about by immigration' (Nugent and King 1979: 42).

Power, then, is realised in both images of, and behavioural responses to, crime. Neither act can be interpreted merely as a common sense strategy invoked to manage danger, despite their appearance as such in folk beliefs. What remains to be explained is how and why social power in the context of inner Birmingham is realised through race more obviously than through other, perhaps more fundamental, societal axes such as those reflecting class or political interest.

Until recently, for much of social theory, race was regarded as something of a spent force, and analysed in terms of class cleavages produced by inequalities in the production or distribution of material wealth. In contrast, social geographers studying segregation have always accorded racial factors primacy – a tendency most explicit in studies attempting to filter out empirically the contri-

bution of class to racial segregation. Class has usually been thought
to 'explain' only a small proportion of segregation (Shah 1979), and
geographers have generally been conceptually prepared to accommodate the salience of race, even when it is not aligned with
class.

Here, the problem is to explain the salience of race as an axis of
the distribution of power in the inner city (in so far as power is
realised in images of, and reactions to, crime). To this end Giddens's
(1981) discussion of the resources drawn upon in the constitution of
power relations provides an appropriate starting point. He draws a
broad distinction between allocative resources (relating to the
control of nature: raw materials, the means of material production
and reproduction, and produced goods) and authoritative resources
(relating to the control of society: the organisation of time–space, of
human production and reproduction and of human life chances for
self-development and self-expression). He argues that in non-
capitalist societies it is the co-ordination of authoritative resources
that determines societal integration and change, whereas under
capitalism it is allocative resources which assume primary
significance in the realistion of power.

I would argue, however, that allocative resources are not readily
available for the realisation of power in the social relations of the
inner city. This is not to claim that the residents are not bound into
power relations constituted through such resources. Rather, I argue
that the working class cannot *initiate* social relations by drawing on
allocative resources, and that the power which gives form to the
social relations played out within the inner city is constituted with
recourse to more traditional *authoritative* resources, particularly in so
far as these refer to the control of life chances for self-development
and expression.

Having acknowledged the relevance of this distinction, it is
necessary to justify divorcing allocative and authoritative resources
analytically to a degree that Giddens may not have intended, and to
explain why the power so realised is both expressed through and
shapes racial identity. My argument rests on a theory of stratification
accounting for the differential distribution of power *outside* the
productive/allocative order, which derives from the political sociology
of Max Weber.

Weber, like Giddens, was concerned with power as a variable
constituting social relations rather than as a pre-given structural
constraint, a non-coercive secondary characteristic of social life, or a
form of stratification (like class or race) in its own right. He describes

his much-quoted structural types – classes, status groups and parties – specifically as 'phenomena of the distribution of power in the commununity' (Weber 1968: 927). Social structure thus derives from and comprises the manipulation of power: 'Power need not be thought of as something which exists over and above the system of material and social rewards; rather, it can be thought of as a concept or metaphor which is used to depict the flow of resources which constitutes the system' (Parkin 1971: 46). What is required to inform the present argument is a means of accruing or wielding social power which does not depend on securing material rewards (since material rewards fall into the domain of Giddens's allocative resources, which, I am arguing, are a less important source of power within the inner city than are authoritative resources).

Although geographers have tended to emphasise the differences between Weber and Marx concerning definitions of class and the distribution of material rewards (when there are, in fact, many similarities between the two authors in this respect), they have paid less attention to Weber's most fundamental refinement of the Marxian model, which was to introduce the concept of social honour or prestige, through which power may be realised in an attempt to secure symbolic rather than material resources (for a fuller discussion of the implications for social geography, see Jackson and Smith 1984).

As a clue to the manipulation of power outside the material order – drawing on authoritative rather than allocative resources – Weber's discussion of status groups is appealing. For symbolic rewards depend on 'the positive or negative social estimation of honour'. Moreover, 'Status honour need not necessarily be linked with a class situation. On the contrary, it normally stands in opposition to the pretensions of sheer property' (Weber 1968: 932). Yet, Weber did not conceive of class and status as wholly independent dimensions of stratification. Rather, he envisaged that one or other would predominate in a society, according to the rate of socio-economic change: status structures would prevail at 'every slowing down of the change in economic stratification' (p.938). Furthermore, while arguing that, theoretically, status may rest on any number of traits or attributes, Weber observed that: 'today the class situation is by far the predominant factor. After all, the possibility of a style of life expected for members of a status group is usually conditioned economically' (p. 935). For much the same reasons as Giddens asserts the primacy of allocative resources over authoritative resources in the realisation of power under advanced capitalism, Weber's own argument seems to deny any real independence of status from class in the present economic system. Parkin explicates this denial while accounting for the distribution of status in modern urban settings. Status is, he argues, 'a system of social evaluation arising from the moral judgements of those who occupy dominant positions in the class structure' (Parkin 1971: 42). He goes on to observe that this interpretation must be true for capitalist societies, because if the distribution of social honour failed to match the distribution of material advantages, the system of economic inequalities would be stripped of its normative support:

How could sharp differences in material rewards be formally justified if it was widely held that all occupations were of equal social value? A major function of the prestige order is to deny this latter premise. It thereby serves to stabilize and legitimize inequalities by harnessing notions of social justice in defiance of existing privileges. (Parkin 1971: 42)

At this level, there is no escaping accountability to the material sphere. Status and class are aligned; prestige and moral righteousness are secured on the basis of qualitative differences in lifestyle conditioned by quantitative differences in income. If, therefore, the concept of status is to be of value in accounting for the form of social relations in the inner city (where, I have argued, the availability of economic and political power in everyday life is limited), (i) a source of status must be found which is sustained by social power realised outside the material order, and (ii) the judgements which preserve such status must be based on something other than material possessions.

The first requirement is fulfilled by Weber's concept of *ethnic* honour. Signified by affiliation to a 'subjectively believed community of descent', it is the only form of social honour which does not typically rest upon economic hierarchy (see Weber 1968: 385–98). Thus Weber described it as the honour of the masses (*Massenehre*), which rests on a 'conception of what is correct and proper' rather than on a position in the occupational order.

The race relations literature, confronting the 'resurgence of ethnicity' in modern societies, contains many arguments which partially fulfil the second requirement, and explain why ethnic identities are sustained in a variety of modern political and economic contexts. My concern, though, is why racial categories are preserved and reproduced in people's reactions to crime; and my conclusion is that, in the inner city, the judgements required to sustain the symbolism and prestige ordering of a racial hierarchy are exercised on the basis of *moral* qualities rather than according to material achievements. I suggest that differences in lifestyle (the definitive characteristic of status groups) are imputed to people from different racial groups by virtue of their supposed deviance or presumed righteousness. It is this practice of moral labelling – the grading of respectability – which sustains processes of racial categorisation (in much the same way as the social grading of occupations sustains the class system). This continual recognition and reaffirmation of racial differences is one consequence of the realisation of social power through reactions to crime. Criminality may not be the only moral label able to legitimate perceptions of racial difference. Within a high-crime neighbourhood, however, where fear is most acute, deviance is the label that is most widely available and frequently used.

Degrees of criminality are variously imputed to racial groups pragmatically and routinely as part of the management of danger in everyday life. The manipulation of social power this represents is not necessarily purposeful. Most often, its realisation in the forms discussed above is unacknowledged and unsuspected by the actors; it lies in the realms of practical rather than discursive consciousness – though its effects, often unintended, are no less potent as a form of racism.

It is not surprising that, in the inner city, status differences are realised first on the basis of racial identity. Here behaviour cannot readily be interpreted as an explicit response to society's political and economic structures. These sources of power are neither significant nor accessible to the actors concerned. Indeed, the final report of the Small Heath Inner Area Study (Department of Environment 1977b) argues that this lack of power is the most fundamental aspect of deprivation and disadvantage in Britain's inner cities generally. What little social power is available is most efficiently used by excluding racial opposites from rewards and life chances. Outgroup labelling and social avoidance are practised in order to preserve status as well as to minimise danger. Reporting, accusing and evading social opposites provides a means of regulating group boundaries as well as aiding the management of danger in a complex environment.

This chapter has examined a range of informal responses to crime and found their effects to be more far-reaching than traditional criminological research has allowed. The public initiate a variety of strategies to minimise risk and distress, sometimes mobilising the formal criminal justice system, but most often drawing on their own resources to avoid the uncertainties associated with suspected deviance. In north central Birmingham, practices from both ends of this behavioural spectrum – from reporting to avoiding crime – varied more noticeably according to racial identity than according to other socio-economic attributes. This had to be explained not only in terms of the pragmatic requirements of the public's routine activities, but also in terms of the distribution and manipulation of power in economically disadvantaged circumstances. The argument suggests that crime does not merely reflect the structure and organisation of society (though at one level, the incidence of crime can usefully be appreciated in these terms); the patterning of crime and its effects also *shapes* the structure of social relations and sustains the process of social reproduction at a local level.

Theoretically intriguing though they may be, the effects of crime have consequences that must also be understood in terms of the quality of human life. In economically, politically and locationally marginal settings, environments are vulnerable, potential offenders are most at risk (from tempting opportunities and from discriminatory police activity), crime rates are highest and fear is most acute. These factors combine to prompt reactions to crime which inhibit personal freedom, discourage many forms of social interaction and impair the quality of local social relations. Spatial inequalities in the incidence and effects of crime will persist; their consequences are wide-ranging and invite greater concern, not only from social theorists but also from the decision-makers and power-brokers of a democratic welfare state.

8

Conclusion

Minimising risk in urban society

Within modern capitalist democracies (the political and economic context framing most of the discussion in this book), crime is an issue penetrating all levels of social life. I have chosen to focus on crime in working-class areas generally, in the inner cities specifically, and in north central Birmingham in particular, to examine the effects of crime where it bites hardest, at the declining edge of the British economy.

In chapter 2 it was argued that although progress in the analysis of deviance requires an understanding of the minutiae of events and relationships in particular social settings, the significance of intensive case studies can fully be appreciated only in terms of their wider political and economic contexts. At the broadest scale, important statements have been made concerning relationships between crime rates and global economic trends (the advance of urban industrialism, the internationalisation of capital, the marginalisation of migrant labour, and so on). However, a sounder empirical base is guaranteed to research situated within the political economy of a single nation or state. Accordingly, the touchstone for observations made about crime and its effects in this volume has been the democratic welfare state of industrial Britain.

Of the many intriguing correlates of crime in advanced industrial democracies, relations between crime rates and socio-economic inequality deserve particular attention, given the important role of inequality in the development of capitalist economies. Taking the example of England and Wales, it was suggested in chapter 3 that national crime rates do reflect spatial inequalities in a number of social and economic indicators, both between regions and within cities.

I have argued that crime rates, the risks of victimisation, and the debilitating effects of fear are greatest in the inner cities (though I

190

acknowledge that much work remains to be completed on the plight of the poorer, more peripheral, council estates). In these areas, offenders travel only short distances to commit generally petty crimes. The environment itself contains abundant opportunities for such offences, since ageing buildings are difficult to secure, and residents are not usually in a position to bear the expense of effective locks, bolts and other security devices. Victimisation rates are high in the inner cities and are related not only to lifestyle and activity patterns but also to the disadvantage of a location in which acceptable risk is unacceptably compounded by an insecure environment, over-burdened statutory services and a police force that does not always seem co-operative. For similar reasons, high levels of fear threaten the quality of social life in such areas.

At a political level, the response to rising crime rates has been swift and extensive. A law-and-order platform contributed to the Conservative Party victory of 1979, and massive public investment has attempted to increase the efficiency and effectiveness of the police service and bring down the crime rate. As a national response to public concern, the gesture has been politically effective, but in chapter 6 I questioned the ability of such blanket measures to confront the issue of crime as a problem *locally* perceived and experienced. If the lifestyle/exposure-to-risk thesis discussed in chapter 4 is correct, it may be impossible and even undesirable to reduce crime rates *overall*; what seems more appropriate is a reduction of risks in areas and amongst groups where particular types of crime are disproportionately severe in their effects.

I have suggested that, in order to achieve this end of securing locally sensitive strategies to control crime and its effects, there are at least two fundamental requirements. First, an attempt must be made to depolarise the accountability debate, securing the basis for an acceptable degree of local democratic participation in the policing process. In this, political geographers' interests in the role of the local state make a valuable contribution. Secondly, a multi-agency approach to policing might be encouraged, such that the responsibility for crime is genuinely shared by the organisations and institutions serving particular neighbourhoods.

Of perhaps greatest concern amongst the residents and observers of British (and indeed American) inner cities is the extent to which the problem of crime has impinged on the quality of race relations (Taub et al. 1984 discuss the experience of the USA). I suggested in chapter 5 that the public's tendency to conflate race relations with the problem of crime reflects the content of a provincial press which routinely combines the two themes. 'Race' and 'crime' are topics valued by journalists as the most newsworthy and enduring constituents of national politics; they are always available to make a story, and they can be endowed with the kind of sensationalism that sells newspapers. Their regular association is worked into the received wisdom of daily life wherever it is able to inform the conversations about *local* crime which take place within culturally bounded social networks. The consequences of this become apparent when social and environmental stress is severe enough to exacerbate anxieties about neighbourhood crime rates. When anxiety is acute in a socially heterogeneous setting, racial stereotyping – the labelling of easily identifiable others – becomes a convenient and ostensibly plausible means of coping with the uncertainty associated with perceived risk.

In chapter 7, while documenting a range of reactions to crime, I attempted to account theoretically for the association of crime with processes of racial stereotyping. It was suggested that uncertainties about the quality of social life, engendered by the prospect of crime, help, through the behavioural responses they elicit, to secure the *local* reproduction of social relations. This place or context-specific element of social reproduction is often neglected in social theory, yet it is at this level that the popular legitimacy of the entire process is established. I argued that racial cleavages – part of a national ideology in Britain – are locally sustained because much of the power struggle within the inner city must take place over the symbolic rewards of status. Such rewards are secured by combining racial or cultural identities with a moral label – in this instance, criminality or innocence. Thus, through an appeal to morality and respectability, do the effects of crime impinge upon the distribution and manipulation of what limited social power accrues to inner-city residents. As a consequence, racial category and cultural affiliation become important criteria upon which to base social action. The effects of crime necessarily play a part in the negotiation of social identities in racial terms, largely, it seems, because of the scarcity of the other effective sources of power in the inner city. Were more resources of a political or economic kind to be made available in such areas, it would be interesting to trace their impact on the racial overtones of today's 'social reality' of deviance.

Many of the arguments presented in this book, particularly those in chapters 5, 6 and 7, pursue crime and its ramifications into a much wider societal context than has been usual in criminological research. It is worth considering, therefore, the limitations and implications of this particularly broad conception of a 'social geography of crime'.

Social theory and the geography of crime

There are numerous modern geographies of crime. Keith Harries (1973, 1974, 1976b, 1980) continues skilfully and methodically to chart the dynamics of inter-regional variations in crime and justice in the United States. David Herbert (1976a, 1976b, 1977, 1979, 1980, 1982), with his students David Evans (1980) and Stephen Hyde (1982) have made important statements on the organisation of delinquency areas, the structure of crime-prone environments, and the future of 'geographical criminology' in Britain. David Smith (1974) has evaluated the contribution of crime rates to the social indicator movement, while Hakim and Rengert (1981) have explored the spatial economics of crime, and Peet (1975, 1976) in his polemical debate with Harries (1975, 1976a) has sketched a radical geography of deviance.

The list might continue, but, as Herbert (1981: 62) rightly observes, a carefully constructed and up-to-date review of ongoing research in the geography of crime is 'about the last thing that is needed at present'. This book, therefore, has partly been a response to Herbert's challenge to 'be much more explicitly concerned with theories which have broader social science bases', and to examine 'scales of analysis in which much more interesting and relevant answers may lie'.

My suggestion has been that an innovative perspective on crime can proceed from the common ground cleared by large-scale realist analyses of crime and space on the one hand, and by detailed phenomenologies of deviance on the other. In response to the former, such a geography will be contextualised in terms of specific political economies; in response to the latter, it will focus on the processes of social interaction that give rise to official crime patterns, the experience of victimisation and the tenor of public fear.

Some definition of the political and economic setting is crucial, in that this conditions the majority of factors responsible for the manifestation of crime: the polarisation of wealth and consequent degrees of inequality and deprivation; changes in lifestyle and increased opportunities for routine and social activities; demographic changes, particularly those related to the volume and disposition of migrant labour; changes in the definition and sanctioning of crime. Detailed analyses of the processes of social interaction in which crime is nested are equally important if the effects of crime are to be assessed in terms relevant to those who experience it most. Such effects include not only quantifiable damage to persons and property but also an unmeasurable impact on the quality of life in some urban neighbourhoods. For this reason recommendations made in the text have often been coloured by my experience as a resident of the studied community. This experience sometimes questions the wisdom of traditional crime-prevention policy – a liberty worth taking if it helps introduce a human dimension to the technical prescriptions of empirical–analytical enquiry which usually inform planners and politicians.

My aim, therefore, has been to analyse crime both as a contingency of a national structure of political and economic relations and as contributory to a local structure of social relations. Policy implications notwithstanding, it is no coincidence that much of the discussion has been theoretical. For although Britain has a long history of criminological research, the impact of this on social policy has always surpassed its contribution to social theory. One notable consequence of bringing a geographical perspective to bear on the study of crime is the possibility it offers to strengthen the weak theoretical base of British criminology in general, and of victimology in particular. To this end, an important requirement is that crime is analysed as an integral part of a more extensive set of social relations, and that it is not compartmentalised as a discrete urban pathology. While this is not a requirement appropriate to all geographical analyses of crime, it is central to the view presented in this book. This view demands that geographers adopt an increasingly interdisciplinary perspective in their analyses of crime. In return, it offers them the prospect of making significant contributions to more general debate in social theory.

I have argued that criminological knowledge can be appreciated in terms of the interests it expresses and in terms of the theories of reality it assumes. There exists such a diversity of approaches that criminological theory appears to share the disarray attributed by Giddens (1979) to social theory in general. The responses of sociologists to such disarray also have their parallel in criminology: disillusionment with theory and capitulation to the practicalities of empirical analysis (a move epitomised in the rise of factorial ecology); reversion to the dogmatism of holistic and politically circumscribed systems of thought (as evinced by some of the left idealists); uncritical acceptance of diversity as the mark of a flourishing discipline (a form of liberal pragmatism which currently has much appeal). Giddens rejects all these solutions, demanding that theory finds its test in empirical research, that scepticism and openness be preserved, and that eclecticism be sacrificed to a search for connections between, and transcendence of, divergent positions.

A first attempt at such transcendence in the criminological litera-ture must be attributed to the Chicago School. Here, a concerted attempt was made to combine the practical interests of empathetic ethnography with the technical interests of systematic empirical– analytical science in order to implement policy-relevant findings sensitive to the needs of the public. The School transcended the philosophical dualism of neo-Kantian formalism and North American pragmatism by concentrating on the practical require-ments of research in a welfare-orientated discipline. The work remained trapped, however, in the unchallenged context of a laisser-faire economy and a capitalist political democracy. The world of commonsense deviancy was experienced and communicated; it was set into the wider geographical structure of the city; but its unac-knowledged sources and unintended consequences were rarely considered, and never tied into the differential distribution of power which permeates all social life.

Drawing inspiration from modern structuration theories, I have attempted in this book to move beyond the conciliatory beginnings of the Chicago School. My aim has been to draw from interpretative, critical and empirical–analytical perspectives, exploring some important links between the first two of these, but evaluating *en route* a number of policy decisions demanded by the social, economic and political realities of crime in a modern democracy. The approach I have followed is one which, while focussing on the impact of crime, has been able to follow the effects of structured inequality into the organisation of daily life in neighbourhood settings. It recognises the authenticity of folk perceptions and behaviours without capitulating to the circumscribed world of discursive consciousness; and while acknowledging that power is integral to all forms of social behaviour, it draws attention to the different ways in which power is realised according to specific relationships between the local context of social relations and the operation of a wider political economy in which they are set.

The introduction to this volume was concerned with the necessary relationship between knowledge and interests. My concluding chap-ters contain observations on a theory of society required to tran-scend the compartmentalisation of knowledge such a relationship implies. The intervening pages have attempted to show how crime impinges on the many spheres of social life which currently interest social geographers. Theoretical concerns notwithstanding, it is to be hoped that these chapters have not ignored the practical requirements of inner-city communities still seeking their share of rewards and life chances dispensed by the British economy.

References

Abrams, P. 1968. *The origins of British sociology*. Chicago, University of Chicago Press.

Akers, R. 1968. Problems in the sociology of deviance. *Social Forces*, 46: 445–65.

Alderson, J. 1982. The case for community policing. In *Policing the riots*, eds. D. Cowell, T. Jones and J. Young, pp. 135–46. London, Junction Books.

Alison, A. 1840. *The principles of population, and their connection with human happiness*. 2 volumes. Edinburgh, William Blackwood.

Allison, J. 1972. Economic factors and the rate of crime. *Land Economics*, 48: 193–6.

Anning, N. and Ballard, B. 1981. The elusive firebombers. *New Statesman*, 102: 6–7.

Antunes, G. E., Cook, F. L., Cook, T. D. and Skogan, W. G. 1977. Patterns of personal crime against the elderly: findings from a national survey. *The Gerontologist*, 17: 321–7.

Apel, K-O. 1981. *Charles S. Peirce. From pragmatism to pragmaticism*. Trans. J. M. Krois. Amherst, University of Massachusetts Press.

Apple, N. and O'Brien, D. J. 1983. Neighborhood racial composition and residents' evaluation of police performance. *Journal of Police Science and Administration*, 11: 76–84.

Archer, D. and Gartner, R. 1976. Violent acts and violent times: a comparative approach to postwar homicide rates. *American Sociological Review*, 41: 937–63.

Ardrey, R. 1966. *The territorial imperative*. New York, Atheneum.

Ariés, P. 1962. *Centuries of childhood: a social history of family life*. Trans. R. Baldick. New York, Alfred A. Knopf.

Armstrong, G. and Wilson, M. 1973. City politics and deviancy amplification. In *Politics and deviance*, eds. I. Taylor and L. Taylor, pp. 61–89. Harmondsworth, Penguin.

Athens, L. H. 1974. The self and the violent criminal act. *Urban Life and Culture*, 3: 98–112.

1977. Violent crime: a symbolic interactionist study. *Symbolic Interaction*, 1:56–70.

1980. *Violent criminal acts and actors*. London, Routledge and Kegan Paul.

Austin, R. L. 1983. The colonial model, subcultural theory and intragroup violence. *Journal of Criminal Justice*, 11: 93–104.

Axenroth, J. B. 1983. Social class and delinquency in cross cultural perspective. *Journal of Research in Crime and Delinquency*, 20: 164–82.

Bagot, J. H. 1941. *Juvenile delinquency.* London, Cape.

Baker, M. H., Nienstadt, B. C., Everett, R. S. and McCleary, R. 1983. The impact of a crime wave: perceptions, fear, and confidence in the police. *Law and Society Review*, 17: 319–35.

Baldwin, J. 1974a. Social area analysis and studies of delinquency. *Social Science Research*, 3: 151–68.

1974b. Problem housing estates – perceptions of city officials and criminologists. *Social and Economic Administration*, 8: 116–35.

1975. British areal studies of crime: an assessment. *British Journal of Criminology*, 15: 211–27.

1979. Ecological and areal studies in Great Britain and the United States. In *Crime and justice: an annual review of research*, eds. N. Morris and M. Tonry, pp. 29–86. Chicago, University of Chicago Press.

Baldwin, J. and Bottomley, A. K. eds. 1978. *Criminal justice: selected readings.* London, Martin Robertson.

Baldwin, J. and Bottoms, A. E. 1976. *The urban criminal.* London, Tavistock.

Baldwin, J. and McConville, M. 1977. *Negotiated justice: pressures on defendants to plead guilty.* London, Martin Robertson.

Baldwin, R. and Kinsey, R. 1982. *Police powers and politics.* London, Quartet.

Balkin, S. and Houlden, P. 1983. Reducing fear of crime through occupational presence. *Criminal Justice and Behaviour*, 10: 13–33.

Batta, I. D., McCulloch, J. W. and Smith, N. J. 1975. A study of juvenile delinquency amongst Asians and half-Asians. *British Journal of Criminology*, 15: 32–42.

Baumer, T. L. 1978. Research on fear of crime in the United States. *Victimology*, 3: 254–67.

Beasley, R. and Antunes, G. 1974. The etiology of urban crime: an ecological approach. *Criminology*, 11: 439–61.

Bechdolt, B. 1975. Cross-sectional analyses of socio-economic determinants of urban crime. *Review of Social Economy*, 33: 132–7.

Becker, H. 1963. *Outsiders.* New York, Free Press.

1966. Introduction. In *The jack-roller* by C. R. Shaw, pp. v–xvii. Chicago and London, University of Chicago Press.

Bell, D. 1962. *The end of ideology.* New York, Free Press.

Bennett, J. 1981. *Oral history and delinquency: the rhetoric of criminology.* London and Chicago, University of Chicago Press.

Bennett, T. 1984. Burglary prevention and the offender. Report of a seminar, British Society of Criminology Newsletter no.1, p.2.

Berg, W. E. and Johnson, R. 1979. Assessing the impact of victimization. In *Perspectives on victimology*, ed. W. H. Parsonage, pp. 58–71. Beverly Hills and London, Sage.

Berger, R. J. 1980. The social economy of street crime. Unpublished PhD thesis, University of California, Los Angeles.

Biderman, A. D. 1967. Surveys of population samples for estimating crime incidence. *Annals, American Academy of Political and Social Science*, 374: 16–53.

Biderman, A. D. and Reiss, A. J. 1967. On exploring the 'dark figure' of crime. *Annals, American Academy of Political and Social Science*, 374: 1–15.

Biderman, A. D., Johnson, L. A., McIntyre, J. and Weir, A. W. 1967. Report on a pilot study in the district of Columbia on victimization and attitudes toward law enforcement. President's Commission on Law Enforcement and Administration of Justice, *Field Surveys 1*. Washington, DC, US Government Printing Office.

Birmingham Education Department Careers Service. 1979. *Statistical summary of unemployed persons on the register*. Unpublished monthly tabulations.

Birmingham Inner City Partnership. 1978. *Inner city partnership programme 1979–82*. Birmingham, HM Government, Birmingham City Council, West Midlands County Council.

Blau, J. R. and Blau, P. M. 1982. The cost of inequality: metropolitan structure and violent crime. *American Sociological Review*, 47: 114–29.

Block, R. 1974. Why notify the police? *Criminology*, 11: 555–69.

1979. Community, environment and violent crime. *Criminology*, 17: 46–57.

1981. Victim–offender dynamics in violent crime. *Journal of Criminal Law and Criminology*, 72: 743–61.

Blum-West, S. 1983. Calling the cops: a study of why people report crimes. *Journal of Police Science and Administration*, 11: 8–15.

Boal, F. W. 1972. The urban residential sub-community: a conflict interpretation. *Area*, 4: 161–8.

1981. Ethnic residential segregation, ethnic mixing and resource conflict: a study in Belfast, Northern Ireland. In *Ethnic segregation in cities*, eds. C. Peach, V. Robinson and S. Smith, pp. 235–51. London, Croom Helm.

Boateng, P. 1982. Democratic accountability and the metropolitan police. In *The future of policing*, ed. T. Bennett, pp. 163–9. Cambridge, Institute of Criminology.

Boggs, S. L. 1971. Formal and informal crime control: an exploratory study of urban, suburban and rural orientations. *Sociological Quarterly*, 12: 319–27.

Bohm, R. M. 1982. Capitalism, socialism and crime. In *Rethinking criminology*, ed. H. E. Pepinsky, pp. 49–60. Beverly Hills and London, Sage.

Bonger, W. 1916. *Criminology and economic conditions*. Boston, Little, Brown and Co.

Boostrom, R. I. and Henderson, J. I. 1984. Crime prevention models and police community relations. *The Police Journal*, 57: 373–81.

Booth, C. 1902–3. *Life and labour of the people in London*. First series: poverty; second series: industry; third series: religious influences; final volume: notes on social influences and conclusions. 3rd ed. 17 volumes. London, Macmillan.

Bordieu, P. 1972. *Outline of a theory of practice*. Trans. R. Nice. Cambridge, Cambridge University Press. (First published in French.)

Bottomley, A. K. 1979. *Criminology in focus*. Oxford, Martin Robertson.

Bottoms, A. E. 1967. Delinquency amongst immigrants. *Race*, 8: 357–83.

1973. Crime and delinquency in immigrant and minority groups. In

Psychology and race, ed. P. Watson. Harmondsworth, Penguin.

Bottoms, A. E. and Wiles, P. 1975. Race, crime and violence. In *Racial variation in man*, ed. F. J. Ebling. Oxford, Blackwell.

Bottoms, A. E. and Xanthos, P. 1981. Housing policy and crime in the British public sector. In *Environmental criminology*, eds. P. J. Brantingham and P. L. Brantingham, pp. 203–25. Beverly Hills and London, Sage.

Bradley, P. 1984. *A review of community policing*. London, Centre for Contemporary Studies.

Braithwaite, J. 1979. *Inequality, crime and public policy*. London, Routledge and Kegan Paul.

1981. The myth and social class and criminality reconsidered. *American Sociological Review*, 46: 36–57.

Brake, M. 1980. *The sociology of youth culture and youth subcultures*. London, Routledge and Kegan Paul.

Brantingham, P. J. and Brantingham, P. L. 1975. Residential burglary and urban form. *Urban Studies*, 12: 273–84.

1981. *Environmental criminology*. Beverly Hills and London, Sage.

Brantingham, P. L., Brantingham, P. J. and Butcher, D. 1982. Perceived and actual crime risks: an analysis of inconsistencies. Paper presented to the twenty-first annual meeting of the Western Regional Science Association, February. Santa Barbara.

Braungart, M. H., Hoyer, W. J. and Braungart, R. G. 1979. Fear of crime and the elderly. In *Police and the elderly*, eds. A. Goldstein, W. Hoyer and P. Monti, pp. 15–29. New York, Pergamon Press.

Brenner, M. H. 1976. Time-series analysis-effects of the economy on criminal behaviour and the administration of criminal justice. Part 1 in United Nations Social Defense Research Institute, *Economic crises and crime*. Publication no. 15, May. Rome.

1978. Impact of economic indicators on crime indices. In *Unemployment and crime*, US Congressional subcommittee on crime of the committee of the judiciary. Washington DC, US Government Printing Office.

Bridges, L. 1982. Racial attacks. *Legal Action Group Bulletin*, January: 9–11.

1983a. Extended views: the British left and law and order. *Sage Race Relations Abstracts*, 8: 19–26.

1983b. Policing the urban wasteland. *Race and Class*, 25: 31–47.

Brogden, A. 1981. 'Sus' is dead: but what about 'Sas'? *New Community*, 9: 44–52.

Brown, C. 1984. *Black and white Britain*. The third Policy Studies Institute Survey. London, Heinemann.

Brown, D. and Iles, S. 1985. *Community constables: a study of a policing initiative*. London, HMSO.

Brown, J. 1977. *Shades of grey: a report on police–West Indian relations in Handsworth*. Cranfield, Cranfield Institute of Technology.

1982. *Policing by multi-racial consent*. London, Bedford Square Press.

Burgess, E. W. 1923. The study of the delinquent as a person. *American Journal of Sociology*, 28: 657–79.

Butler, A. J. P. 1982. Effectiveness, accountability and management: the challenge of contemporary police work. In *The year book of social policy in*

Britain 1980–1981, eds. C. Jones and J. Stevenson, pp. 89–111. London, Routledge and Kegan Paul.

Bynum, T. S., Cordner, G. W. and Greene, J. R. 1982. Victim and offense characteristics. *Criminology*, 20: 301–18.

Cain, M. 1973. *Society and the policeman's role*. London, Routledge and Kegan Paul.

Calhoun, J. B. 1962. Population density and social pathology. *Scientific American*, 206: 139–48.

Capone, D. and Nichols, W. Jr. 1976. Urban structure and criminal mobility. *American Behavioral Scientist*, 20: 119–213.

Carlen, P. 1976. *Magistrates' justice*. London, Martin Robertson.

Carr-Hill, R. A. and Stern, N. H. 1979. *Crime, the police and criminal statistics*. London, Academic Press.

Carroll, L. and Jackson, P. I. 1983. Inequality, opportunity and crime rates in central cities. *Criminology*, 21: 178–94.

Carter, R. L. 1974. *The criminal's image of the city*. Unpublished PhD thesis, University of Oklahoma.

Carter, R. L. and Hill, K. Q. 1980. Area images and behavior: an alternative perspective for understanding urban crime. In *Crime: a spatial perspective*, eds. D. E. Georges-Abeyie and K. D. Harries, pp. 193–204. New York, Columbia University Press.

Cashmore, E. 1979. *Rastaman*. London, George Allen and Unwin.

Castells, M. 1977. *The urban question. A Marxist approach*. London, Edward Arnold.

1978. *City, class and power*. London, Macmillan.

Chambers, G. and Tombs, J. 1984. *The British crime survey: Scotland*. London, HMSO.

Chatterton, M. 1976. Police in social control. In *Control without custody*, ed. J. F. S. King, pp. 104–22. Cambridge, Cambridge Institute of Criminology.

Chilton, R. J. 1964. Continuity in delinquency area research: a comparison of studies for Baltimore, Detroit and Indianapolis. *American Sociological Review*, 29: 71–83.

Choldin, H. M. ed. 1975. Urban density and crowding. *American Behavioral Scientist*, 18 (6) (whole issue).

Cicourel, A. V. and Kitsuse, J. I. 1963. *The educational decision makers*. Indianapolis, Bobb-Merrill.

Clark, G. L. 1984. A theory of local autonomy. *Annals, Association of American Geographers*, 74: 195–208.

Clarke, R. 1980. Situational crime prevention: theory and practice. *British Journal of Criminology*, 20: 136–47.

1984. Opportunity-based crime rates. *British Journal of Criminology*, 24: 74–83.

Clarke, R., Eckblom, P., Hough, M. and Mayhew, P. 1985. Elderly victims of crime and exposure to risk. *The Howard Journal*, 24: 1–9.

Clarke, R. V. G. and Mayhew, P. eds. 1980. *Designing out crime*. London, HMSO.

Clay, J. 1855. On the effect of good or bad times on committals to prison. *Journal of the Statistical Society of London*, 18: 74–9.

Clayton, R. and Tomlinson, H. 1984. Bad history and dubious law. *Police Review*, 92: 2314–16.

Clelland, D. and Carter, T. J. 1980. The new myth of class and crime. *Criminology*, 3: 319–36.

Clemente, F. and Kleiman, M. B. 1977. Fear of crime in the United States. *Social Forces, 56:* 519–31.

Clinard, M. B. 1978. *Cities with little crime: the case of Switzerland.* Cambridge, Cambridge University Press.

Cloward, R. A. and Ohlin, L. E. 1960. *Delinquency and opportunity.* Glencoe, The Free Press.

Cohen, A. 1980. Drama and politics in the development of a London carnival. *Man*, 15: 65–87.

  1982. A polyethnic London carnival as a contested cultural performance. *Ethnic and Racial Studies* 5: 23–41.

Cohen, A. K. 1955. *Delinquent boys.* Glencoe, The Free Press.

Cohen, L. E. and Cantor, D. 1980. The determinants of larceny: an empirical and theoretical study. *Journal of Research in Crime and Delinquency*, 17: 140–59.

Cohen, L. E. and Felson, M. 1979. Social change and crime rate trends: a routine activity approach. *American Sociological Review*, 44: 588–608.

Cohen, L. E., Kluegel, J. R. and Land, K. C. 1981. Social inequality and predatory criminal victimisation: an exposition and test of a formal theory. *American Sociological Review*, 46: 505–24.

Cohen, P. 1979. Policing the working-class city. In *Capitalism and the rule of law*, eds. B. Fine, R. Kinsey, J. Lea, S. Picciotto and J. Young, pp. 118–36. London, Hutchinson.

Cohn, E. S., Kidder, L. H. and Harvey, J. 1978. Crime prevention is victimization prevention: the psychology of two different reactions. *Victimology*, 3: 285–96.

Conklin, J. E. 1975. *The impact of crime.* New York, Macmillan.

Corden, J. 1983. Persistent petty offenders: problems and patterns of multiple disadvantage. *Howard Journal of Penology and Crime Prevention*, 22: 68–90.

Corsi, T. M. and Harvey, M. E. 1975. The socio-economic determinants of crime in the city of Cleveland. *Tijdschrift voor Economische en Sociale Geografie*, 66: 323–36.

Critcher, C., Sondhi, R. and Parker, M. 1975. Race in the West Midlands Press. Unpublished manuscript, Centre for Contemporary Cultural Studies, University of Birmingham.

Critchley, T. A. 1967. *A history of police in England and Wales.* London, Constable.

Croft, S. and Beresford, P. 1984. Patch and participation: the case for citizen research. *Social Work Today*, 17 September: 18–24.

Cronin, T. E., Cronin, T. Z. and Milakovich, M. E. 1981. *U.S. v. crime in the streets.* Bloomington, Indiana University Press.

Crutchfield, R. A., Geerken, M. P. and Gove, W. R. 1982. Crime rates and social integration. The impact of metropolitan mobility. *Criminology*, 20: 467–78.

Damer, S. 1974, Wine alley: the sociology of a dreadful enclosure. *The Sociological Review*, NS 22: 221–48.

Danziger, S. and Wheeler, D. 1975. The economics of crime: punishment or income redistribution. *Review of Social Economy*, 33: 113–31.

Davidson, R. N. 1977. Spatial bias in court sentencing. Paper presented to the urban studies group, IBG, Leicester.

1981. *Crime and environment*. London, Croom Helm.

Davis, F. J. 1952. Crime news in Colarado newspapers. *American Journal of Sociology*, 57: 325–30.

Dean, M. 1982. Making the link between unemployment and crime. *Guardian*, May 17, p. 17.

Dear, M. 1981. A theory of the local state. In *Political studies from spatial perspectives*, eds. A. D. Burnett and P. J. Taylor, pp. 10–31. Chichester, Wiley.

DeFleur, L. B. 1967. Ecological variables in the cross-cultural study of delinquency. *Social Forces*, 45: 556–70.

DeFronzo, J. 1983. Economic assistance to impoverished Americans. *Criminology*, 21: 119–36.

Denzin, N. K. 1974. The methodological implications of symbolic interactionism for the study of deviance. *British Journal of Sociology*, 25: 269–82.

Department of the Environment, 1977a. *Policy for the inner cities*. Cmnd. 6845. London, HMSO.

1977b. *Unequal city: final report of the Birmingham Inner Areas Study*. London, HMSO.

Dingemans, D. J. 1978. Defensible space design in the California townhouse. *The California Geographer*, 18: 95–110.

Doerner, W. G. 1975. A regional analysis of homicide rates in the United States. *Criminology*, 13: 90–101.

Downes, D. and Rock, P. 1982. *Understanding deviance*. Oxford, Clarendon Press.

Duncan, S. S. and Goodwin, M. 1982. The local state and restructuring social relations. *International Journal of Urban and Regional Research*, 5: 231–54.

Durkheim, E. 1947. *The division of labour in society*. New York, The Free Press of Glencoe. (First published 1893, Paris, Felix Alcan.)

1951. *Suicide*. New York, The Free Press of Glencoe. (First published 1897, Paris, Felix Alcan.)

Ealing Community Relations Council 1981. *Racialist activity in Ealing 1979–81*. London, Ealing CRC.

Eberts, P. and Schwirian, K. P. 1968. Metropolitan crime rates and relative deprivation. *Criminologica*, 5: 43–52.

Elion, V. H. and Magargee, E. I. 1979. Racial identity, length of incarceration and parole decision making. *Journal of Research in Crime and Delinquency*, 16: 232–45.

Elliot, D. S. and Huizinga, D. 1983. Social class and delinquent behaviour in a national youth panel. *Criminology*, 21: 149–77.

Elliot, M. 1985. *Preventing child sexual assault*. London, Bedford Square Press.

Elliott, J. F. 1983. *Interception patrol*. Springfield, Illinois, Charles Thomas.

Engels, F. 1845. *The condition of the working class in England*. Trans. and ed.

W. O. Henderson and W. H. Chaloner. Stanford, Stanford University Press (1958).

Ennis, P. H. 1967. Criminal victimization in the United States: a report of a national survey, President's Commission on Law Enforcement and Administration of Justice, *Field Surveys II*. Washington DC: US Government Printing Office.

Erikson, K. T. 1964. Notes on the sociology of deviance. In *The other side*, ed. H. S. Becker, pp. 9–21. New York, Free Press.

Evans, A. and Eversley, D. eds. 1980. *The inner city: employment and housing*. London, Heinemann.

Evans, D. 1980. *Geographical perspectives on juvenile delinquency*. Farnborough, Gower.

Faris, R. E. L. 1967. *Chicago sociology 1920–1932*. California, Chandler.

Farrington, D. P. and Bennett, T. 1981. Police cautioning of juveniles in London. *British Journal of Criminology*, 21: 123–35.

Fenn, G. 1984. The need for a victims' charter. *Police Review*, 92: 2311–13.

Feyerherm, W. H. and Hindelang, M. J. 1974. On the victimization of juveniles: some preliminary findings. *Journal of Research in Crime and Delinquency*, 11: 40–50.

Field, S. 1984. *The attitudes of ethnic minorities*. London, HMSO.

Finestone, H. 1976. *Victims of change*. Westport, Connecticut, Greenwood Press.

Fisher, C. J. and Mawby, R. I. 1982. Juvenile delinquency and police discretion in an inner city area. *British Journal of Criminology*, 22: 63–75.

Fishman, G. 1979. Patterns of victimisation and notification. *British Journal of Criminology*, 19: 146–57.

Fishman, M. 1978. Crime waves as ideology. *Social Problems*, 25: 531–43.

Flango, V. and Sherbenous, E. 1976. Poverty, urbanization, and crime. *Criminology*, 14: 331–45.

Fleisher, B. M. 1966. The effects of income on delinquency. *American Economic Review*, 56: 118–37.

Fletcher, J. 1849. Moral statistics of England and Wales. *Journal of the Royal Statistical Society of London*, 12: 151–81, 189–335.

Forrest, R., Lloyd, J., Rogers, N. and Williams, P. 1978. *The inner city: in search of the problem*. Centre for Urban and Regional Studies, Working Paper 64, University of Birmingham.

Fowler, F. J. and Mangione, T. 1974. *The nature of fear*. Survey research program, University of Massachusetts, Boston and Joint Center for Urban Studies of MIT and Harvard University.

Freedman, J. L. 1975. *Crowding and behavior*. San Francisco, Freeman.

Fryer, P. 1984. *Staying power. The history of black people in Britain*. London, Pluto.

Gabor, T. 1981. The crime displacement hypothesis: an empirical examination. *Crime and Delinquency*, 27: 390–404.

Gaier, E. L. 1976. Shifts in delinquent behavior, 1951–1973. *Juvenile Justice*, 27: 15–23.

Garofalo, J. 1981a. The fear of crime and its consequences. *Journal of Criminal Law and Criminology*, 72: 829–57.

1981b. Crime and the mass media: a selective review of research. *Journal of*

Research in Crime and Delinquency, 18: 319–50.

Gastil, R. D. 1971. Homicide and a regional culture of violence. *American Sociological Review*, 36: 412–27.

Giddens, A. 1979. *Central problems in social theory*. London, Macmillan.

1981. *A contemporary critique of historical materialism*. Berkeley and Los Angeles, University of California Press.

1982. *Profiles and critiques in social theory*. Berkeley and Los Angeles, University of California Press.

1984. *The constitution of society*. Cambridge, Polity Press.

Gill, O. 1977. *Luke street. Housing policy, conflict and the creation of the delinquent area*. London and Basingstoke, Macmillan.

Gladstone, F. 1979. *Voluntary action in a changing world*. London, Bedford Square Press.

Glaser, D. 1968. Crime in a great society. In *Critical issues in the study of crime*, eds. S. Dinitz and P. Reckless, pp. 19–22. Boston, Little, Brown and Co.

Glyde, J. 1856. Localities of crime in Suffolk. *Journal of the Statistical Society of London*, 19: 102–6.

Goffman, E. 1971. *Relations in public*. New York, Basic Books.

1981. *Forms of talk*. Philadelphia, University of Pennsylvania Press.

Goldthorpe, J. H. 1980. *Social mobility and class structure in modern Britain*. Oxford, Oxford University Press.

Goldthorpe, J. H. and Hope, K. 1974. *The social grading of occupations: a new approach and scale*. Oxford, Oxford University Press.

Gordon, D. M. 1973. Capitalism, class, and crime in America. *Crime and Delinquency*, 19: 163–86.

Gordon, M. T. and Heath, L. 1981. The news business, crime and fear. In *Reactions to crime*, ed. D. A. Lewis, pp. 227–50. Beverly Hills and London, Sage.

Gordon, P. 1983. *White law*. London, Pluto.

Gordon, R. A. 1967. Issues in the ecological study of delinquency. *American Sociological Review*, 32: 927–44.

Gottfredson, M. R. 1981. On the etiology of criminal victimization. *Journal of Criminal Law and Criminology*, 72: 714–26.

1984. *Victims of crime: the dimensions of risk*. London, HMSO.

Gottfredson, M. R. and Hindelang, M. J. 1981. Sociological aspects of criminal victimization. *Annual Review of Sociology*, 7: 102–28.

Gould, L. C. 1968. The changing structure of property crime in an affluent society. *Social Forces*, 48: 50–9.

Greater London Council. 1984. *Racial harassment in London*. Report of a panel of inquiry set up by the Greater London Council Police Committee. London, GLC.

Greater London Council Police Committee Support Unit. 1983a. *Policing by coercion*. London, GLC.

1983b. *A new police authority for London*. London, GLC.

Greenberg, D. F. 1977. Delinquency and the age structure of society. *Contemporary Crises*, 1: 189–223.

Greenberg, M. S., Ruback, R. B. and Westcott, D. R. 1982. Decision making by crime victims: a multimethod approach. *Law and Society Review*, 17: 47–84.

Greenstein, M. 1977. An invitation to law enforcement: fear and non-reporting by elders. *The Police Chief*, 44: 30–1.

Gubrum, J. 1974. Victimization in old age. *Crime and Delinquency*, 29: 245–50.

Guerry, A. M. 1833. *Essai sur la statistique moral de la France avec cartes.* Paris, Crochard.

Gurr, T. R. 1977. Crime trends in modern democracies since 1945. *International Annals of Criminology*, 16: 41–85.

Gurr, T. R., Grabosky, P. N. and Hula, R. C. 1977. *The politics of crime and conflict. A comparative history of four cities.* Beverly Hills and London, Sage.

Habermas, J. 1968. *Knowledge and human interests.* Trans. J. J. Shapiro. Boston, Beacon Press (1971).

Hagan, J. L. 1974. Conceptual deficiencies of an interactionist perspective on 'deviance'. *Criminology*, 11: 383–404.

Hakim, S. and Rengert, G. F. eds. 1981. *Crime spillover.* Beverly Hills and London, Sage.

Hakim, S., Ovadia, A., Sagi, E. and Weinblatt, J. 1979. Interjurisdictional spillover of crime and police expenditures. *Land Economics*, 55: 200–12.

Hall, P. ed. 1981. *The inner city in context.* London, Heinemann.

Hall, S. and Jefferson, T. eds. 1975. *Resistance through rituals.* London, Hutchinson.

Hall, S., Critcher, C., Jefferson, T., Clarke, J. and Roberts, B. 1978. *Policing the crisis.* London, Macmillan.

Hamnett, C. 1979. Area-based explanations: a critical appraisal. In *Social problems and the city*, eds. D. T. Herbert and D. M. Smith, pp. 244–60. Oxford, Oxford University Press.

Hannerz, U. 1969. *Soulside.* New York, Columbia University Press.
  1980. *Exploring the city.* New York, Columbia University Press.

Harman, H. 1982. Civil liberties and civil disorder. In *Policing the riots*, eds. D. Cowell, T. Jones and J. Young, pp. 39–51. London, Junction Books.

Harries, K. D. 1973. Social indicators and metropolitan variations in crime. *Proceedings, Associations of American Geographers*, 5: 97–102.
  1974. *The geography of crime and justice.* New York, McGraw-Hill.
  1975. Rejoinder to Richard Peet: 'The geography of crime: a political critique'. *Professional Geographer*, 27: 280–2.
  1976a. Observations on radical versus liberal theories of crime causation. *Professional Geographer*, 28: 100–13.
  1976b. Cities and crime: a geographic model. *Criminology*, 14: 369–86.
  1980. *Crime and the environment.* Springfield, Illinois, C. C. Thomas.
  1985. The historical geography of homicide in the United States, 1935–80. *Geoforum*, 16 (forthcoming).

Harries, K. D. and Brunn, S. D. 1978. *The geography of laws and justice: spatial perspectives on the criminal justice system.* New York, Praeger.

Harries, K. D. and Lura, R. P. 1974. The geography of justice: sentencing variations in US judicial districts. *Judicature*, 57: 392–401.

Harrison, P. 1983. *Inside the inner city.* Harmondsworth, Penguin.

Hartmann, P. and Husband, C. 1971. The mass media and racial conflict. *Race*, 12: 268–82.

1974. *Racism and the mass media*. London, Davis-Poynter.

Hartnagel, T. F. and Tanner, J. 1982. Class, schooling and delinquency: a further examination. *Canadian Journal of Criminology*, 24: 155–72.

Havilan, J. B. 1977. *Gossip, reputation and knowledge in Zinacantan*. Chicago and London, University of Chicago Press.

Heal, K. 1983. The police, the public and the prevention of crime. *The Howard Journal*, 22: 91–100.

Hellman, D. A. 1981. Criminal mobility and policy recommendations. In *Crime spillover*, eds. S. Hakim and G. F. Rengert, pp. 135–50. Beverly Hills and London, Sage.

Hemley, O. D. and McPheters, L. R. 1974. Crime as an externality of regional economic growth. *Review of Regional Studies*, 4: 73–84.

Henderson, W. O. and Chaloner, W. H. 1958. Editors' introduction. In Engels *The condition of the working class in England*, pp. ix–xxix. Stanford, Stanford University Press.

Henig, J. and Maxfield, M. G. 1978. Reducing fear of crime: strategies for intervention. *Victimology*, 3: 297–313.

Hentig, H. von. 1940. Remarks on the interaction of perpetrator and victim. *Journal of Criminal Law*, 31: 303–9.

1948. *The criminal and his victim*. New Haven, Yale University Press.

Herbert, D. T. 1976a. The study of delinquency areas: a social geographical approach. *Transactions, Institute of British Geographers*, NS 1: 472–92.

1976b. Social deviance in the city: a spatial perspective. In *Social areas in cities*, eds. D. T. Herbert and R. J. Johnston, Vol. 1, pp. 89–121. Chichester, Wiley.

1977. An areal and ecological analysis of delinquency residence: Cardiff 1966 and 1971. *Tijdschrift voor Economische en Sociale Geografie*, 68: 83–9.

1979. Urban crime: a geographical perspective. In *Social problems and the city*, eds. D. T. Herbert and D. M. Smith, pp. 117–38. Oxford, Oxford University Press.

1980. Urban crime and spatial perspectives: the British experience. In *Crime: a spatial perspective*, eds. D. E. Georges-Abeyies and K. D. Harries, pp. 26–46. New York, Columbia University Press.

1981. Review of *Crime and the environment* by K. D. Harries. *Progress in Human Geography*, 5: 628.

1982. *The geography of urban crime*. London, Longman.

Hindelang, M. J. 1978. Race and involvement in common law personal crimes. *American Sociological Review*, 43: 93–109.

Hindelang, M. J., Gottfredson, M. R. and Garofalo, J. 1978. *Victims of personal crime: an empirical foundation for a theory of personal victimization*. Cambridge, Mass., Ballinger.

Hindelang, M. J., Hirschi, T. and Weis, J. G. 1979. Correlates of delinquency: the illusion of discrepancy between self-reports and official measures. *American Sociological Review*, 44: 995–1014.

Hoch, I. 1974. Factors in crime. *Journal of Urban Economics*, 1: 184–229.

Home Office. 1981. *Racial attacks*. London, Home Office, November.

1984. *Crime statistics for the Metropolitan Police District analysed by ethnic group. Supplementary tables 1977–83*. London, Home Office.

Horton, F. and Reynolds, D. 1971. Effects of urban spatial structure on individual behaviour. *Economic Geography*, 47: 36–48.

Hough, M. and Mayhew, P. 1983. *The British crime survey: first report.* London, HMSO.

House, J. W. ed. 1978. *The UK space.* 2nd ed. London, Weidenfeld and Nicolson.

Huff, C. R. and Stahura, J. M. 1980. Police employment and suburban crime. *Criminology*, 17: 461–70.

Humphries, D. 1981. Serious crime, news coverage, and ideology. *Crime and Delinquency*, 27: 191–205.

Hyde, S. 1982. Patterns of residential burglary and local environments. Paper presented to the conference 'Crime and space in interdisciplinary perspective', King's College, London, May.

Jackson, P. and Smith, S. J. 1984. *Exploring social geography.* London, George Allen and Unwin.

Jackson, P. I. and Carroll, L. 1981. Race and the war on crime: the sociopolitical determinants of municipal police expenditures in 90 non-southern US cities. *American Sociological Review*, 46: 290–305.

Jacob, H. and Rich, M. J. 1980. The effects of the police on crime: a second look. *Law and Society Review*, 15: 109–22.

Jacobs, D. 1981. Inequality and economic crime. *Sociology and Social Research*, 66: 12–28.

Jacobson, D. 1971. Mobility, continuity and urban social organization. *Man*, 6: 630–45.

Jefferson, T. and Grimshaw, R. 1981. The accountability of police to law and democracy. Paper presented at the Political Studies Association Annual Conference, University of Hull, April 6–8.

　　1984a. The problem of law enforcement policy in England and Wales: the case of community policing and racial attacks. *International Journal of the Sociology of Law*, 12: 117–35.

　　1984b. *Controlling the constable.* London, Frederick Muller in association with the Cobden Trust.

Jeffery, C. R. 1971. *Crime prevention through environmental design.* Beverly Hills and London, Sage.

John, A. 1972. *Race and the inner city.* London, Runnymede Trust.

Johnston, R. J. 1980. On the nature of explanation in human geography. *Transactions, Institute of British Geographers*, 5: 402–12.

Jones, M. 1980. *Crime, punishment and the press.* London, NACRO.

Jones, P. N. 1979. Ethnic areas in British cities. In *Social problems and the city*, eds. D. T. Herbert and D. M. Smith, pp. 158–85. Oxford, Oxford University Press.

　　1980. Ethnic segregation, urban planning and the question of choice: the Birmingham case. Paper presented to the conference on 'Ethnic segregation in cities', St Antony's College, Oxford.

Jongman, R. W. 1982. Crime as a result of expulsion from the labor process. [Criminaliteit als gevolg van de uitstoting uit het arbeidsproces.] *Tijdschrift voor Criminologie*, 24: 3–20.

Journal of Clinical Child Psychology. 1983. Violence against children reconsidered. *Journal of Clinical Child Psychology*, 12 (3) (whole issue).

Karn, V. 1979. Low income owner occupation in the inner city. In *Urban deprivation and the inner city*, ed. C. Jones, pp. 160–90. London, Croom Helm.

Katzman, M. T. 1980. The contribution of crime to urban decline. *Urban Studies*, 17: 277–86.

Keat, R. 1981. *The politics of social theory*. Oxford, Basil Blackwell.

Keat, R. and Urry, J. 1975. *Social theory as science*. London, Routledge and Kegan Paul.

Kerner, H. J. 1978. Fear of crime and attitudes towards crime: comparative criminological reflections. *International Annals of Criminology*, 17: 83–102.

Kettle, M. and Hodges, L. 1982. *Uprising*. London, Pan.

Kinsey, R. 1984. *Merseyside crime survey first report, November 1984*. Merseyside County Council.

Kinsey, R. and Young, J. 1985. Crime is a class issue. *New Statesman*, 109: 16–17.

Kirby, A. 1981. Geographic contributions to the inner city deprivation debate: a critical assessment. *Area*, 13: 177–81.

Kirmeyer, S. L. 1978. Urban density and pathology: a review of research. *Environment and Behavior*, 10: 247–69.

Kitsuse, J. I. 1964. Social reaction to deviant behaviour: problems of theory and method. In *The other side*, ed. H. S. Becker, pp. 87–102. New York, Free Press.

Klecka, W. R. and Bishop, G. F. 1978. *Neighborhood profiles of senior citizens in four American cities*. Washington DC, National Council of Senior Citizens.

Kleinig, J. 1978. Crime and the concept of harm. *American Philosophical Quarterly*, 15: 27–38.

Knight, B. and Hayes, R. 1981. *Self help in the inner city*. London, London Voluntary Service Committee.

Krohn, M. D. 1978. A Durkheimian analysis of international crime rates. *Social Forces*, 57: 654–70.

Kuykendall, J. L. 1974. Styles of community policing. *Criminology*, 12: 229–40.

Kvolseth, T. O. 1977. A note on the effects of population density and underemployment on urban crime. *Criminology*, 15: 105–10.

Lambert, J. 1970. *Crime, police and race relations*. London, Oxford University Press for the Institute of Race Relations.

Lambeth Working Party into Community/Police Relations in Lambeth. 1981. *Final report*. London, Borough of Lambeth.

Lancashire Constabulary. 1983. *Police/public relations survey. June 1983*. Lancashire, Management Services Branch.

Landau, S. F. 1981. Juveniles and the police. *British Journal of Criminology*, 21: 27–46.

Landau, S. F. and Nathan, G. 1983. Selecting delinquents for cautioning in the London Metropolitan area. *British Journal of Criminology*, 23: 128–49.

Lander, B. 1954. *Towards an understanding of juvenile delinquency*. New York,

Columbia University Press.

Landesco, J. 1929. *Organized crime in Chicago*. Chicago, University of Chicago Press.

1933. Life history of a member of the forty two gang. *Journal of Criminal Law and Criminology*, 22: 964–98.

Lavrakas, P. J. 1981. On households. In *Reactions to crime*, ed. D. A. Lewis, pp. 67–85. Beverly Hills and London, Sage.

Lavrakas, P. J. and Herz, E. J. 1982. Citizen participation in neighborhood crime prevention. *Criminology*, 20: 479–98.

Lavrakas, P. J. and Lewis, D. A. 1980. Conceptualization and measurement of citizens' crime prevention behaviors. *Journal of Research in Crime and Delinquency*, 17: 254–73.

Lawless, P. 1981. *Britain's inner cities problems and policies*. London, Harper and Row.

Lawton, M., Nahemow, L., Yaffe, S. and Feldman, S. 1976. Psychological aspects of crime and fear of crime. In *Crime and the elderly*, eds. J. Goldsmith and S. S. Goldsmith. Lexington, DC, Heath.

Layton-Henry, Z. 1984. *The politics of race in Britain*. London, George Allen and Unwin.

Lea, J. and Young, J. 1984. *What is to be done about law and order?* Harmondsworth, Penguin.

Lee, G. W. 1984. Are crime rates increasing? A study of the impact of demographic shifts on crime rates in Canada. *Canadian Journal of Criminology*, 26: 29–42.

Lemert, E. 1972. *Human deviance, social problems and social control*. 2nd ed. Englewood Cliffs, Prentice-Hall.

Levine, J. P. 1976. The potential for crime over-reporting in criminal victim surveys. *Criminology*, 14: 307–30.

Levine, K. 1978. Empiricism in victimological research: a critique. *Victimology*, 3: 77–90.

Lewis, D. A. 1980. *Sociological theory and the production of a social problem: the case of fear of crime*. Reactions to crime project, Northwestern University, Center for Urban Affairs.

Lewis, D. A. and Maxfield, M. G. 1980. Fear in the neighborhoods: an investigation of the impact of crime. *Journal of Research in Crime and Delinquency*, 17: 140–59.

Lewis, D. A. and Salem, G. 1981. Community crime prevention: an analysis of a developing strategy. *Crime and Delinquency*, 27: 405–21.

Lewis, E. B. 1979. Combating crime and citizen attitudes: a study of the corresponding reality. *Journal of Criminal Justice*, 7: 71–91.

Ley, D. 1974. *The black inner city as frontier outpost*. Washington DC, Association of American Geographers.

1975. The street gang in its milieu. In *The social economy of cities*, eds. G. Gapport and H. Rose, pp. 247–73. Beverly Hills, Sage.

Ley, D. and Cybriwsky, R. 1974. The spatial ecology of stripped cars. *Environment and Behavior*, 6: 53–67.

Lienhardt, P. A. 1975. The interpretation of rumour. In *Studies in social anthropology*, eds. J. H. Beattie and R. G. Lienhardt, pp. 105–31. Oxford, Clarendon Press.

Lindquist, J. H. and Duke, J. M. 1982. The elderly victim at risk. *Criminology*, 20: 115–26.

Liska, A. E., Lawrence, J. J. and Sanchirico, A. 1982. Fear of crime as a social fact. *Social Forces*, 60: 760–70.

Loftin, C. K. and Hill, R. H. 1974. Regional subcultures and homicide: an examination of the Gastil–Hackney thesis. *American Sociological Review*, 39: 714–24.

Lowman, J. 1982. Crime, criminal justice policy and the urban environment. In *Geography and the urban environment*, eds. D. T. Herbert and R. J. Johnston, Vol. 5, pp. 307–41. London, Wiley.

Lyerly, R. R. and Skipper, J. K. Jr. 1981. Differential rates of rural–urban delinquency. *Criminology*, 19: 385–99.

Lyman, S. M. and Scott, M. B. 1967. Territoriality: a neglected sociological dimension. *Social Problems*, 15: 236–49.

Lynch, K. 1960. *The image of the city*. Cambridge, Mass., MIT Press.

McCarthy, J. D., Galle, O. R. and Zimmern, W. 1975. Population density, social structure and interpersonal violence. *American Behavioral Scientist*, 18: 771–91.

McCarthy, T. 1978. *The critical theory of Jurgen Habermas*. Cambridge, Mass., MIT Press.

McConville, M. and Baldwin, J. 1982. The influence of race on sentencing in England. *Criminal Law Review*, October: 652–8.

McPherson, M. and Silloway, G. 1981. Planning to prevent crime. In *Reactions to crime*, ed. D. A. Lewis, pp. 149–66. Beverly Hills and London, Sage.

Mack, J. 1964. Full-time miscreants, delinquent neighbourhoods, and criminal networks. *British Journal of Criminology*, 15: 38–53.

Mankoff, M. 1976. Perspectives on the problem of crime. In *Whose Law? What order?*, eds. W. J. Chambliss and M. Mankoff, pp. 240–56. New York, Wiley.

Marcus, S. 1974. *Engels, Manchester, and the working class*. New York, Random House.

Marlin, J. 1973. City crime: report of council on municipal performance. *Criminal Law Bulletin*, 9: 557–604.

Marx, G. T. and Morton, M. 1978. Police and minorities in England. *International Annals of Criminology*, 17: 167–90.

Matza, D. M. 1961. Subterranean traditions of youth. *Annals, American Academy of Political and Social Science*, 338: 102–18.

1964. *Delinquency and drift*. New York, Wiley.

1969. *Becoming deviant*. Engelwood Cliffs, Prentice Hall.

Mawby, R. I. 1977a. Defensible space: a theoretical and empirical appraisal. *Urban Studies*, 14: 169–79.

1977b. Kiosk vandalism: a Sheffield study. *British Journal of Criminology*, 17: 30–46.

1978. A note on domestic disputes reported to the police. *Howard Journal*, 17: 160–8.

1979a. The victimisation of juveniles. *Journal of Research in Crime and Delinquency*, 16: 98–113.

1979b. *Policing the city*. Farnborough, Saxon House.

1981. Overcoming the barriers of privacy. *Criminology*, 18: 501–21.

Mawby, R. I. and Batta, I. D. 1980. *Asians and crime: the Bradford experience*. Southall, Middlesex, Scope Communication for National Association of Asian Youth.

Maxfield, M. G. 1984a. The limits of vulnerability in explaining crime: a comparative neighbourhood analysis. *Journal of Research in Crime and Delinquency*, 21: 233–50.

1984b. *Fear of crime in England and Wales*. London, HMSO.

Mayhew, H. 1862. *London labour and the London poor*. 4 volumes. London, Griffin.

Mayhew, H. and Binney, J. 1862. *The criminal prisons of London and scenes of prison life*. London, Griffin.

Mayhew, P. 1979. Defensible space. The current status of a crime prevention theory. *Howard Journal of Penology and Crime Prevention*, 18: 150–9.

1981. Crime in public view: surveillance and crime prevention. In *Environmental criminology*, eds. P. J. Brantingham and P. L. Brantingham, pp. 119–34. Beverly Hills and London, Sage.

Mays, J. B. 1963. Delinquency areas: a reassessment. *British Journal of Criminology*, 3: 216–30.

Medalia, N. Z. and Larsen, O. N. 1958. Diffusion and belief in a collective delusion: the Seattle windshield pitting epidemic. *American Sociological Review*, 23: 180–6.

Mehay, S. 1977. Interjurisdictional spillovers of urban police services. *Southern Economic Journal*, 43: 1352–9.

Merricks, W. 1985. Public eye. *New Society*, May 2: 166–7.

Merry, S. E. 1979. Going to court: strategies of dispute management in an American urban neighborhood. *Law and Society Review*, 13: 891–925.

1981a. *Urban danger*. Philadelphia, Temple University Press.

1981b. Defensible space undefended: social factors in crime control through environmental design. *Urban Affairs Quarterly*, 16: 397–422.

Merton, R. K. 1938. Social structure and anomie. *American Sociological Review*, 3: 672–82.

Meurer, E. M. Jr. 1979. Violent crime losses: their impact on the victim and society. *Annals, American Academy of Political and Social Science*, 386: 54–62.

Miles, R. and Phizacklea, A. eds. 1979. *Racism and political action in Britain*. London, Routledge and Kegan Paul.

Miller, W. B. 1958. Lower class culture as a generating milieu of gang delinquency. *Journal of Social Issues*, 15: 5–19.

Mitchell, J. C. 1969. African images of the town: a quantitative exploration. Paper presented to the Manchester Statistical Society, January.

1983. Case and situation analysis. *The Sociological Review*, 31: 187–211.

Moore, C. and Brown, J. 1981. *Community versus crime*. London, Bedford Square Press.

Morgan, R. and Maggs, C. 1984. *Following Scarman?* A survey of formal police/community consultation arrangements in provincial Police Authorities in England and Wales, May 1984. Bath, University of Bath.

1985. Called to account?: the implications of consultative groups for police accountability. *Policing*, 1: 87–95.

Morris, D. 1969. *The human zoo*. New York, McGraw-Hill.

Morris, P. and Heal, K. 1981. *Crime control and the police: a review of research*. London, HMSO.

Morris, T. 1957. *The criminal area*. London, Routledge and Kegan Paul.

Moxon, D. and Jones, P. 1984. Public reactions to police behaviour: some findings from the British Crime Survey. *Policing*, 1: 49–56.

Mukherjee, S. K. 1982. Crime and societal change: a study of twentieth-century Australia. *South African Journal of Criminal Law and Criminology*, 6: 262–77.

Murray, R. and Boal, F. W. 1979. The social ecology or urban violence. In *Social problems and the city*, eds. D. T. Herbert and D. M. Smith, pp. 139–57. Oxford, Oxford University Press.

Nagel, J. H. 1978. *Unemployment and crime*. Washington DC, US Government Printing Office.

Nelson, J. F. 1980. Alternative measures of crime. In *Crime: a spatial perspective*, eds. D. E. Georges-Abeyie and K. D. Harries, pp. 77–92. New York, Columbia University Press.

Newman, K. 1984. *Report of the Commissioner of Police of the Metropolis for the year 1983*. London, HMSO.

Newman, O. 1972. *Defensible space: crime prevention through urban design*. New York, Macmillan.

Norris, G. 1979. Defining urban deprivation. In *Urban deprivation and the inner city*, ed. C. Jones, pp. 17–31. London, Croom Helm.

Nugent, N. and King, R. 1979. Ethnic minorities, scapegoating and the extreme right. In *Racism and political action in Britain*, eds. R. Miles and A. Phizacklea, pp. 28–49. London, Routledge and Kegan Paul.

Ogburn, W. F. and Thomas, D. S. 1922. The influence of the business cycle on certain social conditions. *Journal of the American Statistical Association*, 17: 305–40.

Ohlin, L. E. 1971. The effects of social change on law enforcement. In *The challenge of crime in a free society*, no editor, pp. 24–36. New York: Da Capo.

Ostrowe, B. B. and DiBiase, R. 1983. Citizen involvement as a crime deterrent. A study of public attitudes towards an unsanctioned civilian patrol group. *Journal of Police Science and Administration*, 11: 185–93.

Paris, C. and Blackaby, B. 1979. *Not much improvement: urban renewal policy in Birmingham*. London, Heinemann.

Park, R. E. 1925. Community organization and juvenile delinquency. In *The city*, eds. R. E. Park, E. W. Burgess and R. D. McKenzie, pp. 99–112. Chicago, University of Chicago Press.

1929. The city as a social laboratory. In *Robert E. Park on social control and collective behavior*, ed. R. Turner, pp. 3–18. Chicago, University of Chicago Press (1967).

Parkin, F. 1971. *Class inequality and political order*. London, MacGibbon and Kee.

Paterson, A. A. 1974. Judges: a political elite? *British Journal of Law and Society*, 1: 118–35.

Patterson, A. H. 1978. Territorial behaviour and fear of crime in the elderly. *Environmental Psychology and Nonverbal Behaviour*, 2: 131–44.

Pearson, G. 1976. 'Paki-bashing' in a north-east Lancashire cotton town: a case study and its history. In *Working-class youth culture*, eds. G. Mungham and G. Pearson, pp. 48–81. London, Routledge and Keagan Paul.

1983. *A history of respectable fears*. London and Basingstoke, Macmillan.

Peet, J. R. 1975. The geography of crime: a political critique. *Professional Geographer*, 27: 277–80.

1976. Further comments on the geography of crime. *Professional Geographer*, 28: 96–100.

Pfautz, H. W. 1967. Introduction. In *Charles Booth on the city: physical pattern and social structure*, ed. H. W. Pfautz, pp. 3–170. Chicago and London, University of Chicago Press.

Phelps, H. A. 1927. Cycles of crime. *Journal of Criminal Law, Criminology and Police Science*, 20: 107–21.

Phillips, L. and Votey, H. L. 1975. Crime control in California. *Journal of Legal Studies*, 4: 327–49.

Phillips, L., Votey, H. L. Jr. and Maxwell, D. 1972. Crime, youth and the labor market. *Journal of Political Economy*, 80: 491–503.

Phillips, P. D. 1972. The geography of crime. Unpublished PhD dissertation, University of Minnesota, Minneapolis.

Piepe, A., Crouch, S. and Emerson, M. 1978. *Mass media and cultural relationships*. Westmead, Saxon House.

Pike, R. E. 1979. Citizen involvement in law enforcement: community mobilization against crime or latent vigilantism? Unpublished MA thesis, American University, Washington, DC.

Podolefsky, A. M. 1979. *Reactions to crime papers* (number/title unspecified). Chicago, Center for Urban Affairs, Northwestern University.

Poister, T. H. and McDavid J. C. 1978. Victims' evaluation of police performance. *Journal of Criminal Justice*, 6: 133–49.

Police Foundation. 1981. *The Newark foot patrol experiment*. Washington DC, Police Foundation.

Polk, K. 1967. Urban social areas and delinquency. *Social Problems*, 14: 320–5.

Pope, C. E. 1979a. Victimization rates and neighborhood characteristics: some preliminary findings. In *Perspectives on victimology*, ed. W. H. Parsonage. Beverly Hills and London, Sage.

1979b. Race and crime revisited. *Journal of Crime and Delinquency*, 25: 347–57.

Pratt, M. 1980. *Mugging as a social problem*. London, Routledge and Kegan Paul.

Pred, A. 1984. Place as historically contingent process: structuration and the time-geography of becoming places. *Annals, American Association of Geographers*, 74: 279–97.

Pyle, G. F., Hunten, E. W., Williams, E. G., Pearson, A. L., Doyle, G. and Kwofie, K. 1974. *The spatial dynamics of crime*. Chicago, University of Chicago Press.

Quetelet, M. A. 1842. *A treatise on man*. Edinburgh, William and Robert Chambers.

Ramsay, M. 1982. *City-centre crime: the scope for situational prevention*. London, HMSO.

Randall, J. N. 1979. The changing nature of the regional economic problem since 1965. In *Regional policy*, ed. D. Maclennan and J. B. Parr, pp. 111–31. Oxford, Martin Robertson.

Rawson, R. W. 1839. An inquiry into the statistics of crime in England and Wales. *Journal of the Statistical Society of London*, 2: 316–44.

Reiner, R. 1984. Is Britain turning into a police state? *New Society*, 2 August: 51–6.

Rengert, G. 1977. *Burglary in Philadelphia: a critique of an opportunity model*. Paper presented to the annual meeting of the Association of American Geographers, Utah.

Rengert, G. F. and Müller, P. O. 1972. The diffusion of dangerous drugs in New York State. Paper presented to the annual meeting of the Midstates division of the Association of American Geographers, Geneseo, New York. October.

Reppetto, T. A. 1974. *Residential crime*. Cambridge, Mass., Ballinger.

1976a. Crime prevention through environmental policy. *American Behavioral Scientist*, 20: 275–88.

1976b. Crime prevention and the displacement phenomenon. *Crime and Delinquency*, 22: 166–77.

Rex, J. 1981. Urban segregation and inner city policy in Great Britain. In *Ethnic segregation in cities*, eds. C. Peach, V. Robinson and S. Smith, pp. 25–42. London, Croom Helm.

1984. Disadvantage and discrimination in cities. In *Scarman and after*, ed. J. Benyon, pp. 191–9. Oxford, Pergamon Press.

Rex, J. and Moore, R. 1967. *Race, community and conflict*. London, Oxford University Press for Institute of Race Relations.

Rhind, J. A. 1981. The need for accountability. In *Modern policing*, eds. D. Pope and N. L. Weiner, pp. 42–52. London, Croom Helm.

Rice, S. A. 1931. Hypotheses and verifications in Clifford R. Shaw's studies of juvenile delinquency. In *Methods in social science: a case book*, ed. S. A. Rice. Chicago, University of Chicago Press.

Rock, P. 1979. *The making of symbolic interactionism*. London and Basingstoke, Macmillan.

Roncek, D. W. 1975. Density and crime: a methodological critique, *American Behavioral Scientist*, 18: 843–60.

Rose, H. M. and Deskins, D. R. Jr. 1980. Felony murder: the case of Detroit. *Urban Geography*, 1: 1–21.

Ruback, R. B., Greenberg, M. S. and Westcott, D. R. 1984. Social influence and crime-victim decision making. *Journal of Social Issues*, 39: 51–76.

Rubington, E. and Weinberg, M. S. 1968. *Deviance: the interactionist perspective*. New York, Macmillan.

Sacco, V. F. 1982. The effects of mass media on perceptions of crime. A reanalysis of the issues. *Pacific Sociological Review*, 25: 475–93.

Sack, R. D. 1983. Human territoriality: a theory. *Annals, American Association of Geographers*, 73: 55–74.

Sampson, R. J. and Castellano, T. C. 1982. Economic inequality and personal victimisation. An areal perspective. *British Journal of Criminology*, 22: 363–85.

Savage, S. 1984. The police: political control or community liaison? *Political Quarterly*, 55: 48–59.

Scarman, Lord. 1981. *The Brixton disorders 10–12 April 1981*. London, HMSO.

Scarr, H. A. 1973. *Patterns of burglary*. 2nd edn. Washington, DC, US Government Printing Office.

Schlossman, S. and Sedlak, M. 1983. The Chicago area project revisited. *Crime and Delinquency*, 29: 398–462.

Schneider, A. L. and Schneider, P. R. 1978. *Private and public-minded citizen responses to a neighborhood-based crime prevention strategy*. Eugene, Oregon, Institute of Policy Analysis.

Schneider, A. L. and Sumi, D. 1981. Patterns of telescoping and forgetting. *Criminology*, 19: 400–10.

Schwartz, G. G. ed. 1981. *Advanced industrialization and the inner cities*. Lexington, DC, Heath.

Schwendinger, H. and Schwendinger, J. 1975. Defenders of order or guardians of human rights? In *Critical criminology*, eds. I. Taylor, P. Walton and J. Young, pp. 113–46. London, Routledge and Kegan Paul.

Schwind, H. D. et al. 1975. *Dunkelfeldfurschung in Gottingen 1973/74*. Wiesbaden, BKA-Forschungsreihe (reported in OECD 1976. *Data sources for social indicators of victimization suffered by individuals*. Paris, OECD Social Indicator Development Programme, Special Studies no. 3.)

Scott, P. 1965. Delinquency, mobility and broken homes in Hobart. *Australian Journal of Social Issues*, 2: 10–22.

   1972. The spatial analysis of crime and delinquency. *Australian Geographical Studies*, 10: 1–18.

Scraton, P. 1984. Accountable to no-one: policing Merseyside 1979–81. In *Causes for concern. British criminal justice on trial*, eds. P. Scraton and P. Gordon, pp. 11–42. Harmondsworth, Penguin.

Searchlight. 1982. Violence on London's estates and elsewhere. *Searchlight*, 83: 12–13.

Select Committee on Ageing. 1977. A national perspective on elderly crime victimization. In *Perspective on crime victims*, eds. B. Golloway and J. Hudson, pp. 137–47. St Louis, Mosby.

Select Committee on Home Affairs. 1980. *Race relations and the 'sus' law*. Second report from the Home Affairs Committee, session 1979–80, HC 559. London, HMSO.

Shah, S. 1979. Aspects of the geographical analysis of Asian immigrants in London. Unpublished D Phil thesis, University of Oxford.

Shaw, C. R. 1926. Case study method. *Proceedings of the American Sociological Society*, 21: 149–57.

   1929. *Delinquency areas*. Chicago, University of Chicago Press.

   1930. *The jack-roller: a delinquent boy's own story*. Chicago, University of Chicago Press.

   1931. *The natural history of a delinquent career*. Chicago, University of Chicago Press.

Shaw, C. R. and McKay, H. D. 1931. *Social factors in juvenile delinquency*. Washington, DC, US Government Printing Office.

   1942. *Juvenile delinquency and urban areas*. Revised edn. 1969, Chicago, University of Chicago Press.

Shaw, C. R., McKay, H. D. and McDonald, J. F. 1938. *Brothers in crime.* Chicago, University of Chicago Press.

Shelley, L. I. 1981a. *Crime and modernization. The impact of industrialization and urbanization on crime.* Carbondale and Edwardsville, Southern Illinois University Press.

ed. 1981b. *Readings in comparative criminology.* Carbondale, Southern Illinois University Press.

Shibutani, T. 1966. *Improvised news: a sociological study of rumour.* Indianapolis, Bobbs-Merrill.

Short, C. 1982. Community policing – beyond slogans. In *The future of policing,* ed. T. Bennett, pp. 67–81. Cambridge, Institute of Criminology.

Shotland, R., Hayward, S., Young, C., Signorella, M., Mindingall, K., Kennedy, J., Rovine, M. and Danowitz, E. 1979. Fear of crime in residential communities. *Criminology,* 17: 34–45.

Shumsky, N. L. and Springer, L. M. 1981. San Francisco's zone of prostitution, 1880–1934. *Journal of Historical Geography,* 7: 71–89.

Sim, D. 1984. Urban deprivation: not just the inner city. *Area,* 16: 299–306.

Simey, M. 1982. Police authorities and accountability: the Merseyside experience. In *Policing the riots,* eds. D. Cowell, T. Jones and J. Young, pp. 22–57. London, Junction Books.

1984. Partnership policing. In *Scarman and after,* ed. J. Benyon, pp. 135–42. Oxford, Pergamon Press.

1985. *Accountability.* London, Bedford Square Press.

Simey, T. S. and Simey, M. B. 1960. *Charles Booth, social scientist.* London, Oxford University Press.

Singell, L. D. 1968. Economic causes of delinquency: national versus local control. *Urban Affairs Quarterly,* 4: 225–33.

Singer, S. I. 1981. Homogeneous victim–offender populations: a review and some research implications. *Journal of Criminal Law and Criminology,* 72: 779–88.

Skogan, W. G. 1976. Citizen reporting of crime: some national panel data. *Criminology,* 13: 535–49.

1977. Dimensions of the dark figure of unreported crime. *Crime and Delinquency,* 23: 41–51.

1981. Assessing the behavioral context of victimization. *Journal of Criminal Law and Criminology,* 72: 727–42.

1984. Reporting crimes to the police: the status of world research. *Journal of Research in Crime and Delinquency,* 21: 113–37.

Skogan, W. G. and Maxfield, M. G. 1981. *Coping with crime.* Beverly Hills and London, Sage.

Smith, D. A. and Visher, C. A. 1981. Street-level justice: situational determinants of police arrest decisions. *Social Problems,* 29: 167–77.

Smith, D. J. and Gray, J. 1983. *Police and people in London: IV The police in action.* London, Policy Studies Institute.

Smith, D. M. 1974. Crime rates as territorial social indicators: the case of the United States. Occasional Paper number 1, Department of Geography, Queen Mary College, London.

1976. Comment on 'To what extent is the geographer's world the "real" world?' *Area,* 8: 43–4.

1979. *Where the grass is greener.* London, Croom Helm.

Smith, P. W. and Hawkins, R. O. 1973. Victimization, types of citizen–police contacts and attitudes towards the police. *Law and Society Review*, 8: 134–52.

Smith, S. J. 1981a. Negative interaction: crime in the inner city. In *Social interaction and ethnic segregation*, eds. P. Jackson and S. J. Smith, pp. 35–58. London, Academic Press.

1981b. Humanistic method in contemporary social geography. *Area*, 13: 193–8.

1982a. Victimisation in the inner city – a British case study. *British Journal of Criminology*, 22: 386–402.

1982b. Race and reactions to crime. *New Community*, 10: 233–42.

1982c. Race and crime statistics. *Background Paper No. 2* London, BSR Race, Pluralism and Community Group.

1982d. Police, crime and fear in the inner city. *Police Review*, 90: 534–6.

1983. Public policy and the effects of crime in the inner city. *Urban Studies*, 20: 229–39.

1984a. Negotiating ethnicity in an uncertain environment. *Ethnic and Racial Studies*, 7: 360–73.

1984b. Practising humanistic geography. *Annals, Association of American Geographers*, 74: 353–74.

1984c. Crime and the structure of social relations. *Transactions, Institute of British Geographers*, NS 9: 427–42.

1984d. Crime in the news. *British Journal of Criminology*, 24: 289–95.

1985. News and the dissemination of fear. In *Geography, the media and popular culture*, eds. J. Burgess and J. Gold, pp. 229–53. London, Croom Helm.

Snodgrass, J. 1976. Clifford R. Shaw and Henry D. McKay. Chicago criminologists. *British Journal of Criminology*, 16: 1–19.

1982. *The jack-roller at seventy.* Lexington, Mass., Lexington Books.

Southgate, P. and Eckblom, P. 1984. *Contacts between police and public.* London, HMSO.

Sparks, R. F. 1981. Multiple victimisation, evidence, theory and future research. *Journal of Criminal Law and Criminology*, 72: 762–78.

Sparks, R. F., Genn, H. G. and Dodd, D. J. 1977. *Surveying victims.* Chichester, Wiley.

Spector, P. E. 1975. Population density and unemployment: the effects on the incidence of violent crime in the American city. *Criminology*, 12: 399–401.

Stack, S. 1982. Social structure and Swedish crime rates: a time-series analysis, 1950–1979. *Criminology*, 20: 499–513.

Stack, S. 1984. Income inequality and property crime. *Criminology*, 22: 229–57.

Stafford, M. C. and Galle, O. R. 1984. Victimization rates, exposure to risk, and fear of crime. *Criminology*, 22: 173–85.

Stephenson, L. K. 1980. Centrographic analysis of crime. In *Crime: a spatial perspective*, eds. D. E. Georges-Abeyie and K. D. Harries, pp. 146–55. New York, Columbia University Press.

Stevens, P. and Willis, C. F. 1979. *Race, crime and arrests*. London, HMSO.

Sundeen, R. A. and Mathieu, J. T. 1976. The fear of crime and its consequences among elderly in three urban communities. *The Gerontologist*, 16: 211–19.

Suttles, G. D. 1968. *The social order of the slum*. Chicago, University of Chicago Press.

1972. *The social construction of communities*. Chicago, University of Chicago Press.

Sviridoff, M. and Thompson, J. W. 1983. Links between employment and crime: a qualitative study of Rikers Island releasees. *Crime and Delinquency*, 29: 195–212.

Symanski, R. 1974. Prostitution in Nevada. *Annals, Association of American Geographers*, 64: 357–77.

Taub, R. P., Taylor, D. G. and Dunham, J. D. 1984. *Paths of neighborhood change*. Chicago, University of Chicago Press.

Taylor, I., Walton, P. and Young, J. 1975. Critical criminology in Britain: review and prospects. In *Critical criminology*, eds. I. Taylor, P. Walton and J. Young, pp. 6–62. London, Routledge and Kegan Paul.

Taylor, R. B., Gottfredson, S. D. and Brower, S. 1980. The defensibility of defensible space. In *Understanding crime*, eds. T. Hirschi and M. Gottfredson, pp. 53–71. Beverly Hills and London, sage.

Thomas, D. S. 1927. *Social aspects of the business cycle*. New York, Knopf.

Thomas, W. I. 1928. *The unadjusted girl*. Boston, Little, Brown and Co.

Thomas, W. I. and Znaniecki, F. 1918–1920. *The Polish peasant in Europe and America*. 5 volumes. Chicago, University of Chicago Press.

Thornberry, T. P. and Farnworth, M. 1982. Social correlates of criminal involvement: further evidence on the relationship between social status and criminal behavior. *American Sociological Review*, 47: 505–18.

Thrasher, F. M. 1927. *The gang*. Chicago, University of Chicago Press.

Timms, D. W. G. 1965. The spatial distribution of social deviants in Luton, England. *Australia and New Zealand Journal of Sociology*, 1: 38–52.

Tittle, C. R. and Villemez, W. 1977. Social class and criminality. *Social Forces*, 56: 474–503.

Tittle, C. R., Villemez, W. J. and Smith, D. A. 1978. The myth of social class and criminality: an empirical assessment of the empirical evidence. *American Sociological Review*, 43: 643–56.

Toby, J. 1967. *Affluence and adolescent crime*. President's Commission on Law Enforcement and Administration of Justice, task force report on juvenile delinquency and youth crime. Washington, DC, US Government Printing Office.

Tomasic, R. and Feeley, M. M. 1982. *Neighbourhood justice: assessment of an emerging idea*. New York, Longman.

Townsend, A. R. 1981. Geographical perspectives on major job losses in the U.K. 1977–80. *Area*, 13: 31–8.

United States Congressional Subcommittee on Crime of the Committee of the Judiciary. 1978. *Unemployment and crime*. Washington, DC, US Government Printing Office.

United States Department of Justice. 1975. Law enforcement assistance administration: national criminal justice information and statistics service. *Criminal victimization in the nation's five largest cities*. Washington, DC, US Government Printing Office.

Unnever, J. D., Frazier, C. E. and Henretta, J. E. 1980. Race differences in criminal sentencing. *Sociological Quarterly*, 21: 197–206.

Verbrugge, L. M. and Taylor, R. B. 1980. Consequences of population density and size. *Urban Affairs Quarterly*, 16: 135–60.

Vesterdal, J. 1983. Etiological factors and long term consequences of child abuse. *International Journal of Offender Therapy and Comparative Criminology*, 27: 21–54.

Walmsley, D. J. 1980. Spatial bias in Australian news reporting. *Australian Geographer*, 14: 342–9.

1982. Mass media and spatial awareness. *Tijdschrift voor Economische en Sociale Geografie*, 73: 32–42.

Warr, M. 1982. The accuracy of public beliefs about crime: further evidence. *Criminology*, 20: 185–204.

Weaver, G. J. 1980. Political groups and young blacks in Handsworth. Discussion Paper Series C number 38, Faculty of Commerce and Social Sciences, Birmingham University.

Webb, S. D. 1972. Crime and the division of labor: testing a Durkheimian model. *American Journal of Sociology*, 78: 643–56.

Webber, R. J. 1978. *Parliamentary constituencies: a socio-economic classification*. Occasional Paper 13, OPCS.

Weber, M. 1968. *Economy and society*. Eds. G. Roth and C. Wittich. New York, Bedminster.

West, D. ed. 1985. *Sexual victimisation*. London, Gower.

White, R. C. 1932. The relation of felonies to environmental factors in Indianapolis. *Social Forces*, 10: 498–509.

Whyte, W. F. 1961. *Street corner society*. Chicago, University of Chicago Press.

Wiers, P. 1944. *Economic factors in Michigan delinquency*. New York, Columbia University Press.

Wiles, P. 1976. Introduction. In *The sociology of crime and delinquency in Britain. Volume 2: the new criminologists*, ed. P. Wiles, pp. 1–35. London, Martin Robertson.

Wilson, A. 1983. Racism: conspiracies to assault. *New Statesman*, 105: 8–9.

Wilson, E. 1983. *What is to be done about violence against women?* Harmondsworth, Penguin.

Wilson, J. Q. and Boland, B. 1976. The effect of police on crime. *Law and Society Review*, 12: 367–90.

Wilson, R. J. 1973. British judges as political actors. *International Journal of Criminology and Penology*, 1: 197–215.

Wilson, S. 1978. Vandalism and 'defensible space' on London housing estates. In *Tackling vandalism*, ed. R. V. G. Clarke, pp. 41–65. London, HMSO.

Winchester, S. W. C. 1978. Two suggestions for developing the geographical study of crime. *Area*, 19: 116–20.

Wirth, L. 1910. Ideological aspects of social disorganization. *American Sociological Review*, 5: 472–82.

1939. Social interaction: the problem of the individual and the group. *American Journal of Sociology*, 44: 965–79.

Wolf, P. 1971. Crime and development. An international comparison of crime rates. *Scandinavian Studies in Criminology*, 3: 107–20.

1972. *Violence in Denmark and Finland: a comparison of victims and violence.* Scandinavian Research Council for Criminology.

Wolf, P. and Hauge, R. 1975. Criminal violence in three Scandinavian countries. *Scandinavian Studies in Criminology*, Vol. 5. London, Tavistock.

Wood, D. S. 1983. *British crime survey: technical report.* London, Social and Community Planning Research.

Woods, R. I. 1975. Dynamic urban social structure: a study of intra-urban migration and the development of social stress areas in Birmingham. Unpublished D Phil thesis, University of Oxford.

1976. Aspects of the scale problem in the calculation of segregation indices: London and Birmingham, 1961 and 1971. *Tijdschrift voor Economische en Sociale Geografie*, 67: 169–74.

Woods, R. I. 1980. Migration and social segregation in Birmingham and the West Midlands region. In *The geographical impact of migration*, eds. P. White and R. I. Woods. London, Longman.

Wright, K. N. ed. 1981. *Crime and criminal justice in a declining economy.* Cambridge, Mass., Oelgeschlager, Gunn and Hain.

Young, J. 1979. Left idealism, reformism and beyond: from new criminology to Marxism. In *Capitalism and the rule of law*, eds. B. Fine, R. Kinsey, J. Lea, S. Picciotto and J. Young, pp. 11–28. London, Hutchinson.

Zehr, H. 1974. The modernization of crime in Germany and France, 1830–1913. *Journal of Social History*, 8: 117–41.

1976. *Crime and the development of modern society. Patterns of criminality in nineteenth century Germany and France.* Totowa, New Jersey, Rowan and Littlefield.

Zorbaugh, H. W. 1929. *The gold coast and the slum.* Chicago, University of Chicago Press.

Index

222